GUIDE TO CATALINA

AND CALIFORNIA'S CHANNEL ISLANDS

GUIDE TO CATALINA

AND CALIFORNIA'S
CHANNEL ISLANDS

CHICKI MALLAN
PHOTOS BY
OZ MALLAN

PUBLICATIONS

GUIDE TO CATALINA AND CALIFORNIA'S CHANNEL ISLANDS

Please send all comments, corrections, additions, amendments, and critiques to:

**CHICKI MALLAN
c/o MOON PUBLICATIONS, INC.
722 WALL STREET
CHICO CA 95928, USA**

Published by
  Moon Publications, Inc.
  722 Wall Street
  Chico, California 95928, USA
  tel: (916) 345-5473.

Printed by
  Colorcraft Ltd.

Ⓒ Copyright 1989 Chicki Mallan

Printing History
  First Edition 1984
  Second Edition 1988
  Reprinted 1989

Library of Congress Cataloging in Publication Data

Mallan, Chicki, 1933—
  Guide to Catalina and California's Channel Islands. c1984

  Rev. ed. of: Guide to Catalina Island. c.1984
  Bibliography: p. 258
  Includes index.
  1. Santa Catalina Island (Calif.)—Description and travel—Guide-books. 2. Channel Islands (Calif.)—Description and travel—Guide books. 3. Islands—California—Guide books. I. Mallan, Chicki, 1933- Guide to Catalina Island II. Title.
  F868.L8M27   1988   917.94'93   87-34822
  ISBN 0-918373-18-2

Printed in Hong Kong

To my children:
Barbara, Tony, Denise,
Scott, Beth, Guy,
Patti, and Bryant.
You made each day
a bright challenge.

ACKNOWLEDGEMENTS

Each time a book is finally ready to go to the printer, the realization hits home that it takes the hands, brains, desires, and hard work of many people besides the author. Topping the list is publisher Bill Dalton, a great inspiration to everyone at Moon. His perseverance and desire for accuracy and detail in the early days have brought Moon Publications to the forefront of the travel publishing industry. Thanks Bill for having a dream and hanging on to it.

Thanks also to the entire Moon team. Editors Deke Castleman and Mark Morris never relented in their tireless persistence in making the manuscript "right." Thanks to easygoing Dave Hurst, who still never loses his cool when things don't go right. He quietly continues with artistic layouts, cover design, and overseeing the project as it comes together. Thanks to artist Kathy Escovedo-Sanders for the brilliant banner art at the beginning of most chapters; and Diana Lasich Harper for her line drawings. The maps as usual are line perfection with Louise Foote at the board. To Asha with her constantly calculating, computerized brain cells, who has Moon's "chips" ever moving toward perfection and workability; she's always cheerful despite yet another change to the galleys. "Hurray" for our upfront sales-manager-like-no-other, Donna Galassi. Moon has the knack of finding eager, intelligent interns to help with the finite details that go into the making of a book, thanks to them, and thanks to the rest of the Moon crew who were always ready with a smile and encouragement, Jackie, Rick, Marne.

In my office, thanks Kristin Chambers for all the help with the mundane jobs and especially on the computer. I would also like to acknowledge the help of all the friendly Islanders in Avalon and the Santa Catalina Island Co. for all their help and the use of historic pictures from their archives. Thanks especially to Rudy Piltch and Chris Williamson. Shirley Davey at BBDO who always managed to find a little time in her busy day to answer questions. Thanks to Terry Martin, island naturalist, and Patricia Moore, curator of the Catalina Museum. Also to the friendly folks at the Santa Barbara Museum, the staff of the Channel Islands National Park in Ventura, especially to Cindy Nielsen, chief of interpretation. Thanks AT&T for allowing me to make all those long-distance calls to Catalina. And to Island Express for providing a classy helicopter operation to Catalina.

And I've saved the best for last, the family. Thanks to my youngest daughter Patti who took precious college-vacation beach-time on Catalina to round up the endless nuts and bolts details that a guidebook needs. To Bryant for the endearing smile I always got after class even though I was still at the computer and not fixing dinner. And lastly, to my wonderful, loving, patient, ever-supportive photographer husband who took 95% of the photos for the book. Who doesn't say it, but who proves each day, each month of each year, that he is willing to carry those cameras just about anywhere in the world for a good picture, a good book, a good story, and a good time—together.

PHOTO AND ILLUSTRATION CREDITS

Except where noted, all black-and-white photos and color slides including front cover of Avalon Bay were taken by Oz Mallan. **Photos:** Kevin Bicknell, page 162. Denise Bicknell, pages 76 and 194. Santa Catalina Island Co., pages 15, 18, 19, 21, 46, 47, 48, 49, 93, 96, 106, 122. *Catalina Islander*, pages 38, 50, BBDO page, 89. Ventura Visitors Bureau, pages 220, 221. Santa Barbara Conference and Visitors Bureau, page 159. Newport Visitors Bureau, pages 175, 176, 180. San Diego Convention and Visitors Bureau, pages 184, 186, 187, 188, 192. Channel Islands National Park, pages 224, 231, 236. Bill Meister, pages 10, 74,

Illustrations: Kathy Escovedo Sanders, pages 1, 3, 8, 12, 24, 26, 37, 44, 45, 54, 69, 97, 102, 111, 117, 121, 131, 197. Diana Lasich Harper, pages 6, 40, 77, 82, 83, border 95, lower 120, border 136, 141, 143, 148, 199, 200, 201, 202, border 202, 204, 206, 209, 214, 216, 217, 227, 229, 233, 237, 243, 245, 250, 254, 256, 257. Santa Catalina Island Co., pages, 119, 120.

CONTENTS

INTRODUCTION...1

AVALON...45

CATALINA'S INTERIOR...121

BOATING...141

SOUTHERN CALIFORNIA MARINAS...155

THE CHANNEL ISLANDS...197

BOOKLIST...258

INDEX...259

LIST OF MAPS

LIST OF CHARTS

ABBREVIATIONS

C. —century	**OW** —one way	**RT** —round trip
F —Fahrenheit	**pp** —per person	**tel.** —telephone number

INTRODUCTION

An island is a special place. There's a dream-like quality about a bit of land surrounded by the beautiful sea. Birds, fish, and seals frolic in splashing ocean spray for the benefit of anyone watching — or not watching. Tall peaks give the sun and moon a dramatic stage to perform their magic each day — and the show is always different. For those that have not yet discovered their "special island," may we recommend Santa Catalina.

In Avalon, simple things take on new meaning: walking along the beachfront's serpentine wall, watching the harbor lights when the bay is filled with boats, listening to the special music of a clinking halyard on a mast multiplied by a hundred. Here you'll smell fresh salt air on a breezy morning, sit for hours under the palm trees on Casino Point watching the changing colors of the sea. And even if you're not a fisherman, when the cannon booms across the harbor the infectious excitement will rush you along with other beach-goers to see a marlin winched up to the pier's scales.

That's just part of what Catalina is about, but if that much sounds good, cross the channel and look it over. Take a hike into the interior, see wild buffalo peacefully grazing on a hillside with the Pacific Ocean as a backdrop, study plants that have been extinct on the Mainland for thousands of years, see California as it looked before we discovered cement, or cars, or high-rise buildings. Crossing the channel for the first time, there's a whole set of experiences that you'll remember for a lifetime: watching the porpoises following along, diving in and out of the ship's wake, the surprise of finding your sea-legs while carrying coffee and a sandwich to the upper deck, meeting fellow travelers also curious about islands. But probably the most indelible memory of all is first seeing the white speck on the horizon that slowly becomes Avalon's hallmark, the great white moorish-style Casino building on the bay. Avalon, on the crescent-shaped cove, is a Mediter-ranean-like village, climbing the hillsides dotted with vivid colored bougainvilleas and tall eucalyptus trees lining zig zag roads as they circle into the cleavage of the Island. The Casino presides over it all.

Many people already have that special feeling about Catalina, because there's something of interest for every visitor. Boaters, hikers, campers, horsemen, cyclists, divers, anglers, sun worshippers, and jet setters will find all they're looking for, as will historians, naturalists, archaeologists, and botanists. Vacationers can choose non-stop activities around Avalon town—or in your own boat discover the magic of a small cove and complete solitude, just you and nature's wonders. Parents can relax as their children are happily occupied on the beach, splashing in the water, or with organized play. It doesn't have to be summer; winters are mild, spring is glorious, but there are some that swear the most beautiful time of year is in the fall. Come on over, once is all it takes, and Catalina will become your "Special Island."

SOUTHERN CALIFORNIA COASTLINE AND THE CHANNEL ISLANDS

THE LAND

Santa Catalina Island is one of the eight Santa Barbara Channel Islands stretching along the Southern California coast. Catalina itself has a 120-million-year geological history. Early paleontologists assumed that it was once attached to the Mainland, but recent studies and more modern scientific methods are raising some doubts about this theory (see p. 197). Catalina, only 19 miles from the Mainland at its closest point, sits on the Pacific tectonic plate, while most of California and the rest of the U.S. are on the North American plate. Plate movements and volcanic eruptions are responsible for the formation of Catalina Island, though this is not true of all the other Channel Islands. The two most common types of Island rock are the result of this formation process: igneous (volcanic) and metamorphic (sedimentary rock that has changed under pressure, heat, or chemical action).

The Indians of the Mainland used a descriptive phrase when they spoke of Catalina Island: *Wexaj momte asunga wow*—"mountain ranges that rise from the sea." Most of the Island consists of mountains interspersed with meadows and valleys. Black Jack (2,006 feet) and Mt. Orizaba (2,097 feet) are the two highest peaks. Some of the coastal cliffs fall abruptly to the sea, leaving not even a path's space along the ocean, while in other areas the hills slope gently to sandy beaches below. The 21-mile-long Island has an east-west orientation. On the western (or windward) side, the Pacific crashes against the tall rugged coast. Off the eastern (or lee) coast that faces the Mainland, the sea is calm and placid. Catalina's widest section is at Long Point directly across from China Point on the windward side (approximately seven and a half miles). The Island's east and west sides have a natural cleavage at Two Harbors—a half-mile-wide isthmus six miles from the west end—which is the narrowest point. A deep undersea ledge girdles the land mass of the Island, fostering a rich habitat for marinelife. Catalina's steep canyon walls create a temperature and climate that help sustain types of vegetation that are unique to the Island.

Catalina's inland roads wind around the rugged mountain tops overlooking the sea.

Water

Although surrounded by water, the drinkable kind has always been a problem for Catalina. In the early days the Indians and then the first settlers relied on the few natural springs scattered over the Island for their water needs,

plus the few streams which still run to the sea after a good wet year. Today, the utility company maintains a dam, reservoir, and pipeline to accommodate the Island's freshwater needs.

CLIMATE

Many people mistakenly believe that Catalina is a tropical island. Though the sun shines an average of 267 days a year, its climate is in fact similar to the Southern California coast. Thanks to cooling marine breezes, Catalina is generally moister and cooler in the summer months than the Mainland; in winter, with help from the warm Japanese current, it's generally a few degrees milder. In summer, the average temperature ranges from 70-76 degrees F. Variable in the winter, the temperature ranges from 49-63 degrees F, depending on what the rains bring. The average rainfall is 14 inches per year, but the extremes can be great. Some years (as on the California Mainland), as much as 30 inches of rain fall, while the drought years of 1977-78 brought virtually none. The average sea temperature in the winter is 56-59 degrees F, in the summer 67-70 degrees F. The winter months almost always bring a northeastern (Santa Ana) storm or two. These Santa Ana

An occasional storm hits Catalina Island, pounding her placid shores with a turbulent surf.

conditions can turn the calm Pacific into a raging sea. Its high winds are infrequent but dangerous; sometimes reaching 50 knots, they occur November to March. Fog can be expected in all seasons, but in winter it covers a wider area and lasts longer. In May and June, Catalina hosts the fog till about noon. What many visitors consider Catalina's biggest attraction is the lack of smog. This is due to westerly winds and the Island's distance from the Mainland.

FLORA

Though the plant life is similar to the Mainland, Catalina's resident species are slightly different. Some plants that thrive on the Island today existed on the Mainland 20,000 years ago, but as the Mainland became drier, many of those plants died out. Of approximately 600 species on Catalina, 396 are native.

Some of the wildflowers found on Catalina are:

> bright eyes
> brodiaea (blue dick)
> bush lupine
> bush sunflower
> shore heliotrope
> California bindweed
> California island poppy
> sumac (lemonade berry)
> California lilac
> tree tobacco
> tree poppy
> everlasting flower
> violet nightshade
> fiesta flower
> wild apple
> giant sea dahlia
> wild four o'clock
> ground pink
> wild sweet pea
> Indian paintbrush
> woodland star
> yellow pansy

Trees

Early accounts by miners and settlers mention an abundance of pine trees. Yet, the pines introduced in recent years haven't thrived on Catalina because of the frequent dry seasons. Since Philip Wrigley's Conservancy program was introduced in 1972, hikers to the interior can see seven adult mahogany trees. Some of the trees seen on Catalina are:

> California holly (toyon)
> elderberry
> Catalina ironwood
> greasewood
> Catalina manzanita
> island oak
> Catalina wild cherry
> mountain mahogany
> cottonwood
> scrub oak

PLANT LORE

Indians and pioneers, as well as modern-day herbologists, have told of the culinary and medicinal uses of a number of Catalina's plant species. Some of these may be more lore than fact; others have proven still useful today. One is the **prickly pear,** a common edible fruit found not only in Catalina but in many other parts of the world. A deep purplish/red, it grows on cactus common on the Island. This fruit is sweet and juicy when ripe, and according to some, makes a great fruit pudding. A good way to get rid of the thorns and skin without injury is to leave the fruit attached to the plant and carefully peel. Otherwise, a fork makes a good handle while peeling the nasties off.

The **Catalina cherry** grows well on the Island; a large grove on the west end carries the appropriate name of Cherry Cove. The

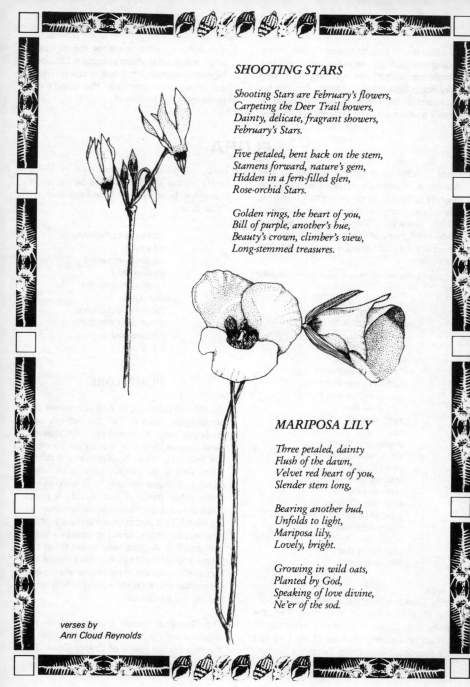

SHOOTING STARS

Shooting Stars are February's flowers,
Carpeting the Deer Trail bowers,
Dainty, delicate, fragrant showers,
February's Stars.

Five petaled, bent back on the stem,
Stamens forward, nature's gem,
Hidden in a fern-filled glen,
Rose-orchid Stars.

Golden rings, the heart of you,
Bill of purple, another's hue,
Beauty's crown, climber's view,
Long-stemmed treasures.

MARIPOSA LILY

Three petaled, dainty
Flush of the dawn,
Velvet red heart of you,
Slender stem long,

Bearing another bud,
Unfolds to light,
Mariposa lily,
Lovely, bright.

Growing in wild oats,
Planted by God,
Speaking of love divine,
Ne'er of the sod.

verses by
Ann Cloud Reynolds

fruit resembles a reddish/black cherry; it has little flesh around its seed, but is quite refreshing. It's said to have been one of the favorite fruits of the Indians. **Sumac** or lemonade berry is said to provide a refreshing drink called lemonade by the Mexicans. **Wild sage,** which grows profusely on the Mainland, is gathered by herbologists for home remedies—it's great added to turkey stuffing and other cooks' specialties. Wild cucumber and radish, beach strawberry, blackberry, and wild currant were most likely eaten by the original inhabitants of the Island, and are a treat when found by today's residents.

Remedies

Two plants used as remedies for rattlesnake bites are the wild carrot and rattlesnake weed. A poultice of the fresh leaves of either is applied to the wound. If, in the course of an illness, copious perspiring was required, a drink was made and administered from the leaves of the large **elder** tree *(Sambucus caerulea).* **Snake cactus** was used to fight high fever. The aborigines were thought to have made a liniment remedy for rheumatism from an extract of the **white willow.**

Narcotics

Historians believe that the Gabrielino Indians took part in Chingichnich religious ceremonies involving jimson weed. This ceremony was a cult of initiation for adolescents entering manhood. The jimson weed *(Datura stramonium)* is a highly effective narcotic. A drink was made from the leaves and given to the young men following a three-day fast. Afterwards, they would dance until they passed out in a stupor. Their dreams during this time were thought to be prophetic and held great significance for the rest of their lives. This ceremony is referred to as the "Toloache Cult." Old-timers described the **yerba santa** as having the power to induce a "gentle sleep," but is found only rarely on the Island today.

Miscellaneous

Long and coarsely fibrous, the tuberous root of the "soap plant" works well as a scrub brush. The *Chenopodium californicum,* a parsnip-like root, also provides a detergent in lieu of soap. **Poison oak** grows on the Island, and if you are sensitive, contact with it can cause discomfort any season of the year. Leaves, bare branches, or even smoke from a burning bush can bring on an itchy rash.

Restoration

Today, the Catalina Conservancy maintains a native plant nursery at Middle Ranch. Here seedlings of plants are coaxed along and then planted throughout the interior. This restoration is an ongoing project that will eventually present the Island as it was 150 years ago.

ANN CLOUD REYNOLDS

From the 1920s into the '50s, the late Ann Cloud Reynolds was a familiar sight in Avalon, with her walking staff, floppy straw hat, rucksack, and beach towel around her shoulders heading into Catalina's hills. She reveled in nature's offerings, from Cottonwood Canyon, to Silver Peak, and all in between. As others know the floor plan of their homes, Ann knew Catalina's interior: every rock, mountain, valley, and wildflower. She wrote three small books, all including poetry and a feeling that she was part of the land and the Indians from the past. "Hiker," whom Ann always referred to in her books, was herself. Hiker found Indian caves with ancient markings, spent nights under the stars long before others did, fed the ravens, spoke to the goats, took pictures of wildflowers, and sang from the hilltops:

> Echoing across the years,
> Comes the call,
> Brings the tears,
> Of joy, to know the Indians all,
> Listen ever for the call— *Yo te hoy!*

FAUNA

LAND CREATURES

Buffalo

In 1924, when William Farnum, a Western movie maker, was filming Zane Grey's *The Vanishing American,* 14 buffalo were brought to the Island for the film. Rounding up the buffalo afterward proved to be too difficult, so in the end they were left to roam. By 1934, the herd had increased to 19, then 30 as additional buffalo were brought from Colorado to supplement the herd. Today's population is held to 400-500 — ideal for the ecosystem. When the herd gets too large, buffalo are culled; the carcasses are sent to the Mainland to be butchered and frozen, then shipped back as expensive hamburger — buffalo chili and buffalo burgers are sold at the Airport-In-The-Sky.

When an old bull is challenged by a younger one a fierce battle generally follows. In most cases the old bull is run out of the herd. Considered a rogue, he thereafter roams the hills alone. Fencing at every road entry into Avalon from the interior and a large metal bump gate for cars ordinarily keep the animals in the hills and out of town, but there are excep-

tions. When a bull finds entry into Avalon it always causes unusual excitement. Early one morning in 1978 the town woke to see a rogue wandering down the beach in Avalon. Before anyone could do anything, he had trotted up Sumner Street and darted onto the Pitch and Putt golf course adjoining Avalon's elementary school. The whole affair soon turned into a noisy roundup with cheering children and a siren-blaring police car chasing the running bull back and forth the length of the golf course, trying to guide him through the gate, missing at least eight times. Finally, he fled toward the peaceful environment of the interior.

Goats

The hills of Catalina Island are lined with a network of narrow paths. These are mostly goat trails. Since goat bones have not been found in the Indian kitchen middens, it's assumed that they arrived after the Spanish era. Some historians claim Spanish explorers brought goats to insure a supply of meat for their travels. Though naturalists now disagree with that theory, another has yet to be suggested. Today the goats number in the thousands. Their coats vary from white to brown to black or a mixture of all three; the most common is the shaggy black goat. Some billies have large horn-spreads measuring three feet and more. These ornery animals command the sheerest cliffs, and frequently climb down to the water's edge to lick salt from the ocean-sprayed rocks. You're sure to spot Catalina goats in the interior. Sometimes a whole herd will be scattered across the brow of a hill—dark dots against the golden grass. Often they'll be grazing along with a herd of buffalo.

Wild Boar

The wild boar (pig) was introduced to Catalina in the mid-1920s to hold down the rattlesnake population. These huge pigs are mean, and have multiplied into the thousands. Though generally anxious to escape a human confrontation, they will almost always fight to protect their young. They occasionally come into Avalon and damage the golf course by digging up the greens, but for the most part they stay in the backcountry to run loose on the roughly 42,000 acres at their disposal. To keep the herds down, boar and goat hunts are organized through the Camp and Cove Agency at Two Harbors.

Deer

Although anthropologist Alfred L. Kroeber briefly mentions deer on Catalina in his 1925 *Handbook of Indians of California,* many historians date the introduction of deer to the Island to 1930, when 18 mule deer were brought for refuge by the California Fish and Game Commission. They too have adapted to the environment, multiplying to the point where deer hunts must be organized periodically to keep the population down. In years of little rain the deer come into town to feast on rose buds, pansy blossoms, and other garden delicacies. During one severe drought, they did considerable damage. To avert total devastation, many of the animals were trapped in huge cages, shipped to the Mainland, and set free in a wild area where ample forage was available.

Catalina Island Fox

The small Island fox seen on Catalina as well as many of the other Channel Islands is a diminuation of the Mainland gray fox. Its color is variegated gray, black, rust, and white. It is seldom seen by the casual observer. However, it has been said that on a summer evening if you study the shoreline when the flying-

Buffalos spend time roaming the hills; here a small herd is gathered around a welcome waterhole.

fish boat aims its powerful light toward shore, you might see a pair of glowing eyes. Fish often get confused or mistakenly follow the light beam and land on the rocky beach, stranded. They don't remain long, as the small fox with his sharp vision is also watching and waiting for just this opportunity for a fresh seafood snack.

Rodents

The ground squirrel is another native. This small gray/brown squirrel, which lives in subterranean tunnels, has an unmistakable clacketing chatter. Also endemic to Catalina and close relative to the ground squirrel are the harvest mouse and white-footed mouse.

Other Animals

Islanders have their share of house pets — the usual dogs, cats, canaries, and parrots. Thoroughbred Arabian horses are raised at Rancho Escondido, a 1,500-acre private ranch owned by the Wrigley family. At Middle Ranch, now part of the Catalina Conservancy, you'll find a variety of farm animals, including milk cows and chickens. Middle Ranch is also the pony center where kids from Avalon learn to ride, some of whom travel to the Mainland to participate in horse shows, and do quite well.

AIR CREATURES

Like most communities near the Pacific, Catalina hosts an abundance of waterfowl, including the cormorant, many varieties of seagull, the tern, grebe, and pelican. You'll also find many species of common birds of the Mainland such as the sparrow, finch, warbler, hummingbird, and mockingbird. At one time there were hundreds of quail; now, hunting them is limited to years of a good hatch (which is very rare). The black raven and the bald eagle were held sacred by the Catalina Indian. The raven is still plentiful on the Island, but by 1979 the magnificent eagles had all but vanished. For many years, they built their nests on sheer cliffs that

The brown pelican (Pelanicus occidentalis), *among the largest of all birds, was a disappearing species on the West Coast until the use of DDT was banned. On rare occasions the aggressive bird has been known to force into its pouch a large fish that it could neither swallow nor disgorge, thus causing its own death.*

overlooked the sea, but nests are rarely seen now. The Catalina Conservancy and the Institute for Wildlife Studies have undertaken the painstaking task of reintroducing the eagle to the Island. In 1979, a nesting platform was built and 14 eaglets were fed and observed until they were able to fend for themselves. Since then other eaglets have been released, making a total of 33. A 1987 count placed the eagle population at 18. As Island naturalist Terry Martin explains, some of the eagles fly away from the Island and others die of natural causes, although one is known to have been shot. The program is considered successful; in 1987 a nest was built and eggs were laid. None of the eggs hatched, but that first nest was definitely a good sign that the eagles were adapting to their new home on Catalina. Nesting eagles care for their young for up to a year. At that age they're nearly the size of an adult. The nest (of necessity) is large, and it's not unusual to see an eagle carrying a stick as big around as a human arm through the air for the building process. One of the largest nests on record weighed a ton and was six feet across.

When hiking in the interior, you may glimpse them soaring on updrafts along the cliff sides or over the sea or reservoirs watching with a keen eye for an errant fish, an important part of their diet. Thanks to the Conservancy these birds are the beginning of a new community of bald eagles on Catalina Island.

Peregrine
Another bird originally native to Catalina is the peregrine falcon. The Conservancy has released these into the interior as well and to date there are one male and several females.

WATER CREATURES

Sea Lions
Herds of this "circus seal," intelligent and easily trained, range the California waters and are protected by law from hunters; some specimens live as long as 35 years. Ranging in color from tan or gray to almost black, the California sea lion cow may be more than six feet long and weigh over 300 pounds, while the bulls can grow to nine feet and 1,000 pounds. A large male usually has a prominent crest on its forehead. These enormous bulls battle for favorite locations for their breeding harems, even while the cows are still birthing. Pups are usually born in June, though some

are born as early as May and as late as July. The pups then have the summer — a gentle season of mild weather — and an abundant supply of fish to encourage their rapid growth. The sea lions return to the place of their birth to mate each year in late spring or early summer. At one time hundreds flocked back to Catalina; many still do, but not in the same numbers as in the past. Naturalists are studying the Catalina area to understand why the seal population has decreased so radically. If you have any interest in the habits of these intelligent, inquisitive pinnipeds ("finfooted" ones), the ideal way to observe their habits is from a boat and with a pair of binoculars. The experience of watching them lolling on the rocks in the summer sun or gently nudging their pups into the water for a swimming lesson is well worth the time.

Seals enjoy summer fun and frolic near Catalina's Seal Rocks.

HISTORY

Prehistory

Catalina Island has a mysterious and complex history. For the last 30,000 years, no less than five aboriginal cultures have occupied the Santa Barbara Channel Islands, but the history of man is clouded; there are few definite answers to long-asked questions. For a brief period, there was wild speculation that Catalina's first inhabitants may have been a cultured race of white giants, survivors from a sunken continent. Old ships' logs and other written accounts refer to the "white-skinned" Indian communities on Catalina Island, but no evidence exists that whites inhabited the islands. It's now thought that during the Pleistocene Ice Age (50,000 B.C.) when the level of the sea fell, men and animals crossed the Bering land bridge from Asia to the American continent. For nearly 50,000 years, humans made an epic trek southward spreading throughout North, Central, and South America until approximately 1000 B.C., when they reached Tierra del Fuego and could go no farther.

With the possible exceptions of Alaska and remote sections of Canada, the use of stone tools continued on Santa Catalina longer than anywhere else in North America. Perhaps this was because of the unlimited quantities of soapstone and obsidian available for making tools, cooking utensils, and ceremonial objects, as well as the isolation of the Island from outside cultural influences and sources of materials.

Gabrielino Indians

Much of our knowledge about early man in the Channel Islands is speculative. Although deep layers of excavated cultural material from middens (ancient refuse heaps) clearly establish that a sizeable number of people have lived on Catalina Island since 2000 B.C., early anthropologists and archaeologists believed that the more modern Indians of the Channel Islands (referred to variously as "Chumash" and "Shoshonean") can be traced as far back as 500 B.C. A.L. Kroeber, an anthropologist distinguished for his studies of early California Indians, wrote that the "remains" found on the majority of the Channel Islands show all the characteristics of Chumash civilization in its most perfect state. However, the Indians on Catalina called themselves "Pimugnans" (they called the Island "Pimu" or "Pimugna") and enjoyed a lively interaction with the Chumash. Their ancestors were from the early Shoshonean linguistic group that migrated from the Great Plains. At the peak of their civilization, 2,500

Indians lived on the Island at three major sites, Little Harbor, Avalon, and Two Harbors. Hundreds of other sites have been found; some were permanent and others were temporary bases for hunting and gathering expeditions. Since the sea supplied the major part of the Indian diet, the permanent sites were located near a freshwater supply that was reasonably close to the shoreline. The Two Harbors area had the largest community, while the site at Little Harbor was the oldest.

The Pimugnans were later called Gabrielinos. This and other names for natives were taken from the missions that eventually became the homes of the last survivors of the Southern California tribes: the Obispeno, Purismeno, and Diegueno, from San Luis Obispo, La Purisma Concepcion, and San Diego. As time passed, these coastal and Island Indians intermingled and developed a shared culture due to an ongoing trade between the people of the Channel Islands and the Mainland. They have since all come to be called "Canalinos."

Friar Torquemada, interpreter for Friar Ascension, the adventurous missionary who accompanied the Vizcaino expedition in 1602, described the Indians as a warm, friendly people and physically hardy. The Indian houses on Catalina were described by Miguel Costanso, an engineer with the 1769 Portola expedition, as circular, thatched, domed structures 60 feet in diameter, spacious enough to hold three to four families. Men and children usually went naked; the women

wore aprons of otter skins. At night robes of otter skins were also used as blankets. The Gabrielinos or Pimugnan of Catalina were energetic traders with a flourishing stoneware trade: archaeologists have found Catalina obsidian carvings in Indian sites as far away as Nevada and New Mexico. Many artifacts were removed from the Island in the early 1900s, and are now exhibited at the Heye Foundation's Museum of American Indians, located at Broadway and 155th Street, New York, NY 10032.

Religious Beliefs

Many of the Islanders' customs differed from the Gabrielinos on the Mainland. According to Bernice Eastman Johnston, noted author associated with the Southwest Museum of Los Angeles, the Mainland Gabrielinos found something sinister in the isolation granted their tribesmen by the rough waters of the channel. Even though brisk trading went on between them, and the Mainland Indians had learned from the religious genius of the men of Santa Catalina many of the elements of their vigorous Chingichnich cult, it was whispered that the Islanders were fierce wizards. Legends tell of a mysterious temple complex where the Indians from all the Channel Islands gathered once a year to worship Chingichnich, their sun god. Their highly formalized and ritualized religion involved temples called *yuva'r,* sacred open-air enclosures with elaborate poles and banners decorated in feathers. An image of Chingichnich was placed in the *yuva'r* and only old men possessing great "power" could enter. Lengthy and involved ceremonies were performed for every important event in life: birth, puberty, marriage, and death. Offerings of food and goods were presented not only to Chingichnich but also to the owl, raven, crow, and eagle.

THE SPANISH ERA

Early Explorers

The first known white explorer to visit the Indians of Catalina was Juan Rodriguez Cabrillo, a Portuguese navigator sailing under the Spanish flag. He claimed the Island in 1542, and called it San Salvador. Sixty years later a Spaniard, Sebastian Vizcaino, believing he was the Island's discoverer, claimed it for King Philip III. Because his arrival on November 24, 1602, coincided with the Catholic feast of St. Catherine (Catalina) of Alexandria, Vizcaino and his men named the island Santa Catalina in her honor. The Indians gave the crew an enthusiastic, hospitable welcome, and the ship remained in various Catalina harbors for several days. Much has been learned from their logs about the Catalina Indians. We know that they caught fish on barbless hooks and kept dogs as pets — dogs that "do not bark, but howl like coyotes." After Vizcaino's visit, however, the Channel Islands were ignored for more than 150 years. In 1769 an expedition headed by Gaspar de Portola and Friar Junipero Serra claimed all of California for Spain. Catalina was considered as a possible mission location, but the shortage of missionaries and the Island's distance from the Mainland made this impractical. So time and outsiders continued to pass Catalina by.

At the end of the 1700s the Catalina Indians still enjoyed a peaceful, primitive lifestyle, though this was not to last much longer. As Spain established presidios, missions, and pueblos along the California coast, ships discovered the safe harbors of Catalina — and the sea otter. This small, intelligent mammal furnished the most valuable fur found on the entire coast from California to Alaska. Violent competition began among ships and crews to monopolize the feeding grounds of these animals, which had gamboled freely for centuries in the waters of the Channel Islands. Their velvet-like skins, sold regularly to Chinese merchants in Canton, also brought exhorbitant prices from Russian nobility. However, foreign vessels were forbidden by the Spanish colonial government to trade along the California coast. If caught, the ship either had its cargo confiscated or had to pay a 100 percent duty.

The brig *Lelia Byrd* was the first American ship on record to anchor in Catalina waters. Captain William Shaler, his hold loaded with otter skins, put into the Spanish harbor of San Diego desperate for food, water, and repairs. The authorities became suspicious; when they threatened to search the ship, Shaler was forced to make a run for the open sea. He limped into the Bay of the Seven Moons (Avalon Bay) in May 1804. His ship, leaking badly, was careened, and with the aid of the friendly Catalina Indians, he caulked his vessel with lime and tallow. Six weeks later, Shaler sailed on to the Hawaiian Islands and sold his precious cargo of skins to King Kamehameha. From that time on the sea otter was to indirectly cause the extinction of the Catalina Indian.

Final Chapter

The end began in 1806 when a business alliance was formed between the Russian-American Fur Company based in Sitka, Alaska, and two American traders, Joseph O'Cain and Jonathan Winship. With a captive crew of Aleuts and Kodiak Indians, the Russian trappers sailed south along the coast from their colony in Alaska to hunt the sea otter at any risk. The peaceful islanders of Catalina were no match for them. The frenzied hunting lasted for several years, during which not only were the otters almost exterminated, but the Pimugnans were looted, the women raped, and many men slaughtered. By 1832 the population had been decimated, and the few remaining Indians sought refuge with the Mainland missionaries at San Gabriel and San Fernando. Most died within several years, unable to cope with the transition from the Stone Age to the lifestyle and diseases of a more modern civilization.

Pirates And Traders

As early as 1847, a small group of Chinese immigrants entered the United States to make their home in California. Lured from poor towns in China by the stories of high-paying jobs in the gold mines, by 1852 20,000 Chinese were in the state. In those first years California politicians and entrepreneurs welcomed the Chinese as hard-working, dependable laborers willing to work for pennies an hour. They held the lowliest jobs in cigar factories, laundries, kitchens, private homes, railroads, ranches, and gold mines. Resentment against the Chinese developed when, despite their low wages, with enormous frugality and perseverance they often ended up wealthier than their American co-workers.

The Chinese were subjected to a variety of indignities and violent acts ridiculing their dress, almond-shaped eyes, food habits (Chinese ate bamboo shoots, seaweed, salt ginger, and dried duck liver). The queue (a pigtail down his back) was cut by authorities for the slightest infringement of the law. This jingoism fueled anti-immigration legislation.

The cry "California for the Americans" brought about various laws over the years. One enacted during the 1850s stated that an immigration head-tax of $50 was to be paid by every foreigner entering the state. Up till then, many sea captains arranged with landowners and big businessmen to pick up in China and deliver cheap labor—all penniless. Under the new law, the captain would have to pay the fee unless he managed to avoid customs. Corrupt sailing masters arriving from the Orient would avoid customs in the larger northern ports and continue south to

Cabrillo and his crew traveled the Pacific in small ships.

Catalina's first mass
transit system,
the stagecoach

Monterey. If they were unsuccessful in finding buyers for their human cargo, they continued on to Catalina, where the Chinese were secreted in Ironbound Bay, Lobster Bay, or Smuggler's Cove to wait for smaller ships to transport them to San Pedro on the Mainland and new work. Even after the laws were repealed there were still periodic political clean-ups; Chinese operating restaurants and laundries in San Francisco were rounded up and loaded on ships supposedly destined for China. However, most were simply hidden on Catalina and other Channel islands until things settled down once more.

Catalina also was used by pirates as a warehouse for contraband, Spanish *vaqueros* tended sheep on the Island, and fur traders made their secret headquarters there. In those early years, Catalina was the scene of both legal and illegal activities, neither of which benefited its development.

Gold

George Yount, a pioneer and otter hunter in the 1830s, told stories on the Mainland of gold-bearing rock he'd seen on Catalina Island. In 1863, miners from everywhere flocked across the channel in anything that floated, and the purple hills of Catalina became the scene of a turbulent gold-mining boom. For "$2 including grub," optimistic miners traveled on boats already loaded with lumber, tools, and provisions to supply the operating mines. Such sloops as the *Ned Beale,* the *Anna Maria,* and the schooner *Commerce* all plied the waters between San Pedro and Catalina's Two Harbors. Phineas Banning, who was destined to play an important part in the history of Catalina Island, advertised that his steamer *Cricket* and his schooner the *San Diego* were available to those who wished to charter them for trips to the "very rich mines" on Catalina. According to old records at the L.A. County Recorder, most of the mining activity was located in the vicinity of Cherry Valley, Two Harbors, and Silver Canyon. Although operating expenses of mining the gold were too high to make it profitable, dreams of grandeur kept these miners groping. Names of claims were as rich as the hopes of the owners: Gem of the Ocean, Pacific Gold, Silver and Galena Co., Diamond Mining, and General Wright Mining Company. Curiously, the last is the name of the Union general responsible for ordering all miners on the Island to abandon their claims and leave their dreams behind.

AN AMERICAN CALIFORNIA

During this period of development (the mid-1800s), many countries cast a wandering eye to the coast of California. Russia, England, France, and America recognized its potential. The coast was perfect for harboring and stocking ships for the long journey to the Orient. The moderate climate provided a long growing season on fertile farmlands. Mexico had forbidden foreign intrusion but was unable to enforce its laws. As a result, many American clipper ships battled the gales around Cape Horn and made a lively profit bringing manufactured goods to the isolated rancheros along the California coast.

A Silver Saddle

Thomas Robbins, an American from Massachusetts, made his first trip to California in 1823. As mate on the *Rover* he got his first glimpse of the Catalina hills rising from the Pacific. After several subsequent trips to California he settled in Santa Barbara, ran a general store, and continued sailing in Channel waters as captain of the schooner *Santa Barbara*. In 1834, he married Encarnacion, the daughter of a rich Santa Barbara landowner, Carlos Carrillo. Known as a good friend to Mexican as well as American officials, Robbins' general store became a gathering place for seafarers who stopped at Santa Barbara.

In the service of Mexican Governor Alvarado, Robbins later commanded the government schooner *California*. In 1839, he asked the governor for possession of Catalina Island. Alvarado did not issue the grant to Robbins or any of the other petitioners for the Island. But in 1846, at the close of the Mexican War when American victory was imminent, provisional Governor Pio Pico signed away Catalina Island to Robbins as a last gesture of his authority. The favorite story of the event suggests that on the 4th of July, with the Americans about to take full control, Governor Pio Pico passed through Santa Barbara in his flight to the Mexican border. The long-sought Catalina grant was swapped with Robbins in exchange for a silver saddle and a fresh horse. After Robbins, many title changes affected the fortunes of Catalina Island.

Guadalupe Treaty

In 1848, with the signing of the Guadalupe Treaty which ended the Mexican War, Catalina was annexed to California, along with Santa Barbara, San Clemente, and the Anacapas. In recent years, however, Mexico has discredited the treaty, and some Mexican citizens strongly believe that Catalina still belongs to Mexico.

Civil War

Occupation of the Island by Union Army troops during the Civil War finally put an end

to the mining activities. For years, historians maintained that this action was taken because the Union believed that the miners were actually Confederate sympathizers who planned to seize Catalina to use as a base for illicit pirate activities by southern privateers. However, research shows that the Union Army's Commander of the Department of the Pacific, Brigadier General George Wright, ordered a company of infantry to take possession of Catalina because he had been having trouble with certain Indian tribes that refused to stay on their reservations north of San Francisco, and he wanted to move them to the Island. A letter written during that period by General Wright describes the condition of the Island:

From a special report which I have just received from the commanding officer on the island, I am well satisfied that it is better adapted for an Indian reservation than I at first supposed. It appears that we found on the island some 80 to 100 people, some few of them mining and the others engaged in stock raising. There are twelve or fifteen small valleys embracing an area of 1,000 or 1,200 acres of good fertile land. The island has on it a large number of wild goats estimated at 15,000, besides quail and small game. It has an abundant supply of fresh running water which can easily be conducted to any part of the island.

In 1887, when this rare picture of the Civil War barracks at Two Harbors was taken, the building was already 20 years old. Pictured in front L to R: a fisherman, Mrs. Walter Whitney, Mrs. Shatto, Mr. Shatto (owner of Catalina), two guests of the Hotel Metropole, Walter Whitney (father of Mrs. Shatto). Just five years later, the Shattos were forced to surrender title to the Island because of financial difficulties.

(Army officials in Washington rejected this proposal and the plan was scrapped.) From this letter it would appear that the water situation was well under control. However, the letter that follows describes the problem:

> In continuation of my report of January 19, 1864, I can now say from personal observation that the so-called big spring has not sufficient water to attempt to lead it to this post, there being not more than half an inch of water at most. This being the case we will refer to the only living stream of any size on the island distant from the isthmus in an air line about six miles, but from the broken and rolling nature of the country will take, in my judgment, ten miles of pipe to reach the post.

Water continued to be a problem for years. The war itself never reached Catalina, but while there, the soldiers constructed a barracks. The barracks still stands, and has since been transformed into a privately owned yacht club. Although Wright's letters implied that Catalina belonged to the government, in fact, it was legally deeded at that time to a man named James Lick.

Title History
After Thomas Robbins, Catalina had several owners. Fellow Santa Barbaran Jose Maria Covarrubias bought the Island from Robbins for $10,000. Next, Albert Packard, a lawyer also from Santa Barbara, gained ownership in 1853 for the all-time bargain price of $1,000. James Lick, eccentric founder of the Lick Observatory, was the next owner. He arrived in San Francisco in 1847 with $40,000 in gold. While other newcomers mined, he began to buy choice pieces of real estate in the city. In 1861, he built the magnificent Lick House, then rented it out and lodged alone in one of its cheapest rooms. At a time when his yearly income was $200,000, he traveled around San Francisco in a dilapidated old buggy pulled by an aged horse. While the public laughed he continued augmenting his fortune.

Built in 1904, the "Angel's Flight" railway operated one car up to the summit of Buena Vista and one car down Lovers Cove. The railway was destroyed by the fire of 1915.

In Los Angeles, he acquired Los Feliz Rancho, now the location of Griffith Park, and from 1863-67 he purchased Catalina Island in quarter shares from four separate owners for $23,000 each. (See "Chain of Title" chart.) Much to his credit, he enjoyed using his money for others, and he funded an old ladies' home, an orphan shelter, a library association, a society for the prevention of cruelty to animals, free public baths, and a memorial to his mother. James Lick died in 1876, and was buried beneath the dome of his powerful telescope on Mt. Hamilton near San Jose, which later developed into the Lick Observatory.

The SCI Company
Lick's trustees sold Catalina in 1887 to the ambitious George R. Shatto for $200,000. Shatto was the first to create and subdivide the town of Avalon. However, he was unable

CHART OF OWNERSHIP TO SANTA CATALINA ISLAND

KING OF SPAIN
Through Spanish occupation of California begun in 1769

|

MEXICO
Through successful revolt against Spain, accomplished in 1822

|

THOMAS M. ROBBINS
By grant on July 4, 1846, from Governor Pio Pico

|

JOSE MARIA COVARRUBIAS
By deed of August 31, 1850, his title being confirmed by
U.S. Land Commission and U.S. Patent

|

ALBERT PACKARD
By deed of October 13, 1853

¾ ¼

JAMES RAY	**EUGENE L. SULLIVAN**
Deed May 14, 1864	Deed June 9, 1858
WALTER HAWXHURST	**CHAS. M. HITCHCOCK**
Sheriff's deed August 6, 1867	Deed Feb 4, 1864

JAMES LICK
By deeds May 23, 1864; May 23, 1865; June 27, 1866; September 16, 1867

|

TRUSTEES OF JAMES LICK TRUST
By deed June 2, 1874

| **J.B. BANNING** | **Lots in Avalon sold to various** |
| Deed Sept. 30, 1891 | **individuals** |

TRUSTEES OF JAMES LICK TRUST
By Sheriff's Sale

|

WILLIAM BANNING
By deed September 20, 1892

|

SANTA CATALINA ISLAND COMPANY
Incorporated October 16, 1894; by deed of May 7, 1896

The Santa Catalina Island Company now owns approximately 13%
of Santa Catalina Island.

Santa Catalina Island Conservancy owns approximately 86% of total land area,
by deed of February 18, 1975.

University of Southern California—Marine Science Center—Big Fisherman's Cove
By deeds of March 8, 1965 and January 26, 1972

Lots in Avalon sold to various individuals approximately 1%

to keep up the mortgage payments and the Lick trustees took the Island back, reselling it in 1892 to William Banning for $128,740. In 1896, he deeded the Island to the newly formed Santa Catalina Island Company (SCI Co.). The company was family owned, the stock held by three Banning brothers—William, Hancock, and J.B.—and their two sisters—Katherine and Anna. The Banning brothers decided to develop Catalina Island into a pleasure resort, and they turned themselves enthusiastically to this task. However, after some major changes to Avalon (see "Casino Point"), the plan was thwarted by the fire in 1915 that leveled the town. Progress came to a halt for lack of capital.

The Wrigley Era
In 1919, chewing gum magnate William Wrigley Jr. bought the major interest in SCI Company for $3,000,000, announcing that "...the development of Santa Catalina Island will be one of the greatest pleasures of my life." A man of his word, he created a fabulous resort within a few short years. Until his death in 1932, Wrigley indulged his love affair with Catalina. He invested huge amounts of money in building projects such as an enormous ballroom housed in the Casino, the first completely round structure built in Southern California. He created a bird park, and invited the public to visit (free of charge) the literally thousands of extraordinary birds that paraded around the "largest bird cage in the world" (built from the ribs of the old Sugarloaf Casino). He developed a baseball field and brought his Chicago Cubs over every year for spring training. He put in costly new utility systems. Catalina soon became the favored vacation spot for the stars and celebrities of Hollywood's Golden Era, as well as an attainable vacationland for regular people...as it is today. In 1932, his son Philip K. Wrigley assumed control of the company, and continued to improve the town which today still rests in the hands of the Wrigleys. Currently, Philip's son, William

William Wrigley Jr.

Wrigley, is seated as the SCI Company's director.

WW II
This growth cycle was interrupted by WW II, when Catalina became a training area for Merchant Marine, Army, Coast Guard, and Navy personnel, including the mysterious OSS (Office of Strategic Service). From 1941-45, tourists were not permitted on the Island. The St. Catherine Hotel was taken over by the Merchant Marine for a cooking school. It never regained its original beauty or its popularity, and in 1965 the classic old hotel was demolished. Several years passed before Catalina was "rediscovered" once again.

SANTA CATALINA ISLAND CONSERVANCY

The Beginning
Since William Wrigley Jr. bought Catalina in 1919, few changes have affected the interior

Airport-In-The-Sky

of the Island. The Wrigley family, which controlled the Santa Catalina Island Company (SCI Co.), was mainly interested in establishing Avalon as a desirable vacation destination. This was accomplished. Catalina's interior, however, was off-limits to anyone but VIPs visiting the Wrigleys, and Islanders who traveled the private roads with a special permit. All of this changed in 1972 when William Wrigley Jr.'s son Philip created a non-profit foundation, the Santa Catalina Island Conservancy, "to preserve and protect open space, wild lands and nature preserve areas for future generations."

L.A. County Involvement

In 1974, an easement agreement gave Los Angeles County the right to share the use of 41,000 acres of Catalina's interior and part of its coastline for parks, conservation, and recreation purposes for 50 years. In 1975, the Santa Catalina Island Conservancy acquired title to 42,139 acres and other assets from the SCI Co. and now owns about 86 percent of Catalina Island, including the acreage and coastline covered by the agreement with L.A. County. This partnership of Conservancy and County was created to bring the Catalina experience to as many people as the area is able to accommodate. However, only the Conservancy bears the considerable financial responsibility for the preserve, including maintaining roads and paying taxes. To help

meet these substantial financial responsibilities, the Conservancy solicits membership.

Preservation

The Conservancy has worked to halt deterioration of Catalina's natural resources, enabling threatened plant and animal species to reestablish. In the past, domestic sheep were allowed to graze and proliferate freely. Along with goats and pigs, these herbivores depleted many native grasses and plants and encouraged the growth of cactus in their place. The preservation program has begun to replenish many of these plants, and the animal populations are kept at numbers the interior lands are able to support. The sheep have been eliminated entirely.

Airport-In-The-Sky

Until 1946 the only planes that landed at Catalina were small amphibians. Shortly before WW II, the tops of two of the tallest hills near the Island's center were cut off to build a landing strip. During the war years, however, this strip was deliberately wrecked, making it unusable in the event of enemy attack. Because of that, the runway to this day has a slight hump three quarters of the way to the end of the strip. Building resumed immediately after the war and a runway and modern terminal were erected. The airport, today called the Airport-In-The-Sky, overlooks rolling hills to the ocean in the background, and is operated by the Santa Catalina Island Conservancy.

United Airlines flew DC-3s for several years from Los Angeles to Catalina. While there are no regularly scheduled flights to the Airport-In-The-Sky today, several charters are available. The 3,200-foot asphalt runway will still handle planes up to and including DC-3s. The $5 landing fee includes overnight tie-down for the first night; it's $5 for each night after that. Any size private aircraft may land. Many small private planes visit Catalina every year and the number of Islanders that fly and park their planes here continues to grow.

The airport, 10 road miles from Avalon, is served by a shuttle which runs frequently to Avalon ($4) and to Two Harbors ($6). A coffee shop is open for breakfast and lunch daily, served on the lovely red-tiled Spanish patio or inside the Runway Cafe. The airport specializes in (among other things) buffalo

tuna cactus flower

burgers and buffalo chili along with a regular menu; tel. 510-2196. For shuttle-bus information, call (213) 510-2078, airport information, call (213) 510-0143. Private planes are welcome from 8 a.m. to 7 p.m. mid-May to mid-October, 8 a.m. to 5 p.m. the rest of the year.

Natural History Museum

Open to the public, the Conservancy-owned and -operated airport is fast becoming the inland hub of Conservancy activities. A small natural history museum here is scheduled for opening in 1988. The museum will continue to expand and diversify, displaying much of the Indian history of Catalina, along with plant, animal, and geology exhibits. Lectures and seminars are given by Catalina resident-naturalist Terry Martin (Terry's book, *Santa Catalina, an Island Adventure,* is a great pictorial review of the Island and is available at the Sugar Loaf Bookstore in Avalon.) College-student interns assist in interpreting the Island for visitors. They will staff the Catalina Conservancy Natural History Center, on airport grounds. Guided nature hikes are also offered (see "Conservancy Tours" below), including trips to some Indian sites. For more information tel. (213) 510-1421.

Plants are an important concern of the Conservancy.

Education

One of the newer extensions developed by the Conservancy is the education program. In addition to tours which foster direct participation, the Conservancy travels to the Mainland to provide informative slide presentations and lectures. These give up-to-date information about the *real* treasures of Catalina Island. For more information call (213) 510-1421.

Intern Program

University science students participate in a program that brings them to the Island for a summer of study and college credit. These interns bunk at Middle Ranch, and are given a crash course in the native plants and animals of Catalina. They assist naturalist Terry Martin in projects in the interior. For more information call (213) 510-1421.

Membership

There are three Conservancy support groups, organized along special interests. The Catalina Marineros are a group for people interested in boating and sailing along the coastline. Catalina Flyers include people who enjoy flying to the Island. Catalina Caballeros involve members who enjoy horseback riding through the interior. These groups join together for year-round tours of the Island followed by festive barbecues, picnics, and dinners. In the fall of 1981, the First Annual "Buffalo Wallow" was held with an inland tour and golf tournament capped by a deep-pit buffalo barbecue and dancing to a bluegrass band in the old hangar at the Airport-In-The-Sky. A Conservancy membership is a satisfying way to insure that the Island will remain the great untainted open space it is now.

There are many ways to get involved; classes of memberships are based on contribution amounts. All members receive the Catalina Conservancy newsletter and other special mailings. Contributions are tax deductible. For more information contact Doug Probst, President, Santa Catalina Island Conservancy, Box 2739, Avalon, CA 90704, tel. (213) 510-1421.

Conservancy Tours

The Conservancy has initiated a program of

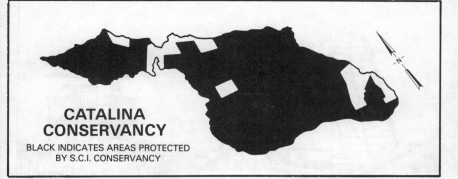

CATALINA CONSERVANCY

BLACK INDICATES AREAS PROTECTED
BY S.C.I. CONSERVANCY

CATALINA CONSERVANCY MEMBERSHIP FEES

Initiation fees:

Student $10

Participating Member $25

Supporting Member $50

Donor $100

Sustaining Member $500

Annual pledge for support groups:

Catalina Caballeros $100

Catalina Marineros $100

Catalina Flyers $100

nature tours to special areas. Reservations must be made by a Conservancy member, but non-members are welcome on the tours. Groups are generally limited to a minimum of 12 and a maximum of 25 persons. Destinations include the Renton Mine area with its abundant animals, plants, and geological formations. The Haypress tour explores the ridge country at Haypress and Toyon Junction, an area of profuse native plant and animal life. Bulrush Canyon tour explores the canyon country, a relatively untouched environment for native flora and fauna. For boaters, the Conservancy provides special nature tours starting from one of the channel-side coves and exploring the country upland from there. Group arrangements are also made from Avalon. These nature treks can last from half a day to three days. Payment is by contribution and covers the cost of transportation. The donation averages from $50 for half day to $200 for the entire group. Tours are conducted by Terry Martin, naturalist for the Catalina Conservancy, or another qualified staff member.

GETTING THERE

There are a variety of ways to get to Catalina Island from Southern California. Several boat lines depart from four handy locations (Newport Beach, Long Beach, San Pedro, and San Diego). You have a choice of two boating destinations on Catalina, Avalon or Two Harbors. If you're in a hurry, there's helicopter and plane service to Pebbly Beach or the Airport-In-The-Sky. Reservations are a must on all transportation to (and from) the Island. Even with reservations you should arrive at all debarkation points at least an hour early to

buy your ticket and check in. If you already have a ticket, it must be stamped before you get in line to board. Being early also allows time to park your car. Parking facilities are ample at each location; the fees vary. You may bring as much luggage as you like, but keep in mind that on all boats passengers handle their own. For a more detailed description of boat rides to Catalina, see "Kidstuff."

FROM ORANGE COUNTY BY SEA

The Holiday
Catalina Passenger Service *Holiday* leaves from Newport Harbor. To get to the terminal, take Pacific Coast Highway (Hwy. 1) to Balboa Drive and follow Balboa Drive to Balboa Pavilion. From April to October, *The Holiday* departs each morning at 9:00 a.m., arrives at 11:15 a.m., departing Avalon the same day at 4:30 p.m. Fares: adult $22 RT, child 12 and younger $11 RT. If you're bringing a bicycle, mention this when making res-

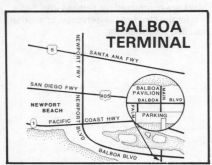

BALBOA TERMINAL

ervations; there's a $3 fee. For reservations call (714) 673-5245. On board are a small snack bar, comfortable inside seats, open deck, and video games.

FROM LONG BEACH BY SEA AND AIR

Catalina Cruise Ships
To get to Catalina Landing in downtown Long Beach, go south on Long Beach Freeway, then turn off at the Downtown Long Beach exit and continue to the Golden Shore exit. Take Golden Shore Blvd. and follow signs that say "Catalina Terminal." The cruise between Long Beach and Avalon on Catalina Cruises takes approximately two hours, part of which is a tour through massive Long Beach Harbor, past the permanently docked *Queen Mary* and the new geodome hangar housing Howard Hughes' giant plane, the *Spruce Goose.*

Fares: adult $21.90 RT, child under 12 $11.70, child under two $1.20. Group rates on request. Bikes are permitted (free), but only at specific sailing times. Wheels must be removed and attached to frame. Each three-deck ship carries 500-700 passengers, with tables and chairs on the inside and wooden benches on the open decks. Two snack bars

sell light snacks and drinks, including beer and wine. During the summer season, there are a minimum of six scheduled round trips a day, with weekend variations. After November, call for the winter schedule. For reservations and schedules, from the Long Beach area call (213) 514-3838; from Orange County (714) 527-7111; from the L.A. area (213) 775-6111. Group rates on request. You'll find a small cafeteria, upstairs restaurant, and gift shop at Catalina Landing in Long Beach.

Special Charters
Seaquest Catalina Charters offers three-day, three-night cruises from Long Beach on luxury sail and power yachts to Avalon and Two Harbors. Private cabins, gourmet meals, dive, fish, etc.; tel. (818) 840-0789.

Helicopter
Island Express Helicopter Service, tel. 1-800 2 AVALON or (213) 510-2525, offers daily flights between Long Beach, the Catalina Terminal in San Pedro, and Avalon. Commuter books are $380 plus tax for 10 one-way rides plus one one-way bonus ride free (good for an entire family), or five one-way rides for $190 plus tax. You're allowed one bag, plus baggage space available. Courtesy van service in Avalon. Commuter books are good for one year. Free parking in Long Beach.

Island Express Helicopter Service.

Catalina Cruise Line passenger ship arriving at Avalon Bay

Catalina Flying Boats

Year-round seaplane service to Catalina Island from Long Beach Airport to Avalon departs Long Beach Airport at Martin Aviation and lands in the ocean at Pebbly Beach seaplane base. The plane is a Grumman Goose, a nine-passenger twin-engine amphibious aircraft. Daily flights are available. Fare: $39.00 OW, $75.00 RT. (Fare does not include FTT tax.) Daily air freight service is available to the Island from 2870 E. Wardlow, Long Beach. For further information and reservations, call (213) 595-5080. **Catalina Flying Boats** is at 4225 Donald Douglas Drive, Long Beach.

Charter Flights

Allied Air Charter has a regular run which leaves Avalon in the early morning (a van fetches you from the hotel) and lands at Long Beach. From there, the return flight departs at 4:15 p.m. Allied also offers twin-engine charters to other Mainland airports. For information, call (213) 510-1163.

FROM SAN PEDRO BY
SEA AND AIR

Catalina Air And Sea Terminal

Catalina Air and Sea Terminal is located under the Vincent Thomas Bridge in San Pedro. Go to the south end of Harbor Freeway, take the Harbor Blvd. turnoff, and continue for a mile. Follow signs to the Catalina Terminal entrance. From here you have the choice of taking either the Catalina Cruise Line, the Express Line, or a helicopter. Outside parking only.

Catalina Cruise Line

During the summer months **Catalina Cruise Line** runs at least five scheduled round trips each day, with many variations on the weekends. After October 1 winter scheduling allows for two scheduled round trips each day during the week, more according to need on the weekend. Call for winter schedule. The trip takes slightly less than two hours. Fare: adult $21.90 RT, child under 12 $11.70, child under two $1.20. Many travelers carry picnic coolers with lunch or beer for the day. Ask for information if you plan to bring a bike; both wheels must be removed and attached to the frame. There's no extra charge on Catalina Cruise Lines for bikes, but they're only allowed at specific times. Snack bars, inside tables and chairs, outside open deck with wooden benches, plenty of walking space. Reservations are a must, especially in the summer. From the Long Beach area call (213) 514-3838, from the Los Angeles area call (213) 775-6111, from Orange County call (714) 527-7111.

Helitrans

From the Catalina Air-Sea Terminal in San Pedro, Helitrans, a commuter jet helicopter service, offers as many as 25 flights daily to Avalon in the summer. Flying time is a swift 18 minutes. Fare: adult $51.84 OW, $92.88 RT; two to three pieces of luggage allowed free. In Southern California call toll-free (800) 262-1472 or (213) 548-1314 for prices, winter schedule, and reservations.

Catalina Express

These boats are fast—90 minutes from San Pedro to Avalon—with individual airline-type seats and a cabin attendant to serve drinks and snacks. On its sister ship, the **Avalon Express,** there's a VIP stateroom available for private parties, $40 (for the cabin) OW over and above adult fare. It accommodates eight passengers with lounge-type seating. Express boats are available to charter for private parties. Both vessels are equipped with stabilizers for a smoother trip. Fare: adult $25 RT, senior $21 RT, child under 12 $15 RT, and child under two $1. The Express line offers an early-morning trip originating in Avalon and Two Harbors during the summer season. There is a $3 charge for bicycles and surfboards. For round-trip reservations and current schedule, call (213) 519-1212 in San Pedro, or tel. (213) 510-1212 in Catalina.

Island Express Helicopter Service

Daily flights between the Catalina Terminal in San Pedro and Avalon. For reservations and more fare information call (800) 2-AVALON or (213) 510-2525.

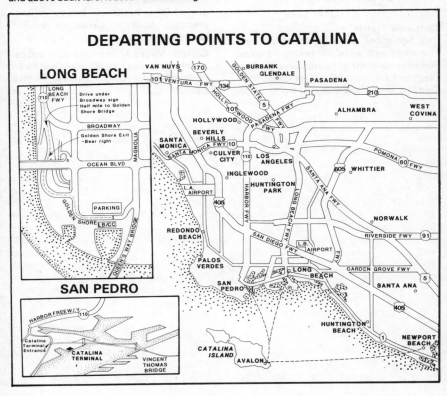

DEPARTING POINTS TO CATALINA

FROM LOS ANGELES BY AIR

Trans World Express
Flights available to Catalina's Airport-In-The-Sky from Orange County Airport and Los Angeles International Airport on weekends only; $19 OW according to availability, regular fare $39 OW. For reservations and schedule call (800) 221-2000.

Allied Air Charter
From Santa Monica to Catalina, $30 per seat. For Catalina information, call (213) 510-1163.

FROM SAN DIEGO BY SEA AND AIR

California Cruisin'
This high-speed passenger catamaran service from San Diego direct to Catalina takes approximately three hours; departs San Diego at 7 a.m. from "B" Street Cruise Ship Terminal, and leaves Avalon at 6 p.m. Complimentary Continental breakfast and afternoon hors d'oeuvres are served and a cocktail and snack bar are on board. Fare: adult $39 RT, senior and military $33, child 12 and under $23. Group tour packages are available. For reservations call (619) 235-8600. Security parking is $4 daily.

Charter Seaplanes
San Diego Sea Planes and surface transportation between airports bring you from San Diego to downtown Avalon and also provide service from San Diego, Orange County, Long Beach, Torrance, and Los Angeles. Direct service also to your boat, camp, or Two Harbors. Call (619) 578-2933.

Also leaving from San Diego is **Southern Wings, Inc.—Sky Limousine,** custom air charter service between Catalina and Montgomery Field, San Diego. One-day tours or overnight. Advance reservations required, tel. (619) 456-1212.

Catalina-Vegas Airline has charter and daily flights between Catalina Island and Montgomery Field, San Diego, California, tel. (619) 292-7311.

Avalon Municipal Hospital

HEALTH AND HELP

Hospital And Paramedics

Avalon Municipal Hospital, 100 Falls Canyon Road, has a highly efficient emergency room, a fully equipped lab, x-ray facility, and an intensive-care unit. Two practicing doctors are permanent residents of Avalon, and at least 20 are on call when in town. In case of a serious emergency, call 911 or 510-0700 for an ambulance to speed you there.

Working hand in hand with the local medical staff, Avalon's highly trained paramedics have saved hundreds of lives with their quick response to emergency situations. *Bay Watch,* the L.A. County lifeguard vessel docked at the Avalon Mole, is manned by paramedics who handle boating and water-related emergencies.

Other Facilities

The Marine Science Center at Two Harbors has one of the few hyperbaric chambers on the Southern California coast, designed to treat divers with the bends (nitrogen poison-

ing). In an extreme situation the Medivac helicopter can transport an emergency case to several hospitals on the Mainland in about 25 minutes. For simple complaints you can be treated at the Avalon Clinic, 204 Metropole, tel. 510-0096. In the event of a sudden toothache that can't wait, call resident dentist Dr. B.A. Calise, 231 Beacon, tel. 510-0322, in Avalon.

HEALTH CARE

Water

Avalon has good clean water straight from the sky. However, if you're hiking through the interior bring water with you. Water at the county campgrounds is potable, but don't drink the water in any streams or lakes. This is good advice wherever you hike since more and more cases of giardiasis are turning up across the States. If you must drink the water—purify it. The easiest way is using purification tablets; Hidroclonozone and Halazone are two, but many brands are available at drugstores. Another common method is to carry a small plastic bottle of liquid bleach (use eight to 10 drops per quart). Whichever you use, let the water stand for 20 minutes to improve the flavor. If you're not prepared with any of the above, boiling the water for 20-30 minutes will purify it. Even though it takes a heck of a lot of fuel when you're carrying it on your back, don't get lazy in this department. You can become very sick drinking contaminated water and you can't tell by looking at it—unless you travel with a microscope!

When camping on the beach where fresh water is scarce, use seawater to wash dishes and even yourself. Liquid Ivory or Joy detergents both suds well in salt water. It only takes a small squirt to do a good job. (A rub of soap on the bottom of pots and pans before use over an open fire makes for easy cleaning of the pots after cooking.)

Sunburn

Sunburn can spoil a vacation quicker than anything else. Approach the sun cautiously. Expose yourself for short periods the first few days; wear a hat and sunglasses. Use a good sunscreen, and apply it to all exposed areas of the body (don't forget your feet, hands, nose, back of the knees, and top of forehead—especially if you have a receding hairline). Remember that after every time you go into the water for a swim, sunscreen lotion must be reapplied. Even after a few days of desensitizing the skin, when spending a day snorkeling, wear a T-shirt in the water to protect the exposed back, and thoroughly douse the back of the neck with sunscreen lotion. PABA (para amino benzoic acid) solutions offer good protection and condition the skin. It's found in many brand names and strengths. The higher the number, the more protection.

If you still get a painful sunburn, stay out of the sun. Cover up with clothes if it's impossible to find protective deep shade (like in the depths of a dark, thick forest). Even in the shade (such as under a beach umbrella), the reflection of the sun off the sand or water will burn your skin. Reburning the skin can result in painful blisters that easily become infected. Soothing suntan lotions, aloe gel, coconut oil, vinegar, cool tea, and preparations like Solarcaine will help relieve the pain. Drink plenty of liquids (especially water) and take tepid showers. Mostly a cure takes just a couple of days out of the sun.

Water Safety

The usual precautions apply: don't swim alone in isolated places, and do take small children to calm surf areas, especially if there isn't a lifeguard. Familiarize yourself with the beach before splashing into the surf. In Avalon the surf is almost always gentle, but at Pebbly Beach and on the Island's back side the surf is much stronger and there are no lifeguards. While swimming, if you feel yourself being pulled out to sea, don't panic, and don't wear yourself out trying to swim to shore. Instead, swim parallel to the beach in either direction, and usually after swimming three or four yards you'll be out of the undertow—then swim to shore. Pebbly Beach especially is noted for undertows, so beware.

Self Help

The smart traveler carries a first-aid kit of some kind with him. If backpacking, at least carry the following:

- alcohol
- adhesive tape
- aspirin
- baking soda
- bandages
- cornstarch
- gauze
- hydrogen peroxide
- iodine
- insect repellent
- Lomotil
- needle

- ✓ pain pills
- ✓ antibiotic ointment
- ✓ pain killer
- ✓ sunscreen
- ✓ tweezers
- ✓ water purification tablets

Even if not out in the wilderness you should carry at least a few bandages, aspirin, and an antibiotic ointment, powder, or both. Keep wounds as clean and dry as possible. If you're planning to backpack in the interior another great addition to your kit is David Werner's book, *Where There Is No Doctor.* It can be ordered for $8.39 from Hesperian Foundation, Box 1692, Palo Alto, CA 94302. Werner drew on his experience living in Mexico's isolated backcountry to create this practical, informative book. Make sure your tetanus vaccination is current before you leave home especially if you're backpacking in isolated regions.

Emergency Telephone Numbers

Ambulance, paramedics, and Fire
Dept. — 911 or 510-2233
Hospital — 911 or 510-0700
Harbormaster — 510-0535
Police — 911 or 510-0174

Emergency Toll-free Mainland Numbers

Pollution and Oil Spills — (800) 424-8802
Runaway Hotline — (800) 448-4663

Emergency Mainland Numbers—Toll

Coast Guard Search and Rescue — (213) 590-2225
FBI — (213) 477-6565
Poison Control Center — (213) 484-5151

Insurance ID Card

Carry proper identification and a medical insurance card with you. If you need to use a medical facility, your card will expedite matters, just as it does on the Mainland.

SIMPLE FIRST-AID GUIDE

Acute Allergic Reaction

This, the most serious complication of insect bites or stings, can be fatal. Common symptoms are hives, rash, pallor, nausea, tightness in chest or throat, trouble in speaking or breathing. Be alert for symptoms. If they appear, get prompt medical help. Start CPR if needed and continue until medical help is available.

Animal Bites

Bites, especially on face and neck, need immediate medical attention. If possible, catch and hold the animal for observation, taking care not to be bitten. Wash the wound with soap and water (hold under running water for two to three minutes unless bleeding is heavy). *Do not* use iodine or other antiseptic. Bandage. This also applies to bites by human beings. In case of human bites the danger of infection is high.

Bee Or Wasp Stings

If available apply cold compresses quickly. Try to remove stinger by gentle scraping with clean fingernail and continue cold applications till pain is gone. Be alert for symptoms of acute allergic reaction or infection requiring medical aid.

Bleeding

For severe bleeding apply direct pressure to the wound with bandage or the heel of the hand. Do not remove clothes when blood-soaked; just add others on top and continue pressure till bleeding stops. Elevate bleeding part above heart level. If bleeding continues, apply pressure bandage to arterial points. *Do not* put on tourniquet unless advised by a physician. *Do not* use iodine or other disinfectant. Get medical aid.

(continued)

Blister On Feet

It is better not to open a blister if you can rest the foot. If you can't, wash foot with soap and water; make a small hole at the base of the blister with a needle sterilized in alcohol or in a match flame; drain and cover with a bandage or moleskin. If a blister breaks on its own, wash with soap and water, bandage, and be alert for signs of infection (redness, festering) that call for further attention.

Burns

Minor burns (redness, swelling, pain): apply cold water, or immerse burned part in cold water immediately. Use burn medication if necessary. With deeper burns blisters develop. Immerse in cold water (not ice water) or apply cold compresses for one to two hours. Blot dry and protect with sterile bandage. *Do not* use antiseptic, ointment, or home remedies. Consult a doctor. With very deep burns skin layers are destroyed; skin may be charred. Cover with sterile cloth; be alert for breathing difficulties and treat for shock if necessary. *Do not* remove clothing stuck to burn. *Do not* apply ice. *Do not* use burn remedies. Get medical help quickly.

Cuts

Wash small cuts with clean water and soap. Hold wound under running water. Bandage. Use hydrogen peroxide or other antiseptic. For large wounds see "Bleeding" above. If a finger or toe has been cut off, treat severed end to control bleeding. Put severed part in clean cloth for the doctor (it may be possible to reattach it by surgery). Treat for shock if necessary. Get medical help at once.

Diving Accident

There may be injury to the cervical spine (such as a broken neck). Call for medical help. (See "Drowning and Fractures" below.)

Drowning

Clear airway and start CPR even before trying to get water out of lungs. Continue CPR till medical help arrives. In case of vomiting, turn victim's head to one side to prevent inhaling vomitus.

Food Poisoning

Symptoms appear a varying number of hours after eating and are generally like those of the flu — headache, diarrhea, vomiting, abdominal cramps, fever, a general sick feeling. See a doctor. A rare form, botulism, has a high fatality rate. Symptoms are double vision, inability to swallow, difficulty in speaking, respiratory paralysis. Get to emergency facility at once.

Fractures

Until medical help arrives, *do not* move the victim unless absolutely necessary. Suspected victims of back, neck, or hip injuries should not be moved. Suspected breaks of arms or legs should be splinted to avoid further damage before victim is moved, if moving is necessary.

Heat Exhaustion

Symptoms are cool moist skin, profuse sweating, headache, fatigue, and drowsiness, with essentially normal body temperature. Remove victim to cool surroundings, raise feet and legs, loosen clothing, and apply cool cloths. Give sips of salt water — one teaspoon of salt to a glass of water — for rehydration. If victim vomits, stop fluids, and take the victim to emergency facility as soon as possible.

Heat Stroke

Rush victim to hospital. Heat stroke can be fatal. Victim may be unconscious or severely confused. Skin feels hot, is red and dry, with no perspiration. Body temperature is high. Pulse is rapid. Remove victim to cool area, sponge with cool water or rubbing alcohol; use fans or air conditioning and wrap in wet sheets, but do not over-chill. Massage arms and legs to increase circulation. *Do not* give large amount of liquids. *Do not* give liquids if victim is unconscious.

Jellyfish Stings
Symptom is acute pain and may include feeling of paralysis. Immerse in ice water from five to 10 minutes or apply aromatic spirits of ammonia to remove venom from skin. Be alert for symptoms of acute allergic reaction and/or shock. If this happens, get victim to hospital as soon as possible.

Motion Sickness
Get a prescription from your doctor if boat travel is anticipated and this condition is a problem. Many over-the-counter remedies are sold in the U.S.: Bonine and Dramamine are two. Medication administered in adhesive patches behind the ear is also available by prescription. If you prefer not to take chemicals or get drowsy, try the Sea Band, a cloth band that you place around the pressure point of the wrists. It works through acupressure, without drugs. For more information write: Sea Band, 1645 Palm Beach Lake Blvd., Suite 220, W. Palm Beach, FL 33401, tel. (305) 684-4508.

Muscle Cramps
Usually a result of unaccustomed exertion. "Working" the muscle or kneading with hand relieves cramp. If in water head for shore (don't panic—you can swim even with a muscle cramp), or knead muscle with hand. Call for help if needed.

Mushroom Poisoning
Even a small ingestion may be serious. Induce vomiting immediately if there is any question of mushroom poisoning. Symptoms—vomiting, diarrhea, difficult breathing—may begin in one to two hours or up to 24 hours. Convulsions and delirium may develop. Go to a doctor or emergency facility at once.

Nosebleed
Press bleeding nostril closed, pinch nostrils together, or pack with sterile cotton or gauze. Apply cold to nose and face. Victim should sit up, leaning forward, or lie down with head and shoulders raised. If bleeding does not stop in 10 minutes get medical help.

Obstructed Airway
Find out if victim can talk. If he can talk, encourage him to try to cough obstruction out. If he can't speak, a trained person must apply the Heimlich Maneuver. If you are alone and choking, try to forcefully cough the object out. Or press your fist into your upper abdomen with a quick upward thrust, or lean forward and quickly press your upper abdomen over any firm object with a rounded edge (back of chair, edge of sink, porch railing). Keep trying till the object comes out.

Poison Oak
After contact, wash affected area with alkali-base laundry soap, lathering well. Cortisone creams are helpful when itching and blisters develop.

Puncture Wounds
They often do not bleed, so try to squeeze out some blood. Wash thoroughly with soap and water and apply a sterile bandage. Check with doctor about tetanus. If pain, heat, throbbing, or redness develop, get medical attention at once.

Rabies
Bites from bats, raccoons, rats, or other wild animals are the most common source of rabies today. If bitten try to capture the animal (avoid getting bitten again) so that it can be observed; do not kill the animal unless necessary and try not to injure the head so the brain can be examined. Even if the animal can't be found, you must see a doc-

(continued)

tor, who may decide to use antirabies immunization. In any case, flush the bite with water and apply a dry dressing; keep victim quiet and see a doctor as soon as possible.

Scrapes
Sponge with soap and water; dry. Apply antibiotic ointment or powder and cover with a non-stick dressing (or tape on a piece of cellophane). When healing starts, stop ointment and use antiseptic powder to help scab form. Ask doctor about tetanus.

Shock
Can be a side effect in any kind of injury. Get immediate medical help. Symptoms may be pallor, clammy feeling to the skin, shallow breathing, fast pulse, weakness, or thirst. Loosen clothing, cover victim with blanket but do not apply other heat, and lay him on his back with feet raised. If necessary, start CPR. *Do not* give water or other fluids.

Snakebite
If snake is not poisonous, toothmarks usually appear in an even row (an exception, the poisonous lizard, the Gila monster, shows even tooth marks; not seen on Catalina). Wash the bite with soap and water and apply sterile bandage. See a doctor. If snake is poisonous, puncture marks (one to six) can usually be seen. Kill the snake for identification if possible, taking care not to be bitten. Keep the victim quiet, immobilize the bitten arm or leg, keeping it on a lower level than the heart. If possible, phone ahead to be sure antivenin is available and get medical treatment as soon as possible. *Do not* give alcohol in any form. If treatment must be delayed and snakebite kit is available, use as directed.

Spider Bites
The black widow bite may produce only a light reaction at the place of the bite, but severe pain, a general sick feeling, sweating, abdominal cramps, and breathing and speaking difficulty may develop. The more dangerous brown recluse spider's venom produces severe reaction at the bite, generally in two to eight hours, plus chills, fever, joint pain, nausea, and vomiting. Apply a cold compress to the bite in either case. Get medical aid quickly.

Sprain
Treat as a fracture till injured part has been x-rayed. Raise the sprained ankle or other joint and apply cold compresses or immerse in cold water. If swelling is pronounced, try not to use the injured part till it has been x-rayed. Get prompt medical help.

Sunburn
For skin that is moderately red and slightly swollen, apply wet dressings of gauze dipped in a solution of one tablespoon baking soda and one tablespoon cornstarch to two quarts of cool water. Or take a cool bath with a cup of baking soda mixed in the water. Sunburn remedies are helpful in relieving pain. See a doctor if burn is severe.

Sunstroke
This is a severe emergency. Skin is hot and dry; body temperature is high. The victim may be delirious or unconscious. Get medical help immediately. (See "Heat Stroke.")

Ticks
Cover ticks with mineral oil or kerosene to exclude air from ticks and they will usually drop off or can be lifted off with tweezers in 30 minutes. To avoid infection, take care to remove the whole tick. Wash area with soap and water.

To Save A Knocked-out Tooth
Rinse tooth in cool water, do not scrub it. If possible, replace tooth in socket and hold it in place. If this cannot be done, put the tooth under the tongue, or wrap it in a wet cloth, or drop it in a glass of milk. See a dentist immediately.

PRACTICALITIES

Chamber Of Commerce

This office is located at the foot of the Pleasure Pier. You can obtain helpful information here on just about any Island-related subject, and they're especially helpful for making hotel reservations. Ask for a free directory of businesses in Avalon. Open daily from 8 a.m. to 5 p.m., tel. 510-1520.

News Media

The local paper, *Catalina Islander,* is published once a week. You can purchase it at Sugarloaf Book Store, 403 Crescent Avenue, the Island Pharmacy, Leo's Drug Store, or at the *Islander* office at 615 Crescent Avenue. This small newspaper is mailed to thousands of Mainlanders who enjoy keeping up with Catalina activities. Seasonal schedule changes for transportation are reported, as well as business information. A classified ad section also lists summer and winter housing rentals. Also buy Mainland newspapers at Sugarloaf Bookstore, tel. 510-0077, at several racks around town, and at the mole.

Mail

The post office (tel. 510-0084), in the Atwater Hotel Building, can be reached either from Metropole Street (across from Safeway) or from Sumner Avenue (next to the Atwater Hotel). If you plan to stay on the Island for more than a day or two and would like to receive mail, have it addressed to you care of General Delivery, Avalon, CA 90704. There's no mail delivery in Avalon; it all comes to P.O. boxes in the post office or the General Delivery window. Mail deposited by 3 p.m. will leave Avalon the same day. Mail drops are on the corner of Crescent and Metropole and in the post office.

Telephone

For all parts of Catalina the telephone area code is 213. Public telephone booths are located in the post office arcade and the plaza. Calls to Orange County and Los Angeles County are usually less than $1 for three minutes. Western Union: tel. (800) 648-4100.

The streets of Avalon get swept daily by Melena Saldana.

Restrooms
Men's and women's public restrooms in Avalon are located at the foot of the Pleasure Pier, Boat Terminal Mole, Bird Park, Casino walkway, Island Plaza, and at Pebbly Beach at the Buffalo Nickel look for the sign that says "Buffalo Heads." A drinking fountain is located on each end of Middle Beach.

Public Showers
At the foot of the green Pleasure Pier, coin-operated showers are open to the public. Bring your own towel, soap, and a quarter for each three minutes of shower you desire. Outside on the beach, saltwater showers are available to rinse the sand off.

Lockers
If you're just visiting for the day and need someplace to leave your gear while swim-

ming or eating, storage lockers are available at the Island Plaza and on the mole.

Groceries
Safeway, 123 Metropole, tel. 510-0280; and Fred and Sally's Market, 117 Catalina Avenue, tel. 510-1199. Both deliver for a small fee, check time schedule at the store.

Health Food Store
Health foods, vitamins, literature, fresh-squeezed juices, and sandwiches are available in the arcade at Catalina Provisions, tel. 510-2214.

Laundromat
Island Wash Laundromat, 113 Metropole Avenue, tel. 510-9109, $2 for a wash and dry.

Dry Cleaners
Catalina Cleaners, 210 Metropole, tel. 510-2480, offers one-day service, 9 a.m. to 5 p.m., closed Sunday. They also do alterations.

Drug Stores
Island Pharmacy, 417 Crescent Avenue, tel. 510-0036. Leo's Drug Store, 401 Crescent Avenue, tel. 510-0189. Both are well stocked with camera supplies and film, and other sundries.

Banks
There are two banks on the Island, both in Avalon: National Bank of Catalina, 303 Crescent Avenue, tel. 510-2265; and Bank of San Pedro, 307 Crescent Avenue, tel. 510-1170. Open 9 a.m. to 3 p.m. daily.

Credit Cards
Business is run much like on the Mainland; most businesses accept credit cards. Many do not accept personal checks, but most shops and businesses will accept well-known travelers checks with proper identification.

Diving Supplies
Catalina Divers Supply, Pleasure Pier, tel. 510-0330. Island Marine, 124 Catalina Ave-

nue, tel. 510-0238. Blue Dolphin House, 603 Beacon, tel. 510-1811.

Fishing Supplies
Avalon Boat Stand, Pleasure Pier, tel. 510-0455. Island Marine, 124 Catalina Avenue, tel. 510-0238.

Children's And Infants' Garments
Melody's, 106 Sumner Avenue, tel. 510-0706. The Sand Box, 519 Crescent Avenue, tel. 510-2130. Catalina Kids, 205 Crescent Avenue, tel. 510-1120.

Department Stores
Catalina Island Department Store, 421 Crescent Avenue, tel. 510-0151, sells men's and women's sportswear and bathing suits. Good selection of sweaters and sweatshirts if you forgot to bring something warm for the boat trip.

Unique Shops
For seashells, try Mermaid's Garden, 203 Crescent Ave., tel. 510-0295, or The Little Shell Shop, 105 Pebbly Beach, tel. 510-2127. Grand Traditions, 523 Crescent Avenue, tel. 510-1278, is a gourmet, bed, bath, educational toy, and wine shop, plus a lot more for the discriminating shopper. Upton's House of Wood, 517 Crescent Avenue, tel. 510-0125, displays many of Avalon artist Bud Upton's oil paintings, along with woodcarvings, the infamous "buffalo gold chip," and other unique gifts from Catalina and South Sea islands. Perico Gallery, in the Metropole Market Place, tel. 510-1342, also displays the work of local artists. You'll find watercolors, pen and inks, and prints of Catalina here, along with colorful Catalina bird tiles. The Gold Shop deals not only in gold, but in diamonds as well.

Secondhand Shop
The Gingerblossom at 125 Metropole, tel. 510-0105, is an old-fashioned general store with a little bit of *everything,* some used and some new.

Government
Many visitors are surprised that Catalina is in America, a tax-paying, sixth-class city of Los Angeles County, state of California. The Los Angeles County Health, Fire, and Building Inspection departments provide services for Avalon and Catalina Island. The city receives its police protection under a contract from the Los Angeles County Sheriff Department. Avalon has jurisdiction for three miles out to sea including moorings, sanitation, and police protection. It functions under a city council with an appointed city manager. The

Avalon's only gas station is located at Pebbly Beach.

mayor is chosen from among the council members; in 1987 Catalina elected its first woman mayor, Irene Strobel.

The Law
Although the police department is run by the Los Angeles County Sheriff's Department, there is a resident judge, and a jail and courthouse administered through Avalon. Drinking of any alcoholic beverage on the beach or city streets is prohibited by city ordinance. This is vigorously enforced.

WHAT TO TAKE

Clothes
Go simple. Dress to suit your lifestyle. There isn't a place on the Island that requires a tie. Sundresses and shorts are acceptable everywhere, as are Levi's and T-shirts. Take at least one swimsuit, and a sweater or a light jacket especially for the boat ride; it can get cool on the water once the sun goes down. Sandals are good for pavement and hot sand and a good pair of walking shoes will carry you comfortably over the hiking trails around Avalon town or the interior. There are laundromats in Avalon, so you needn't take your entire wardrobe.

Winter
If you're visiting Avalon in the winter the weather is much the same as it is along the coast of Southern California: around 56-63 degrees F, often rainy. If you plan to be outdoors a lot, bring warm clothes and a raincoat.

Children
If you have kids, bring them! This is a great place for kids. Take several swimsuits for each; kids live on the beach and spend most of their time in the safe waters of Avalon (all small children need supervision). Bring their favorite beach toys and flotation vests or arm rings for safety. Don't forget beach towels. See "Kidstuff" for more details.

Food
Most visitors choose to buy their food on the Island, where there is a variety of choices, ranging from restaurants to convenience stores (see "Food"). Some, however, prefer to carry a cooler or picnic basket over on the boat; there are picnic areas in a variety of scenic places on the Island. Just remember, you'll be doing a lot of walking so you'll only want to carry what you need. Cooking facilities are limited but there are free barbecue pits on the mole, close to where the boat dis-

Divers can rent equipment or bring it over on the boat.

embarks. There's a 50¢ fee to use the picnic grounds located past the golf course, about a one-mile walk from the mole. Your fire permit, required even for barbecues, can be obtained at the County Parks office at 213 Catalina Street.

Photo Equipment
Catalina is a photographer's paradise. There's a picture to take wherever you look: the bay, the Casino, the purple hills, a buffalo, or sun worshippers on the beach. Bring an ample supply of film—it's cheaper at your favorite discount store on the Mainland. However, if you run short, camera supplies (including rentals) are available at the Island Pharmacy and Leo's Drug Store. (See "Cameras and Picture Taking" for more information.)

Pets
If you plan to bring your pet with you to Catalina, it travels free on the boat but must be leashed and muzzled. On the plane pets require a regular priced ticket. For your convenience and in an effort to keep Avalon as clean as possible, the Avalon Humane Society has provided a fenced-in area for your pet to relieve himself alongside the roadway on the Casino side of the bay. Check the Avalon

map. Avalon also has some regulations pertaining to your pets in town. For a helpful pamphlet containing excerpts of the municipal code concerning animals, ask at the Chamber of Commerce office at the foot of the Pleasure Pier, or write to the Avalon Humane Society, Box 1584, Avalon, CA 90704.

Swimming And Diving Equipment
If you enjoy snorkeling, bring your fins and mask. There are many clear deep coves close by that are alive with colorful fish darting through kelp forests. If you're a diver, you may bring your air tanks with you on the boat; air is available in Avalon on the Pleasure Pier. If you don't want to carry it all, tanks and equipment can be rented on the Pleasure Pier at Catalina Divers Supply, tel. 510-0330 in Avalon.

CAMERAS AND PICTURE TAKING

Bring a camera to Catalina. Land and sea combine to provide unforgettable panoramas, well worth taking home with you on film to savor again at your leisure. Many people find simple cameras such as Instamatics or disc-types easy to carry and un-complicated. Others prefer 35mm, which offer higher-quality pictures, are easier than ever to use, and are available in any price range. They can come equipped with built-in light meter, automatic exposure, self-focus, and self-advancing—with little more to do than aim and click.

On the island, whether in the interior with the magnificent buffalo, or along an isolated coast, or in Avalon, picture taking is a natural. Don't miss this chance, bring your camera!

Film

Reasons to bring film with you are: it's cheaper at discount department stores on the Mainland. Reasons *not* to bring lots of film are: if you're backpacking, space may be

a problem, and heat can affect film quality, both before and after exposure. Even in a car, heat is something to consider. To protect the finished product, carry film in an insulated case, something as simple as a styrofoam cooler (the size that handles a 6-pack). Or you can be more sophisticated by buying (for greater cost) a soft-sided insulated bag sold in some camera shops or ordered out of a professional photography magazine. Ideally, it's best to plan ahead and pick up a limited quantity of film as you need it. Obviously if you're planning a day or two in Avalon and staying at a hotel, your film will be just fine.

If you bring your film from home and travel by air where you must go through an x-ray security device, remember to take precau-

---

CATALINA CALENDAR
OF EVENTS

JAN.	Avalon Benefit 50-mile run	JULY	Dixieland Jazz Jamboree Metropolitan Yacht Club Annual Opening Fourth of July Town Fireworks Fourth of July Casino Dance
MARCH	Catalina 10K Race Catalina Marathon Race Annual Avalon Underwater Clean-Up		
APRIL	Easter Sunrise Service and Pageant	AUG.	Coors U.S. Championship Outrigger Race
MAY	Memorial Dance	SEPT.	Catalina Art Festival Billfish Tournament
JUNE	Catalina Island Chamber Music Festival Del Rey Yacht Club Race in Avalon Exchange Club Fishing Tournament	OCT.	Gold Cup Marlin Tournament
		NOV.	Rotary Club 10K Run
		DEC.	New Year's Eve Dance

For more detailed information and exact dates
for each event, call the Chamber of Commerce, tel. (213) 510-1520.

Shooting the extraordinary art of the Casino often takes extraordinary methods.

tions. Each time film is passed through the machine, a little damage is done, especially in high ASA film. It's cumulative, and perhaps one time won't make much difference, but most photographers won't take the chance. With today's tight security at airports, some guards insist on passing your film and camera through the x-ray machine. But whenever possible, request hand inspection. Another alternative is to place it in protective lead bags and pack it in your checked luggage. Lead-lined bags are available at camera shops in two sizes. The larger size holds up to 22 rolls of 35mm film. The smaller size holds eight rolls. If you use fast film, ASA 400 or higher, buy the double lead-lined bag designed to protect more sensitive film. It's also efficient to have an extra lead-lined bag for carrying your film-loaded camera if you want to drop it into a piece of carry-on luggage (and for non-photographers, it protects medications from x-ray damage).

If you decide to request hand examination make it simple for the security guard. Have the film out of boxes, and plastic containers placed together in one clear plastic bag that you can hand him for quick examination both coming and going. He'll also want to look at the camera; if possible, load it after going through security.

Film Processing

For processing film the traveler has several options. Most people take their film home and have it processed at a familiar lab. However, for the traveler shooting lots of film, another option is to buy prepaid Kodak mailers before you leave home and simply drop the film in the post office in Avalon. Be sure to put postage on the inside envelope that will be sent to your home address. Some photographers don't trust the mail and won't let their film out of sight until they reach their own lab, but with the Kodak label all over the yellow envelopes, problems with the mail are rare. In Avalon good photo processing is done at several locations including Leo's Drug Store, 401 Crescent Ave., tel. 510-0189, and Island Pharmacy, 417 Crescent Ave., tel. 510-0036, and for instant processing go to Zap 30 Minutes Photo, 125 Metropole Ave., tel. 510-0479. Remember, outside of the Zap instant service, film is sent to the Mainland, and therefore takes longer to get back. If on the Island for a short visit, be sure and ask the date it will be back.

Camera Protection

Take a few precautions with your camera while traveling. At the beach remember that a combination of wind and sand can really gum up the works and scratch the lens. On 35mm cameras keep a clear skylight filter instead of a lens cap so it can hang around the neck or over the shoulder always at the ready for that spectacular shot that comes when least expected. And if something is going to get scratched, better an $18 filter than a $300 lens. It also helps to carry as little equipment as possible. If you want more than candids and you carry a 35mm camera, basic equipment can be simple. A canvas bag is lighter and less conspicuous than a heavy photo bag. At the nearest surplus store you can find small military bags and webbed belts with eyelet holes to hang canteen pouches and two clip holders. These are the perfect size to hold one or two extra lenses (safely tucked into a canteen pouch), and another filled with film. They're comfortable hanging on the

hips, and free the hands while on long hikes.

Keep your camera dry; carrying it in a couple of big Ziploc bags is instant protection. If you plan to be in small boats that put you close to the water, keep the cameras temporarily in the zipped bags when not in use. Don't *store* cameras in plastic bags for any length of time, because the moisture that builds up in the bag is the same as being in the rain. It's always wise to keep the cameras out of sight when camping. Put your name and address on the camera. Chances are if it gets left behind or stolen it won't matter whether your name is there or not, and don't expect to see it again; however, miracles do happen. You can put a rider on most homeowner's insurance policies for a nominal sum that will cover the cost if a camera is lost or stolen.

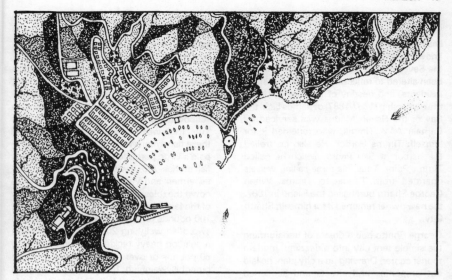

AVALON

INTRODUCTION

HISTORY

In 1987, Avalon turned 100 years old. Though the town has obviously changed in many ways, in 1887 Avalon was a beautiful tent city, where residential lots were auctioned off for as little as $150; today you're lucky to buy one for $50,000 (and at that price you won't see the ocean). In the early days, water was at a premium, sold on street corners by the gallon after being hauled to the Island in barges from the Mainland. Today, the Edison Company and modern technology have it a little easier with reservoirs and pumping stations (but water will always be a problem since its source is unpredictable Mother Nature). The town has cable TV, offering the latest movies, concerts, and soapies, as well as the even more dramatic weekly meetings of the Avalon City Council. New hotels and homes continue to spring up in the one-square-mile town. Vacationers now have the choice of newly built "jet-set" style resorts or historical "quaint" and "charming" old inns—there's even a campground in Avalon.

Most agree that the changes have greatly improved Avalon. But great care has been taken not to destroy the natural beauty of the bay, even though it's loaded most weekends with small boats. The harbor is kept clean, a project in which most boaters are happy to participate. The mountains surrounding the town are as beautiful as ever. There are not now nor will there ever be buildings marring the natural rhythm of the rolling hills.

Timms Harbor And Shatto City

When the first Spanish ships sailed to Catalina Island, the harbor now called Avalon was known by the Pimugna Indians as the Bay of the Seven Moons. Since then, the name has been altered to reflect the changing owners, residents, and destiny of the Island. Under the ownership (1867-1887) of James Lick, the Bay of the Seven Moons was serviced by Captain A.W. Timms, who renamed it for himself: Timms Harbor. He also controlled the harbor at San Pedro, which he called Timms Point. Thus, his three sailing vessels operated from Timms to Timms. When George Shatto purchased the Island in 1887, the new owner renamed it for himself: Shatto City.

George Shatto had a dream of transforming the simple tent city into a dazzling, modern tourist center. Drawing up a city plan, he laid out properties and streets and auctioned them off — from $150 for a 20-foot lot to $2,000 for a larger bayview site. On these small lots people pitched tents or built lean-

tos that could be taken down at the end of their vacations. Small lots were also leased to summer campers for $25 yearly. What's now known as Avalon was the only land on Catalina Island ever sold to private parties. Shatto built the Metropole Hotel, a gathering spot for the social elite, as well as for the sport-fishermen drawn to the harbor for the rich schools of game fish that surrounded it. The Tuna Club was spawned in 1898 by eight of these fishermen who gathered on the Metropole's large porch for long nights of endless fish stories. Along with Fredric Holder, noted fisherman and writer, these sportsmen set down the rules. To belong you had to be one of the few who had taken "...a tuna weighing 100 pounds or over or a swordfish or marlin swordfish weighing 200 pounds or over on regulation heavy tackle; or a tuna weighing 60 pounds or over or a marlin swordfish or broadbill weighing 100 pounds or over on regulation light tackle." This active club's first building, constructed at the turn of the century, was destroyed in the 1915 fire. The

Avalon Harbor in the early days of development, with the tug Falcon pulling into the dock, the elegant Hotel Metropole, the Grand-view Hotel, and the Miramar Hotel located right on the beach next to the bathhouse

A swimming scene from the late 1890s Sugarloaf Rock on the point was later removed and replaced by the Casino in 1929

present structure was built in 1916 at the same location on the edge of the bay. The club goals of the past still apply, and the Tuna Club carries on as a place where gentlemen anglers mingle, as well as honor and protect the sports-fishing waters of Catalina (oh yes, there are women members also).

Avalon

George Shatto's 20-year-old sister, Etta Whitney, christened the harbor "Avalon" from a phrase out of Tennyson's *Idylls of the King*:

> To the island-valley of Avalon:
> Where falls not hail or rain or any snow;
> Nor ever wind blows loudly; but it lies
> Deep-meadow'd happy fair with orchard lawns
> And bowery hollows crown'd with summer sea...

Etta's choice took hold. Soon Avalon was well on its way to becoming the tourist attraction of Shatto's dream, with the completed Metropole Hotel, and his two steamers shuttling people across the channel. There was even the new thrill of glass-bottom boats, invented and perfected by Charley Feige. But

this was not enough for Shatto to meet his financial obligations. After only four years of investment, Shatto's schemes failed and he was forced to sell.

The Banning Family's Avalon

In 1892, the new owner William Banning became the first of his family to realize Catalina's true potential. By 1896 the rest of the family followed, forming the Santa Catalina Island Company (SCI Company) to further develop Avalon as a tourist center. The town grew: beaches were dotted with more and more tents, and hundreds of vacationers swam in Avalon's clear waters, fished for their dinner, and listened to the music of the Metropole orchestra floating over the bay. The adventurous could ride on a stagecoach over the rough back roads of the interior. William Banning was the finest amateur six-in-hand stagecoach driver in the United States. (His father, Phineas Banning, was the builder of quality stagecoaches in Wilmington, California, and a pioneer who ran a stage line along the Southern California coast.) The Bannings also constructed a steep incline railway providing a stunning view of the town and bay from atop Buena Vista Park, as well as a dance pavilion and a public golf course. All of these attractions, along with the glass-bottom boats, were included in the price of the boat ticket to Avalon, or offered for very little extra.

A Growing Town

As more people visited Catalina, the permanent population increased, though the winter population leveled out at 300-400. Other entrepreneurs could see the money to be made, and competition developed over transportation to Avalon. This was the beginning of a nine-year waterfront war, during which barbed-wire fences were raised, torn down, and raised again to keep passengers brought by non-SCI Company transport away from Avalon. Bloody beach-front battles were a common occurrence each summer. The Avalon Freeholders Improvement Association was formed in 1909 to bring peace to the Island community. Though they were unsuccessful, the Municipal Pier (now called the Pleasure Pier) was built under its sponsorship. Turbulent years of civic government followed. Lawsuits were filed and the battle for waterfront rights continued. In 1913, after a hard-fought election—backed by proof that it had 500 residents, Avalon was incorporated as a sixth-class city, the 30th city in Los Angeles County.

However, the Banning Company was still responsible for providing water for the town. Many townspeople felt that the Bannings were not exerting their best efforts to establish a good water system. Much of the water was hauled in on steamers from Torqua Springs, an expensive proposition. The Bannings' dream was coming to life, but profits were slim and the strings of control were inexorably slipping from their hands.

The Fire Of 1915

A devastating fire on November 29, 1915, leveled most of Avalon, horrifically demonstrating the need for a viable water system. For years an aura of suspicion surrounded the mysterious start of the conflagration. Was this someone's way to get rid of the Bannings and perhaps put an end to the ongoing problems of the new city of Avalon? No one knows. After this catastrophe the Bannings implemented an electric plant and saltwater mains for fire protection and sanitation. Drinking water was still hauled in. To replace the fire-gutted Metropole, the SCI Company completed the St. Catherine Hotel in Descanso Bay, by the summer season of 1918. But the financial blow caused by the fire was more than the company could absorb. So after 27 years of Banning management, Wil-

In 1906-07, the Banning family built a fence known as the "Freeholders Fence," trying to control non-paying yachtsmen and "scab" steamers.

liam Wrigley Jr. purchased the Santa Catalina Island Company in 1919. Wrigley proceeded to build and broaden Catalina above and beyond the wildest dreams of either George Shatto or the Banning family.

Wrigley's Island

From 1919 until the beginning of WW II, Avalon's facilities and popularity did nothing but grow. It was the "in place" for Southern Californians to visit. Wrigley was a wise and daring businessman, not afraid to spend money advertising the Island. The Wrigley $10 package deal included round-trip transportation from Los Angeles, a night at the luxurious St. Catherine Hotel, four meals, and an excursion in a glass-bottom boat. He built the Island Villas to replace the tent city that had grown larger every summer during the Bannings' ownership. The villas were small canvas-topped bungalows lined up in close rows where families could stay inexpensively. He sponsored the Wrigley Ocean Marathon in January 1927, awarding $25,000 to the winner of a swimming race from Two Harbors to the San Pedro shore (22 miles). A 17-year-old Canadian, George Young, had bicycled from Toronto, Canada, to take part, and out of 103 contestants only he completed the swim. His official time of 15 hours, 46 minutes, was made in 56-62 degree waters. Over and above the $25,000, Wrigley had offered a special prize of $15,000 to any woman who finished. Hours after Young had landed, two determined women were forcibly removed from the water and awarded $2,500 each for their efforts. Since then, many swimmers have both succeeded and failed. On September 21, 1952, Florence Chadwick swam the channel in 13 hours, 42 minutes. In 1958, Greta Anderson swam both to and from the Mainland in a 26-hour period.

P.K. Wrigley

After the death of William Wrigley Jr. in 1932, his son Philip K. Wrigley ("P.K.") assumed the leadership of the family-owned SCI Company, carrying on the Wrigley tradi-

Philip K. Wrigley, son of William Wrigley Jr., was instrumental in making Avalon a "total resort for Mainland families."

tion of making Avalon an exciting place to visit and an ideal place to live. Everyday utilities taken for granted on the Mainland improved on the Island. Dams were built; pipes were connected; cables were laid. Today, the Southern California Edison Company provides electricity and water.

COMMUNICATIONS

Early Methods

Signal fires between the Island and the Mainland Indians were the first means of communication across the channel. Later, it became common to send messages on infrequently passing boats. By the 1850s, letters arrived by boat once or twice a month. During the gold rush, the miners kept homing pigeons; records show that as late as 1899, carrier pigeons were sent to Los Angeles in as little as 45 minutes! In contrast, a letter sent in 1864 from Two Harbors was 10 days reaching Wilmington, a stagecoach stop on the

Southern California coast. Today, Avalon's post office still cannot match the record of feathered "air mail."

Telephones

In 1902, the world's first commercial wireless radio station was opened in Avalon. In 1903, the Banning Company built a telephone line from Avalon to Two Harbors via Middle Ranch and Little Harbor. Pacific Telephone and Telegraph installed the first commercial telephone system in 1919 at Pebbly Beach, with a sister station at San Pedro. In 1923, Pacific T&T laid two 23-mile-long, 300-ton submarine cables to the Mainland. The Avalon telephone system, one of the longest-lived "number please" systems in operation in the country, wasn't replaced by direct dialing until 1979. Retired Avalon operators still tell stories about the personal-style communication that lasted for so long. If, for instance, an Islander was spending the evening at a friend's but was expecting an important phone call, he'd just lift the receiver and ask the operator to transfer it — today you pay for that same service, called "call forwarding."

The operators knew which numbers were those of the elderly and infirm. Would-be catastrophes were averted by an operator quickly sending a police car to check out an irregularity of a light on her switchboard. One little old lady, a regular patient at the hospital, in spite of repeated instructions on how to use the buzzer to get a nurse, insisted on using her phone to tell the operator to "get that nurse in here right now!" With small-town care and concern the telephone operator would in turn call the hospital main office to pass on the request. Today, Catalina has direct dialing like everywhere else in the United States.

Broadcasting

The first radio broadcasting station on Catalina, little more than a crystal set, was built in 1921 by Lawrence Gordon Mott at his residence on Clarissa Avenue. During the winter of 1922-23, he maintained contact with the McMillan Expedition at the North Pole — for three weeks, he was the only contact the expedition had with the outside world. In the late '20s and '30s, radio shows were com-

Avalon's "number please" operators shortly before the system was abandoned for a telephone service installed in 1979, at the time one of the most sophisticated in all of North America.

mon on the Island, either of random street interviews with vacationers (strolling announcer Gary Breckner was a familiar sight in Avalon, especially when the big white steamer was about to dock) or guests on the SS *Catalina,* and regular broadcasts of big-band music from the Casino. One of the world's first civilian microwave radio systems was installed in 1946, and in 1952 a 10,000-watt radio station, KBIG, was built in the interior of the Island.

Newspapers

The first newspaper printed in Avalon was the *Catalina Wireless,* a small daily published by the *Los Angeles Times* in 1903, which used a wireless radio to communicate news between Avalon and the Mainland. This, however, proved unprofitable and lasted only a short time. Another short-lived paper was a summer tabloid published in the early 1900s by Ernest Windle and George Channing. In 1912, a new *Catalina Wireless* appeared, surviving as a weekly until the big fire of 1915. In 1913, Ernest Windle founded the *Catalina Islander,* which is now produced weekly by the most modern computerized technology.

EDUCATION

From two students in 1888, the Avalon school system has grown to 370-400 children in grades kindergarten through 12. Over the years the "schoolhouse" has been located in a variety of buildings, including the old Sugarloaf Casino, the Congregational Church, and the present Casino. In 1902, the first election was held to approve funds to buy property for a schoolhouse. Fourteen votes were cast, all in favor. In 1923, Avalon Schools were affiliated with the Long Beach School System. William Wrigley Jr. donated a six-acre lot in Falls Canyon, the current site of the elementary and high schools. The 370 current students are taught by 20 teachers. A handful of students are bused from the Two Harbors-coastal area of the interior daily, a

---

MUSIC AND STORIES

Many people who have been impressed by Catalina's natural beauty have communicated this awareness in songs and stories. Al Jolson's "Avalon" continues to perpetuate the town's popularity, and in the '50s the Four Preps' popular "26 Miles Across the Sea" was heard repeatedly on pop radio stations. Catalina has inspired fictitious Indian legends as well as contemporary stories. Even Leroi, the well-fed and much-loved town cat usually found napping in the sun on the Pleasure Pier, had his story written and published by local Avalon author Elizabeth Grieson.

45-minute trip each way. A new, red, one-room schoolhouse at Two Harbors run by the Long Beach School System now makes it possible for the youngest children, kindergarteners to fourth graders (about 14 students), to be instructed close to home.

Reunions

Graduates have always considered themselves a special group of people, fortunate to have grown up in the homey, small-town atmosphere of Catalina Island. Class reunions are held regularly. The largest was held in 1982, open to all students that had ever attended Avalon schools. It was a tremendous turnout; 1,500 people of all ages came from all over the world for a weekend of street parties, barbecues, picnics, and informal get-togethers. It culminated in a grand dinner dance at the Casino Ballroom. The proceeds were donated to the Avalon School to buy modern computer equipment. Businesses like Eric's Hamburger Stand, an institution and student hangout on Pleasure Pier, dropped prices to the "old days" level. Treasured momentoes such as old photos, school sweaters, yearbooks, athletic awards, and trophies were displayed in shop windows.

Houses step up the sides of steep hills, reminiscent of sunny Mediterranean villages.

ISLAND LIVING

Life has its trade-offs, and the pleasant things about living on Catalina Island may not all be measurable in the usual terms. Perhaps the nicest thing about Avalon is its small town warmth combined with the bonus of the Island's natural beauty. Everyone knows everyone else. Some of the families on the Island trace their roots back to the early settlers, and the Catalina Museum presents special certificates to long-time Island residents. Islanders value their history and old timers' memories are guarded carefully on taped oral interviews. In Avalon, social activities abound. Mom isn't a taxi since the kids can walk everywhere. Crime is rare. When tragedy hits, the whole town rallies. And the most amazing thing is that all this is less than an hour from L.A.

Of the million people that travel to Santa Catalina Island every year, there are always a few who decide that this is the way of life they would like to pursue permanently. So the year-round population (about 2,500) of Avalon grows—but not rapidly. Because space is limited; housing is a major problem in Avalon. Because the town is small, there's a restricted number of dwellings, and the cost of housing is very high.

The hardier pioneer-types will adapt to island living, and it will be a joy; but those people who aren't flexible should dismiss the thought. What's considered an adventure for one person could turn into a nightmare for another. Everything that is eaten, drunk, worn, built, or driven must be brought from the Mainland by barge. And though freight service is excellent 90 percent of the year, the barge is occasionally halted by a raging wind or an irate sea. Rarely do two days in a row go by, however, that the barge or boat can't make it. When this does happen, grocery store shelves start to empty and the fresh milk and bread supply gets very low. There's no outgoing or incoming mail, no Mainland newspapers, and of course if you happen to be on the Mainland when this happens, you are stuck there until the storm subsides. Sometimes the sea will crash over the beaches and rush across the road and sidewalk on Crescent Avenue. In 1982, the ocean really flexed its muscles, tearing out part of the sea wall around the Casino, and almost destroying the road and boardwalk to Pebbly Beach.

Water Troubles

Other times it's the rain that affects the Islanders—or the lack of it. Avalon depends almost entirely on rainfall for fresh water; dams and reservoirs capture rainwater before it runs into the sea. Thompson Reservoir holds 326 million gallons. Two pumping stations and eight miles of pipeline are required to convey the water 800 feet up over "The Summit" and back down to Avalon town. During the drought years of 1977-78 the

Islanders were forced to learn a new way of life. Each family was allowed to use only a given amount of water each month; after two warnings their water was turned down to a dribble by the Edison Company. This didn't happen to many; for most the water shortage was dealt with effectively. Five-minute Navy showers became the norm, and faucets were never left to run for any chore. Households learned the easiest ways to recycle their washing machine water—pumping or hand-dipping it into the garden. If toilets weren't already hooked up to a saltwater line, they were converted then. All fire hoses use salt water, and during the drought the streets were hosed down with salt water. If one had a swimming pool and wanted to keep it filled, water was brought from the Mainland in huge tanks on a barge at the pool-owner's expense. These measures proved effective, and many insiders have continued this frugality with water as a way of life.

On the other hand, some years the skies open and water comes in a nonstop deluge. The streams get high, all the reservoirs fill to capacity, and overflow plays havoc with the interior roads. Children who live in any one of the many coves around the Island need to travel to and from school in Avalon by boat when interior roads get washed out. The houses in Avalon are built up the sides of the hills; surprisingly none has ever slid down, as in some Mainland areas.

Shopping

Avalon has a great selection of small shops that carry almost everything needed for day-to-day living. You can buy TVs, refrigerators, and other appliances, but for large furniture and specialty items you go to the Mainland. Goods cost more on the Island since everything must come over on the barge and freight costs are steep. Most Islanders feel though, that the slight increase in price balances their diminished auto expense. A very few people go to the Mainland for groceries and haul them back to Catalina on the boat. (There are even those who refuse to pay freight charges. One man carried most of an automobile to the Island on the boat every week, piece by piece, secreted in boxes and suitcases. Eventually he did have to ship the motor and a few large parts, but he put his car together, content to have saved a lot of money.) Avalon clothing shops carry top-line sportswear, and at summer's end put on a very popular sale. Such crowds turn out (even from the Mainland) that bargain-hunters are admitted into the shops only a few at a time. Like most small towns, there are one or two of everything: two top-quality children and infant shops; two flower and plant shops as well as a garden nursery; two pharmacies; two hardware stores; a stationery shop; two grocery stores. There's even a health food store in the arcade.

CASINO POINT

From prehistory, a large, loaf-shaped rock has jutted out into the sea, around which the Bay of the Seven Moons curved in a gentle crescent. Though the profile and name have changed, from this spot, once known as Sugarloaf Point, you can clearly see the hills of the Mainland on a crystalline day.

A Second Sugarloaf

In the 1890s, when Catalina was owned by the Banning brothers, they tried blasting a tunnel between Avalon Bay and Descanso Bay (at that time known as Banning Cove). The cove was to be the site of the Bannings' home and the tunnel through Sugarloaf Point would provide easy access. The Banning house was built in the cove in 1895; the tunnel collapsed in 1906. However, what appeared to be a setback provided a firm foundation for a new road which followed the coastline from Casino Point to Descanso Bay. The collapse of the tunnel, the first of several changes to the skyline at the Point, left two distinct rock formations instead of one: Big Sugarloaf and Little Sugarloaf.

Big Sugarloaf Bites The Dust

In the devastating fire of 1915, many of Avalon's premier buildings were destroyed. One of the victims was the large, gracious Hotel Metropole on Crescent Avenue, then considered one of the finest hotels in Southern California. By 1917, the Metropole had yet to be rebuilt, and the Bannings decided that Big Sugarloaf should be leveled, with the new hotel constructed in its place. They blasted the rock completely away with black powder—a tricky demolition job in those times. After removing the last of the rock in 1918, the long-awaited hotel, called the St. Catherine, was finally built—not on Sugarloaf Point but in Banning Cove (renamed Descanso Bay). At that time, Little Sugarloaf was still a landmark for sailors because it could be seen from great distances. It was also the location of a treacherously steep stairway built to the top in 1896 where enterprising Island boys offered a steady arm (for 25 cents) to the less hardy who wished to climb to the peak. It was also the favored place to shoot off fireworks on the Fourth of July.

More Construction

The next alteration to the Point took place in 1920, with the addition of a building called the "Sugarloaf Casino" (not to be confused with the present-day Casino). The first was an octagonal, steel-framed stucco building surrounded by a large wood-planked deck. The dance floor, large enough for 250 couples, was also used as a roller-skating rink. One of its two wings once housed a Chinese Tea Room, as well as an elementary school, until the Falls Canyon School was completed in 1925.

Ocean Access

In 1921, a freight wharf was added on the Avalon side of the Point. Shortly after that a ramp and float were installed to receive passengers flying into Avalon from Wilmington on Curtiss Flying Boats and bi-motored Sikorskys. This continued until 1931 when the

Hamilton Beach Amphibian Airport was completed.

The Casino

The destiny of Sugarloaf Point was decided in 1928, when William Wrigley Jr. chose it as the location for a mammoth new casino. The smaller Sugarloaf Casino was dismantled and its octagonal steel frame was placed well up into Avalon Canyon to become the world's largest birdcage, subsequently expanding into the Catalina Bird Park. In March 1929, the last of Little Sugarloaf was blasted away, and the spectacular new Casino began to take shape. Over the years there have been other changes. Landfill added a parking lot. During WW II a battery of anti-aircraft guns was mounted there and a large wooden armory was constructed. Merchant seaman trainees practiced maneuvers on a wooden ship's bow that had been constructed on the

When determining the design of the Casino, William Wrigley Jr. imposed several restrictions before construction began: that Sugarloaf Rock on the point and Mrs. Wrigley's flower garden at the base of the cliff be preserved. The spit of land, being triangular in shape, dictated a circular building as the most logical. Wrigley envisioned a Moorish-style structure with a theater on the bottom level and a large ballroom above. Today the Casino stands alone. Sugarloaf Rock was ultimately removed during the construction.

wharf. It was quite common to see the gleeps (as the trainees were called by the Islanders) marching in their white or navy-blue uniforms along the Casino Road. The wartime buildings have since been removed.

Diving

In 1951, the new attraction on the Point was a diving bell. Viewers descended in a metal tank surrounded with small windows that looked out upon darting fish and undulating giant brown kelp in the clear waters of Catalina. The bell was removed 10 years later, though divers continue to enjoy exploring in this underwater park. Only now they dive with the aid of wetsuits and compressed air tanks.

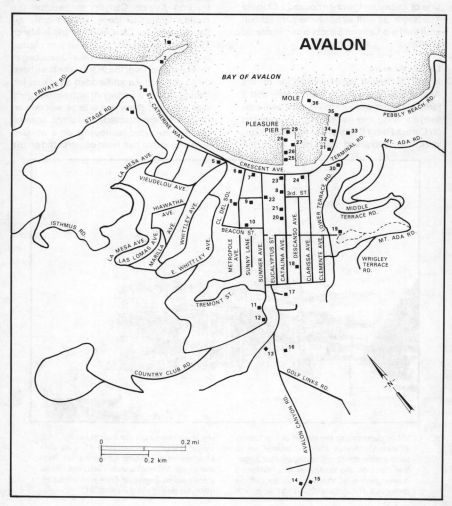

Storms

In 1964, the sea wall was reinforced and a short breakwater was built with rocks from the Pebbly Beach quarry. This protects Avalon during the northeastern storms each winter. The Catalina Channel can turn vicious on occasion. In February 1982, Casino Point bore the fury of one of the worst storms ever recorded on the Island. All through the night giant chunks of cement were torn from the sea wall and hurled onto the area as though they were toy blocks. The ocean crashed repeatedly over the sea wall and breakwater. Fortunately, outside of some water seepage in the lower-level rooms, the Casino—staid lady of Avalon—suffered no harm.

THE CASINO BUILDING

The present Casino is basically the same as the day it was completed in 1929. The years have proved it a sturdy monument to the builders of the past. Large enough to hold Catalina's entire year-round population, it is the city's civil defense shelter. Stored in its many corners and caverns are enough water and emergency supplies to last two weeks. The Casino has become a landmark. Its image *is* Catalina. It gleams white against the sea in the brilliant sunshine and at night lights create dramatic shadows on its walls. Building the Casino was a tremendous engineering feat. A cantilevered structure, two 178-foot girders weighing 50 tons each span the building at right angles. Steel and concrete columns and beams support the main weight of the roof and all floor weight except that of the ballroom. The exterior buttresses carry a vertical load. With its 40-foot-deep foundation, 100,000 sacks of cement and 25,000 yards of concrete, it's a monolith that has already stood for over 50 years, and it will continue its constant vigil over Avalon Bay for many years to come.

Avalon Theater

The main floor of the Casino holds the Avalon Theater, the Catalina Island Museum and the art gallery. The movie theater was designed in the late '20s, around the time "talking pictures" were introduced. Though Wrigley, along with most, didn't have much faith in the success of the talkies, he insisted on perfect acoustics for the theater's sound system. His system was so well designed that in 1931, when the Radio City Music Hall

AVALON

1. underwater park
2. Casino
3. Chimes Tower
4. Zane Grey Hotel
5. El Encanto
6. Metropole Market Place
7. bank
8. grocery store
9. Post Office Arcade
10. Community Church
11. Country Club Tennis Ct., Golf Club
12. Avalon Municipal Hospital
13. Pitch & Putt Golf Course
14. Bird Park Campgrounds
15. picnic grounds
16. golf links
17. La Casitas tennis courts
18. Catalina Bible Church
19. St. Catherine's Catholic Church
20. shuttle bus
21. County Parks Office
22. Island Plaza
23. Catalina Visitor's Center
24. Grand Tradition's Shop
25. Pleasure Pier
26. Chamber of Commerce
27. boat rentals
28. dive shop
29. Fish Market
30. playground
31. basketball court
32. volleyball court
33. Holly Hill House
34. picnic area
35. boat tickets (Mainland boats)
36. Cabrillo Mole

was being built in New York City, engineers involved in that project visited the island to study the acoustics of the Avalon Theater.

A large Page organ was installed in the theater to provide musical accompaniment to the silent movies that, as fate had it, soon faded into the past. Still, the Page was used for several years to add drama and excitement to early talkies shown in the Casino. Organ music itself was popular entertainment in the '20s and '30s, and free concerts were given every day in the summer. Today, the Page organ has great historical value. During the spring of 1979, six men from the Los Angeles Chapter of the American Theatre Organ Society performed the tedious, time-consuming task of replacing leather and felt parts that had been gnawed away by mice that lived in the vast mechanism of the organ during its many years of non-use. They repaired electrical connections and gave the organ a general overhaul for the 50th anniversary of the Casino when, once again, the organ came to full vibrant life.

Today's Theater
The grand-scale art-deco murals in the auditorium have survived the past 55 years intact. They were painted in 1929 by John Gabriel Beckman, a well-known young artist, who also painted Grauman's Chinese Theater in Hollywood. Beckman went on to become an art director for Columbia Studios. In 1986, Beckman was found and commissioned to complete the tile mural along the box office wall. It had been designed in 1929, but never finished. Over 50 years later the tile was set. These theater walls have an intrinsic history and value, which is probably why they have never been replaced or painted over. Although the theater was primarily designed to show movies, many live stage productions have also been performed. During WW II, the theater was used as a classroom for merchant seamen as well as for USO shows, alive with Hollywood's finest stars: Bob Hope, Alice Faye, Kate Smith, Danny Kaye, and Spike Jones, to name a few. Boxing was

a weekly event for the servicemen along with band concerts and radio shows. Today, community groups use the theater regularly for local entertainment, as do convention groups from all over. The theater shows a first-run single feature twice nightly during the summer. The first feature begins at 7:15 p.m. and the second starts at about 9:15 p.m.; adult $5, child $2.50.

The Catalina Museum
This growing museum is well worth visiting. Its three primary areas of interest are archaeology, history, and natural history. Its displays of Indian artifacts from various parts of the Island chronicle the history of Catalina from the days of earliest Indian habitation. See photographs from the 1880s and listen to taped interviews of Catalina old-timers—

John Gabriel Beckman, who did the original art for the Casino Building in 1929, returned in 1987 to add more tile-work above the theater box office.

The museum is a step into Catalina's past. Among Indian artifacts and changing exhibits, various vignettes of the past hundred years include such memorabilia as this from the SS Catalina *and SS* Avalon, *which made thousands of crossings between the Mainland and the Island.*

priceless history if you have time to tune in. Quartered in the Casino's bottom level, the museum's entrance is on the south side of the building. Admission is free.

The Museum Society is a private, nonprofit corporation. It conducts research, offers free lectures on Island-related topics, stages slide shows with taped commentary, and organizes tours of the historical Holly Hill House. Membership is invited; donations and other financial support (tax deductible) are welcomed. For more information write to Catalina Island Museum, Box 366, Avalon, CA 90704.

Art Gallery And Festival

Next to the museum, also on the lower level, is the entrance to the Catalina Art Gallery, admission free. The exhibits, which change frequently, represent both Island and visiting artists. The active Catalina Art Association initiated the Art Festival more than 20 years ago. Held in late September, this event has since become one of the most prestigious art festivals in Southern California and beyond. The Casino ballroom is the scene of the Invitational Exhibit on the first night of the three-day show. Artists that have formerly been awarded prizes for their work are invited to take part in this judging. The streets of Avalon become an outdoor gallery hosting an array of international artists and art enthusiasts. Avalon is proud to have many local artists represented in winning categories. Cash prizes are awarded for the best art entered. For more information, write to the Catalina Art Association, Box 235, Avalon, CA 90704.

Ballroom

The top floor of this Moorish-flavored structure is the world-famous Casino ballroom, scene of massive crowds during the golden era of the big bands. In those days the big white steamer SS *Catalina* carried thousands of passengers to the Island to hear such greats as Glen Miller, Benny Goodman, and Kay Kyser. Designed to give the largest unobstructed dancing area possible, the engineering allowed for 20,000 square feet of dance floor. Built to accommodate 1,500 couples, it very often did. The dance floor is surrounded by a 14-foot open balcony that provides a romantic setting from which to view the lights of town at night. In 1929, when the Casino was opened, only soda and ice cream sundaes were offered at the bar, in the tradition of Wrigley's attitude that Avalon would provide wholesome entertainment for the entire family. Even after Prohibition was repealed, it was not until immediately after WW II that the Casino ballroom began serving liquor.

In 1987, the Casino ballroom was refurbished: new paint, new carpet, new drapes, a new stage, and new kitchen. It is again run by the Santa Catalina Island Company, which encourages the public (both on the Mainland and in Avalon) to rent the ballroom for the evening or afternoon for weddings, receptions, banquets, dances, or other private events. For more information call (213) 510-2000. Catering is available through Ristorante Villa Portofino, known for gourmet food.

Building Maintenance

Maintenance of the Casino is a major expense of the Santa Catalina Island Company. About 570,000 gallons of water a month are used during peak season and the monthly electricity usage has reached as much as 66,000 kilowatts. A resident maintenance man lives in an apartment at the top of the east wing. This apartment has been occupied by only three families since 1929. Bill Bowman was the early maintenance man from 1929 to 1947. Next, Dale Eisenhut was hired as the electrical engineer. He and his wife, Donna (now the librarian at the Avalon County Library), moved in with their 3 young daughters. The giant building—as unique a home to grow up in as one could imagine—became the romping backdrop for the unfolding lives and energies of growing kids. These little girls tricycled around a balcony, which by night metamorphosed into a splendid promenade filled with romance-minded young couples. There was an occasional attempt at "tightrope" walking across a 10-story-high balustrade, and with the passing years the roar of motorcycles was frequently heard as they climbed the broad indoor ramps to the front door of the Eisenhut apartment. Today, Frank Buck holds the position. One important duty is the special cleaning and waxing of the 59-year-old dance floor. Not only has the floor been constantly maintained, but it has actually been enhanced by continuous use. The late Dale Eisenhut commented that the floor was the cleanest and brightest he'd ever seen after a crowd of 4,835 people had danced on it all evening.

Catalina Casino

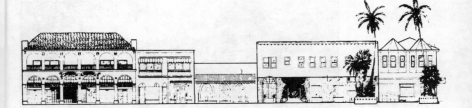

ACCOMMODATIONS

The variety of accommodations on Catalina can be as luxurious or as spartan as your wallet and taste dictate. You can stay on top of a hill with its invigorating walk and views, or you can remain on the flats—close to all downtown activities and just a short walk from the beach. Note: the only lodgings on the island are within the city limits of Avalon; outside the city your only choice is camping. (The only exception to that is the hunting lodge at Two Harbors.) Many hotels and motels offer package deals. During summer months most require a two-day weekend minimum stay and on holiday weekends, a three-day minimum. Condominiums and houses, which offer cooking facilities, are also available. Make reservations as early as possible for summer stays and don't hesitate to visit Avalon in the winter. Winter rates, which begin the middle of October, are considerably cheaper, the weather is usually beautiful, and you'll find fewer tourists, giving Islanders more time to show you what their Island is really like. A local city ordinance states that minor children (under 18) cannot occupy an overnight accommodation unless accompanied by a parent or guardian.

Camping

The cheapest way to stay in Avalon is to bring your tent and camp at the Bird Park Campgrounds for $5 per night. It's a one-mile walk from the Avalon Mole past the golf course on Avalon Canyon Road. There are toilets, cold showers, fire rings, picnic tables,

and barbecue pits. Reservations are necessary; talk to the County Office in the Plaza, tel. (213) 510-0688.

Rock Bottom

If money is a serious consideration, try the Hermosa Hotel, Catalina Beach House, or El Rancho Hotel.

Budget

The Westbrook welcomes divers and longtime Islander owner Blackie is full of Island lore and always ready with a joke. Bayview Hotel is a budget inn and also welcomes divers. At Casa Mariquita, if they know you're on your honeymoon, you'll find a bottle of champagne in your room. These older hotels are few in number so make summer reservations as early as possible; many rooms have shared bathroom facilities.

Picturesque

El Terrado Terrace stretches across a small canyon, each unit with complete cooking facilities. There's a stunning view from Zane Grey Hotel, the historical former home of the late western novelist and big-game fisherman. Glenmore Plaza Hotel, built in 1881, is charming; for a special occasion stay in the unique suite in the cupola (round bed included). The Catalina Island Inn was built in 1906, and the turn-of-the-century flavor has been tastefully preserved. Another with yesteryear charm, the Hotel Catalina has its own small movie theater (seats 30).

Located above town in a lovely canyon, the Catalina Canyon Hotel offers visitors a secluded resort with a Continental restaurant on the grounds.

Modern

Some of the more modern accommodations are Hotel Vicentes, where all rooms have king beds, refrigerators, color televisions, heat and fans. Suites have ocean view. Seaport Village is very new, attractive, from small rooms to suites, and with all the conveniences including a jacuzzi; some have lovely views of the harbor. When you call, ask about their package deals, including transportation from the Mainland. Hotel Villa Portofino has a beachfront location, queen and king beds, some suites with ocean view; downtown and close to all activities. Excellent restaurant and bar on premises.

Luxury

Avalon luxury hotels are not that much more expensive than the average hotel. The pink Hotel St. Lauren was designed to resemble the old circular building that was built on the same spot at the turn of the century. This lovely new structure, built in its place has things the old homestead probably never dreamed of, such as jacuzzi tubs, rooms for the handicapped, elevator, smoking and non-smoking rooms, color TV, phones, honeymoon suites, conference rooms, and all are invited to partake in a Continental breakfast with an ocean view, all a half block from the beach. Rates change depending on the room

and the season. No pets. Catalina Canyon Resort Hotel is built into a beautiful canyon a couple of miles from downtown. The hotel offers modern Mainland touches such as telephones, pool, conference rooms, and terrific restaurant on the premises; a complete resort hotel. Courtesy transportation takes guests back and forth to town or it's a beautiful walk beyond the Catalina Island Golf Club.

Services And Reservations:

Many of the hotels serve complimentary coffee, some provide courtesy transportation one way to or from the mole or airport, and some have jacuzzis, patios, and barbecues. During the summer reservations will insure a room; during the winter you could chance it and probably get a room that suits you. A simple one-call system is handled through the Avalon Chamber of Commerce, tel. (213) 510-1520; they have a good list of current reservations available and will in turn transfer your call to the hotel of your choice. Rates are quite fluid in today's economy and Catalina is definitely affected by the seasons—use the following prices to give you a rough idea of what to expect, or call and double check for the most current prices. Rates do not include a seven percent city bed tax, and all rates are based on double occupancy.

Other Rentals

Another way to save on lodging costs is to rent a house or condo and share it with another family or group. The condos are all fairly new and in many cases offer a swimming pool. Most of the rental cottages are older, but some are larger than some of the condos. If you're interested in this option, buy a copy of the *Catalina Islander* (Editor Don Haney, Box 428, Avalon, CA 90704, tel. 213-510-0500) and check the classified ads, or deal through one of several property managers:

All American Realty, 510-1559.
Beach Realty, 510-0039.
Century Twenty-One Realty,
    510-2112.
CPS Property Services, 510-2242.
Davis-Baker Realty Co., 510-2276.

Loskamp Realty, 510-0480.
Provincial Realty, 510-1495
Santa Catalina Island Co., 510-2000

BED AND BREAKFAST

When planning a vacation, everyone has a fantasy to find dreamlike accommodations. Some fantasies star high-rise hotels with lush rooms, room service, nightclub, color TV, sauna, spa, pool, breathtaking views, and an assortment of gourmet dining rooms. But wait! These daydreams are changing in the U.S. More and more people are choosing to stay in a homey place that offers cushy quilts, a touch of simplicity, clean air away from the bustle of the city, a view of glittering stars at night, a chance to meet warm and friendly

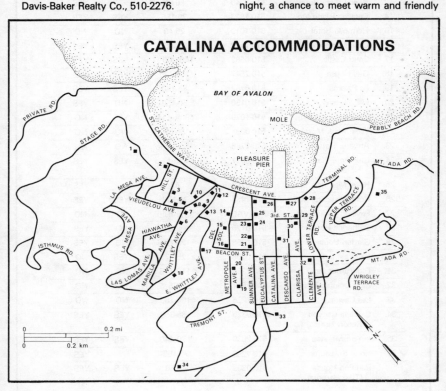

CATALINA ACCOMMODATIONS

Area Code:
(310)

ACCOMMODATIONS

#	Name	Phone	Rates	Transport	Ocean View
✓ 1.	Zane Grey Hotel	510-0966	70-110	YES	YES
2.	Snidow Hotel	510-0746	125-150	YES	NO
3.	Seaport Village Inn	510-0344	74-174	YES	YES
4.	Marilla Inn	510-1651	50-80	NO	NO
5.	El Rancho Hotel	510-0603	40-75	NO	YES
6.	El Terrado Terrace	510-0831	60-100	NO	NO
7.	Catalina Beach House	510-1078	45-70	YES	YES
8.	Hotel Vincentes	510-1115	95-200	NO	YES
9.	Hotel Catalina	510-0027	65-95	NO	YES
10.	Cloud 7	510-0454	75-150	YES	YES
11.	Hotel Villa Portofino	510-0555	70-120	YES	YES
12.	Bayview Hotel	510-0600	60-70	NO	YES
13.	Buena Vista Hotel	510-0340	50-95		YES
14.	Catalina Island Inn	510-1623	75-155	YES	YES
15.	Hermosa Hotel	510-1010	25-49	NO	NO
16.	Casa Mariquita	510-1192	80-220	YES	YES
• 17.	Sand Castle	510-0682	**140-200**	YES	YES
• 18.	Gull House	510-2547	100-125	YES	NO
• 19.	La Paloma	510-0737	85-120	YES	YES
20.	Ida Gardens	510-0150	50-150	NO	YES
21.	Catalina Lodge	510-1070	69 and up	YES	NO
22.	Westbrook Motel	510-0091	50-55	NO	NO
23.	Atwater Hotel	510-1788	49 and up	NO	NO
24.	Glenmore Plaza Hotel	510-0017	69 and up	YES	YES
25.	Hotel Mac Rae	510-0246	42		YES
26.	Hotel Vista Del Mar	510-1452	75-150	YES	YES
27.	Pavilion Lodge	800-4-AVALON	93 and up	NO	NO
28.	Catherine Hotel	510-0170	50 and up	NO	YES
29.	Garden House Inn	510-0356	125-220	NO	YES
30.	Seacrest Inn	510-0196	125-175	YES	NO
31.	Old Turner Inn	510-2236	**110-175**	NO	NO
32.	Blue Dolphin House	510-1811	135	NO	NO
33.	Las Casitas	510-2226	100-180	NO	NO
34.	Catalina Canyon Resort Hotel	510-0325	135-350	YES	YES
35.	Inn on Mt. Ada	510-2030	**170-440**	YES	YES
✓ 36.	Hotel St. Lauren	510-2299	70-165		YES
	Banning House (Two Harbors)	510-0303	45-60	YES	YES

ACCOMMODATIONS

#	Name	Patio	Pool	Restaurant	Cont. Breakfast	Credit Cards
1.	Zane Grey Hotel	YES	YES	NO	YES	YES
2.	Snidow Hotel	YES	NO	NO	YES	NO
3.	Seaport Village Inn	YES	NO	NO	NO	YES
4.	Marilla Inn	YES	NO	NO	NO	YES
5.	El Rancho Hotel	YES	NO	NO	NO	YES
6.	El Terrado Terrace	NO	NO	NO	NO	YES
7.	Catalina Beach House	YES	NO	NO	YES	YES
8.	Hotel Vincentes	YES	NO	NO	NO	YES
9.	Hotel Catalina	YES	NO	NO	NO	YES
10.	Cloud 7	NO	NO	NO	YES	YES
11.	Hotel Villa Portofino	YES	NO	YES	YES	YES
12.	Bayview Hotel	YES	NO	NO	NO	YES
13.	Buena Vista Hotel	YES	NO	NO	NO	NO
14.	Catalina Island Inn	YES	NO	NO	YES	YES
15.	Hermosa Hotel	NO	NO	NO	NO	YES
16.	Casa Mariquita	YES	NO	NO	NO	YES
17.	Sand Castle	YES	NO	NO	YES	YES
18.	Gull House	YES	YES	NO	YES	NO
19.	La Paloma	YES	NO	NO	NO	YES
20.	Ida Gardens	YES	YES	NO	YES	YES
21.	Catalina Lodge	NO	NO	NO	NO	YES
22.	Westbrook Motel	NO	NO	NO	YES	NO
23.	Atwater Hotel	NO	NO	YES	NO	YES
24.	Glenmore Plaza Hotel	NO	NO	YES	NO	YES
25.	Hotel Mac Rae	YES	NO	YES	YES	YES
26.	Hotel Vista Del Mar	YES	NO	YES	YES	
27.	Pavilion Lodge	YES	NO	NO	NO	YES
28.	Catherine Hotel	YES	NO	NO	NO	YES
29.	Garden House Inn	YES	NO	YES	YES	
30.	Seacrest Inn	NO	NO	NO	YES	YES
31.	Old Turner Inn	NO	NO	NO	YES	YES
32.	Blue Dolphin House	NO	NO	NO	NO	YES
33.	Las Casitas	YES	YES	NO	NO	YES
34.	Catalina Canyon Resort Hotel	YES	YES	YES	NO	YES
35.	Inn on Mt. Ada	YES	NO	YES	YES	YES
36.	Hotel St. Lauren	NO	NO	NO	YES	YES
	Banning House (Two Harbors)	YES	NO	NO		YES

fellow guests, and waking to the aroma of coffee and cinnamon rolls in the morning. Put all of this together and you come up with something called a bed and breakfast.

For years the low-key bed and breakfast has been popular in Europe, but it's only in the past 10 years or so that it's really caught on in the States. Bed and breakfast aficionados are the first to tell you though that all B&Bs are not the stuff that fantasies are made of. The "Continental breakfast" which many offer, for example, can mean a number of things. It can be a stale, packaged sweet roll and a cup of weak coffee. Or it can be a wonderful farm-style offering that is enough to hold you all day. The building itself can be a converted old farmhouse, a stately old home, or it can be an old hotel that doesn't live up to the standards of a chain. The newest surprise on Catalina Island is the emergence of five lovely bed and breakfast establishments, which can all be handily recommended.

The Sand Castle
This lovely old house has a view of both the ocean and Avalon Valley surrounded by mountains. The house is one of the oldest on Catalina, built by Count Robert Conrad Mankowski in 1929. Looking for just the right spot for his wife the contessa, he chose this

Sand Castle Bed and Breakfast

lovely knoll overlooking the sea. His instructions to the builder were simple: "Make every room with a view."

Today the old Spanish-style villa is available to a discriminating few; three rooms on the second floor, each with private bath, are open for guests. There's a choice of king, queen, or twin beds. Gardens, terraces, sun decks, and balconies are available to guests

"Jennifer's Room" at the Sand Castle

for relaxation or sunning in private with a good book. The bedrooms are cozy with plush quilts, private baths (some with the original tiles of 1929), and small baskets of fragrant flower petals, fresh flowers, and plants. Visitors are encouraged to use the sundecks that overlook Avalon town and the ocean. The living area, with a fireplace, is on the first floor, breakfast is served in the dining room, and guests are free to dine on the terrace or in the garden. Continental breakfast is fresh orange juice squeezed every morning, along with a choice of hot beverage, and unique recipes of homemade pastries and other goodies (the caramel French toast is wickedly scrumptious). After-noon snacks and occasional dinners are of-fered (like a Fourth of July chili feed on the sun deck while watching fireworks over the bay). The Sand Castle is on the top of a hill (219 East Whittley), a short walk from downtown and the activities of Avalon. Guests have courtesy transportation when arriving and departing. Owner Guy Sanders and his wife Janis go out of their way to wel-come guests. Winter room rates begin at $140 to summer high of $240 (depending on the room); no smoking and no children. Credit cards accepted; for more information and reservations call (213) 510-0682; mailing address is P.O. Box 53, Avalon, CA 90704.

The Inn On Mount Ada

This lovely white "mansion" on a hill overlooking Avalon Bay was formerly the home of the William Wrigley Jr. family. At night the building is lit and gives the impres-sion of floating over the bay. The home was built in 1919 after the Wrigleys bought the island. Totally refurbished and renovated to accommodate visitors of the 1980s, Marlene McAdam and Susie Griffin have created a luxurious, pleasant bed and breakfast. Each bedroom is comfy and attractive; some have fireplaces. The house is beautifully decorated with antiques that fit the era. The views are spectacular; Ada Wrigley loved it because she could watch the sun rise and set. The public rooms are many and spacious, in-cluding a formal living room and dining room, a cozy sun room, and expansive terrace; the butler's pantry is always stocked for do-it-yourself snacks including homemade cook-ies. Wine and hors d'oeuvres are served at cocktail hour. Reservations must be made for dinner (limited seating). A hearty "Ca-talina" breakfast is included with the price, as is the use of a golf cart.

All six rooms have beautiful views and dif-ferent prices; winter rates begin at $140, summer high $440. No smoking or kids un-der 14. Want to have a wedding party? The

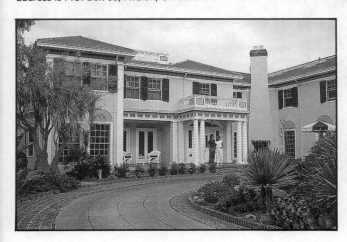

entrance to the Inn on Mt. Ada

entire Inn rents for $1800 to $2500. The surprises at the Inn on Mt. Ada will all be good ones. For reservations call (213) 510-2030 or write to P.O. Box 97, Avalon, CA 90704.

The "Old" Turner Inn

Located downtown near everything, the Old Turner Inn has five guest rooms (four with wood-burning fireplaces), handmade linens, and lovely antique furniture. Breakfast is "upgraded" Continental; wine and snacks are served in the afternoon. Rates are $110 to $165. Located at 232 Catalina Ave., the mailing address is P.O. Box 97, Avalon, CA 90704, tel. (213) 510-2236.

Garden House Inn

Built in the early 1900s, the three-story building has eight rooms with lovely early '30s decor, queen-size beds, private terraces, some rooms with a harbor view. The Inn offers phones and TV, Continental breakfast, afternoon snacks, evening sherry and cookies. Rates begin at $125 to $220; winter discounts are given. No children under 16, no pets, and no smoking. The Inn is located on the corner of Third and Clarissa, one block from the beach. Mailing address is P.O. Box 1881, Avalon, CA 90704, tel. (213) 510-0356.

Gull House

Gull House offers two suites with separate entrances, living room, small pool, spa, and barbecue located on the lower level of owners' Hattie and Bob Michalis' home. The roomy suites are comfortable and offer much privacy. A Continental breakfast is served each morning under an umbrella on the cheery patio. Special attention is given to anniversary and honeymoon couples. Winter rates begin at $70 to summer rates of $110; closed January and February. Gull House is located at 344 Whittley Avenue. For more information and reservations call (213) 510-2547 or write to P.O. Box 1381, Avalon, CA 90704.

dining room at the Inn on Mt. Ada

FOOD

In Avalon, eating can be a gratifying dining experience or merely the exercising of a necessary daily habit. The town offers walk-away hot-dog stands, carry-out tacos, fresh shrimp cocktails in paper cups, and chocolate-covered frozen fruit, as well as culinary treats at a variety of first-class restaurants. As of this printing the big chain burger take-outs haven't yet invaded the Island. There's little difference in price between Catalina's and comparable Southern California's restaurants. If in some instances you notice the price is slightly higher on Catalina, remember that you're on an island; everything you eat starts out on the Mainland and must be barged across the channel.

Choice Places

There are several good Mexican restaurants with atmosphere to match. Mi Casita serves excellent Mexican food. For a family-style cafe and a quick spicy lunch try Saldana's Taco Shop. Some coffee shops like Joe's Place and Dodie's Country Kitchen open for the early fishermen. Several outdoor cafes like the Busy Bee (overlooks the bay, boats, and Casino) and Metropole Market Place offer good food and crowd-watching tables where the pigeons strut close by hoping for a small crumb. Two restaurants — Armstrong's and The Upstairs Place — specialize in fresh seafood and provide a lovely spot to view the ocean while you eat. Italian food lovers have several choices: Antonio's, which serves tasty pizza and creative sandwiches; Prego, with its soft, candle-lit interior, and luscious Italian dishes (try the eggplant parmesan and baseball-sized meatballs); and Villa Portofino, serving outstanding Continental food in lovely, tranquil surroundings. The meat-and-potato fan has many choices for good steak dinners, some with salad bar. For a lively evening and a good steak, go to El Galleon on Crescent Avenue. For a more elegant atmosphere try The Palms on the lower level of the Country Club. *(continued on p. 72)*

EATERIES OF AVALON

Name	Address	Telephone	Meals	Comments
Antonio's Pizzeria	114 Sumner Ave.	510-0060	L,D	Lively atmosphere with Italian food, pizza delivered.
Armstrong's Fish Market & Seafood Restaurant	306 Crescent Ave.	510-0113	L,D	Good seafood, pleasant dining by the sea.
Avalon Seafood	Pleasure Pier	510-0197	L,D	Fish market/fast food, shrimp cocktails to go or watch Rosie cook your abalone steak.
Buffalo Nickel	Pebbly Beach Rd. at airport	510-1323	L,D	Rooftop patio, Continental dinner, call for courtesy transportation.
Busy Bee	304 Crescent Ave.	510-1983	B,L,D	Patio by the sea, great burgers and evening cocktails.
Cafe Metropole	107 Metropole	510-0302	L	Outdoor patio— great sandwiches.
Cafe Prego	603 Crescent Ave.	510-1218	L,D	Sunday brunch.
Canyon Restaurant and Lounge	883 Las Lomas Rd.	510-0327	B,L,D	Continental dinners, tropical drinks.
Casino Restaurant	Casino Point	510-2000	D	Special seasonal dinners.
Catalina Donut Shoppe	122 Catalina Ave.	510-0361	B	Coffee and the freshest donuts.
Catherine Hotel	708 Crescent Ave.	510-0170	D	Happy hour, champagne brunch.
Channel Hopper	4 Cabrillo Mole where the boat leaves	510-1971	L	Carry-out sandwiches, call ahead to have sandwiches ready at boat time.
Channel House	205 Crescent Ave.	510-1617	B,L,D	Great Belgian waffles, patio.

B = Breakfast, L = Lunch, D = Dinner

Descanso Beach Club	Follow palm trees beyond Casino.	510-0484	L,D	Private club open to public, on the beach, good sandwiches. Weekly barbecue.
Dodie's Country Kitchen	125 Sumner Ave.	510-0081	B,L,D	Homemade pies.
Doug's Harbor Reef Restaurant	Two Harbors	510-0303	L,D	Tropical atmosphere.
El Encanto Patio Restaurant	101 Marilla Ave.	510-0883	L,D	Enjoyable Mexican patio.
El Galleon	411 Crescent Ave.	510-1188	L,D	Good steaks, lively atmosphere, good music in summer, sidewalk cafe.
Eric's	Pleasure Pier	510-0894	L	Homemade chili.
Harbor Grill	313 Crescent Ave.	510-0171	B,L,D	Good salad bar.
Joe's Place	510 Crescent Ave.	510-0491	B,L	For the early riser.
J.L.'s Locker Room	126 Sumner Ave.	510-0258	D	Gathering place for the young at heart.
Lori's Good Stuff	501 Crescent Ave.	510-2489	L	Fresh fruity shakes, vegetable sand- wiches (seasonal).
Lloyd's of Avalon	315 Crescent Ave.	510-0541	L	Walk-away ham- burgers and fries, homemade candy.
Mi Casita	111 Clarissa	510-1772	D	Spanish food.
Mt. Ada	398 Wrigley Terrace Rd.	510-2030	L,D	Reservation only, one seating for each meal.
The Palms	Country Club Rd.	510-2766	D	Continental food.
Pancake Cottage	118 Catalina Ave.	510-0726	B,L	Great breakfast house.
Pete's Snack Bar	132 Sumner Ave.	510-0523	B,L	Patio, great omelettes.
Picnic Fry	104 Clarissa Ave.	510-0587	L	Budget (take-out only) refreshing frozen chocolate- dipped bananas.
Ristorante Villa Portofino	209 Crescent Ave.	510-0508	L,D	First-class Continen- tal food.

(continued)

EATERIES OF AVALON (CONT.)

Name	Address	Telephone	Meals	Comments
Runway Cafe	At the airport	510-2196	B,L	Good buffalo burgers.
The Sand Trap	Pitch and Putt Golf Course	510-1349	L	Terrific sandwiches.
Saldana's Taco Shop	113 Catalina Ave.	510-1176	L,D	Authentic home-style Mexican food.
Sally's Waffle Shop	505 Crescent Ave.	510-0355	B,L	Great waffles.
Solomon's Landing	El Encanto Upstairs	510-1474	D	Oyster bar, large upstairs patio with ocean view.
Sunset Buffet Cruise	On board MV *Phoenix*	510-2000	D	Reservations, seasonal dinner cruise.
Tom Cat's Liquor & Deli	417 Crescent Ave.	510-0345	L	Good after-hours snacks.
Top Of The Island Dinner Tour	Airport-In-The-Sky	510-2000	D	Reservations required, transportation provided.
Twilight Dining Tour	Two Harbors	510-2000	D	Reservations required, boat trip included.

B = Breakfast, L = Lunch, D = Dinner

DESSERT

Are you just looking for something sweet? Try Lloyd's (an Island institution), on the corner of Crescent Avenue and Sumner, and watch real taffy being pulled on machines that have been operating since before WW II. There's a difference between real saltwater taffy and the imitation. The real stuff is rather hard to bite into at first and tastes like old-fashioned candy. The imitation has wax added, making a soft, slick texture that is easy to bite down on. Try a bag and you'll be an expert. Lloyd's also sells freshly made chocolate fudge, divinity, and pralines. All can be mailed to anywhere in the world. Catalina Ice Cream and Donut Shoppe, 122 Catalina Ave., makes fresh donuts every day and sells quality ice cream cones and super-deluxe banana splits to go. In the Metropole Market Place you'll find the Catalina Cookie Co. with mouth-watering home-style cookies, and Olaf's, serving ice cream in giant waffle

Take a one-mile walk from the waterfront through Avalon Valley to the Avalon picnic grounds.

cones. The Sweet Shoppe, next to Mi Casita, has a complete soda fountain along with a tantalizing display of pastries and candy.

PICNICS

There are barbecue pits the visitor can use free of charge along the mole. A pleasant one-mile walk past the horse stables on Avalon Canyon Road brings you to another picnic area (50 cents pp) with tables and large barbecue pits. Toilet facilities are available. Ask at the Visitor's Information Center, 605

Crescent, across the street from the Pleasure Pier, or call 510-2500 for information. Bring your picnic basket or cooler over on the boat, or shop at one of the two grocery stores in Avalon: Fred and Sally's Market, 117 Catalina Ave., tel. 510-1199; and Safeway, 123 Metropole, tel. 510-0280. Fred and Sally's sells tasty barbecued chicken and ribs; call early — they sell out fast. Both of these markets are not only well stocked with food, but also with crowds of people in the narrow aisles. Tom Cat Liquor Store, 417 Crescent, tel. 510-0656, offers tasty deli sandwiches and trimmings.

KIDSTUFF

Catalina is a family kind of place, where parents bring their young children year after year, generation after generation. This is an island of adventure and learning for children, who then grow up and often return with their own children. This chapter deals with the many things you can bring, show, and do with your children, as well as the many activities they can do on their own. However, this information is pertinent to "kids-at-heart" of any age, who are certain to get a childlike thrill from a trip to Catalina.

What To Take

For summer travel, bring beach towels and a couple changes of swimwear. Small children should have a hat to protect their heads from the sun, along with sunscreen. Even when the sky is overcast the sun's rays will burn; the reflection from water and the white sand increases the danger. If you forget to bring these necessities from home, drugstores and giftshops carry lotions and sunhats. Take 10 or 20 small plastic sandwich bags and 20 small plastic garbage bags; these come in handy for stashing wet bathing suits and dirty clothes, as well as toting and saving a variety of things during your vacation.

THE TRIP

Flying

Getting to your destination is a large part — if not the largest part — of a child's visit to Catalina. If your youngster hasn't yet had the opportunity to travel on a small plane or helicopter, you might choose to fly to Catalina. This adds to the thrill of the trip, and is a quick way to get there — only about a 20-minute flight from San Pedro Harbor or Long Beach to the Island or a little longer from Los Angeles, San Diego, and Las Vegas. However, flying is expensive for a family (see "Getting There"); boats are an economical way to go.

Boat Travel

Depending on which boat you choose to cross the channel to Catalina, the trip can take one-and-a-half to two hours. Do your children get car-sick? If so, you may presume your child will get an upset stomach at sea. And if not, it's still wise to be prepared. Many over-the-counter remedies are available for motion sickness. Ask the druggist to give you one that doesn't cause drowsiness (unless you *want* him/her to sleep the two hours crossing the channel). To be effective the medication should be taken at least an hour before departure. Seasick pills are sold on-board, but by the time you decide you need it (usually outside of the breakwater) it's too late to do any good.

The best place to sit during a rough crossing is in the center of the lower deck. However, fresh breezes will often help allay queasiness; outside seating is available. On a clear summer day, sitting on the open deck it's easy to get sunburned in two hours, so use protective lotions freely and sun blockers for sensitive skin. Being sunburned can really take the zest out of a vacation. Windburn should also be considered. A good coating of lotion prevents chapping. When you travel in the winter months remember that even though the sun may be shining in the harbor, warm jackets and hats are recommended; the winter wind off the ocean can get very chilly in mid-channel. There are two enclosed decks with tables and chairs; bring a deck of cards or other amusements in case it's the kind of day you want to spend inside.

SIGHTS

The Harbors

If leaving from Long Beach or San Pedro by boat, along with the activities described in this part of the book, there are many guided tours (with reduced fares for children), as well as movies (child $2.50) and game arcades. The first part of the trip from the Mainland takes you past harbors full of ships and many fascinating landmarks. Later, you'll cross channel waters teeming with sealife. If you depart from Long Beach Harbor, you'll pass the permanently docked *Queen Mary*. The *Queen Mary* is one of the largest of the old passenger ships that regularly crossed the Atlantic Ocean between New York and Great Britain. She not only carried passengers paying for luxury service, but also brought thousands of immigrants from Europe to this country. Their quarters were on the lower

It's fun for kids to travel across the channel on a boat. They might see flying fish, seals, porpoise, or even a gray whale.

decks deep within the ship below the water-line. The deeper the deck, the lower the class, and the cheaper the fare. Today, the *Queen Mary* is used as a tourist complex with a hotel (the original staterooms), a variety of trendy shops, or you can buy a ticket and tour the large ship. Its many cafes are open to the public for breakfast, lunch, and dinner on-board. The colorful ceremony of the chang-ing of the guard, with their bright red uni-forms and tall fur hats, takes place several times a day, just as it's done in London. These guards add a touch of old England to the seaside community of Long Beach. For hotel reservations call (213) 432-6964.

Spruce Goose

After passing the *Queen Mary*, you'll see the **Spruce Goose** Geodome hangar in Long Beach Harbor. Airborne only once, the *Goose* was built by Howard Hughes of spruce wood—the largest plane of its time. Besides the plane, there are many exhibits in the hangar and movies are shown all day of the *Goose* on its one and only flight with Howard Hughes in the cockpit. The geodome was de-signed and constructed to give the impres-sion that the huge plane is sitting in the out-doors with a night sky overhead. Climb the stairway to get a closer look into the cockpit. The plane is immense and well worth a trip to take a look. Informational books, souvenirs, and snacks are sold in the geodome. Admis-sion to the complex includes both the *Spruce Goose* and the *Queen Mary;* $14.50 adult, $10.50 juniors $8.50 child under 12. Hours are 9 a.m. to 8 p.m. Good wheelchair access; lots of parking available at the south end of the Long Beach Freeway, $3 cars, $5 over-sized vehicles. Transportation is available be-tween Catalina Landing and the *Queen Mary* and *Spruce Goose* complex; tel. (213) 435-3511.

Shipping

As you pass through either the Long Beach or San Pedro harbors, you'll see many lårge ships from all over the world. Some are giant tankers bringing oil from as far away as the Middle East and North Atlantic. Other ships are enormous "container craft" carrying goods and flying flags from the far-flung cor-ners of the globe. See giant cranes handling these containers quickly and efficiently. Help your kids guess what country the ships hail from by trying to identify the flags and the language the names are written in.

The Breakwater

Looking much like a stone wall, this break-water for many miles parallels the Long Beach and San Pedro coastline, shielding the working part of these harbors from heavy

Leaving Long Beach Harbor the Catalina Cruise Ship passes the Queen Mary *and the* Spruce Goose *Geodome.*

winter storms. The storms can bring rain and powerful winds that turn the Pacific Ocean into a churning, heaving body of water. The breakwater is a deeply planted barrier. Thousands of huge rocks were hauled on large flat barges by tugboats (from Catalina's quarries) and piled on the bottom of the ocean until the wall grew high enough to make the harbors safe and calm. Because of the action of the waves upon the breakwater, it needs constant repair.

From the boat you're traveling on, you may actually see some rock-loaded barges being pulled by a tugboat from Catalina's two rock quarries, one very close to Avalon just beyond Pebbly Beach, and the other at Empire Landing toward the west end of the Island just before Two Harbors. These rock quarries are located near mountains of stone. With dynamite and mechanical equipment, the mountains are broken up into smaller chunks of rock (some weighing as much as a couple of tons) which are then loaded onto barges with giant cranes, taken across the channel, and dumped at the spot where the breakwater is being built or repaired. Projects like this take years to complete.

On The Boat
While you motor through the breakwater, the boat obeys the speed limit within all harbors. Fast moving boats leave a wake (couple of big waves with deep ditches in the water) behind and a small boat caught in that wake could flip over. When you pass through the entrance to the breakwater, you'll see a large flashing light that warns ships traveling at night or in fog that they're near the harbor. Once the boat leaves the protection of the sea wall, it picks up speed. Sometimes it's difficult to get your "sea legs" if the deck is pitching. If it's a calm sea the deck won't move much, but don't be surprised if it's still hard to stand!

Sealife
Watch the water for fish. Different sealife swims the channel depending on the time of

year and the currents. In the winter months, you'll see the mammoth gray whales traveling south to Mexican waters to bear their young in Scammon's Bay off Baja California. Every year they travel 6,000 miles from their summer feeding grounds in the Bering Sea to Mexico and then back. When you see a whale blow a tall stream of water straight up into the air and then dive to the bottom with a flap of its giant tail, it's called "sounding." Often you'll see several of the huge mammals traveling together.

In the summer, you might see porpoises playing in the wake of your boat. They leap out of the water, jump the waves, and dive back into the wake as they follow along. These popular mammals seem to enjoy showing off. At the end of the summer, look for flying fish skimming over the top of the waves. You might see a translucent, bubble-like tube or balloon floating in the water, this is a jellyfish. If you encounter one while swimming, don't touch it and don't stick around; it can give you a painful sting. As you get closer to the Island, you might see a seal that strayed from the rookery (seal colony) located near the east end of the Island. The seals that live on Catalina are California sea lions; intelligent and playful, this is the variety that's trained for circus acts. Sometimes the brown pelicans put on a show if they find a school of fish. Attacking the sea like divebombers, they fill their pouch-like bill with as many of the small shiny fish as possible. A flock of squawking seagulls meets the arriving passenger boats in the harbor every day, waiting for the free lunch thrown by the galley crew.

Docking In Avalon

Depending on the weather, the mountains of the Island will be visible rising out of the sea during most of the trip. From several miles away the white Casino is apparent. As the ship approaches the harbor, the speed is reduced and the captain carefully negotiates the large boat snugly against the dock. Deck hands throw the lines ashore as waiting departing passengers watch. The gangplanks are put into position and you've arrived at Catalina's Cabrillo Mole. If you're traveling on Catalina Cruises, follow the ticket seller's instructions, and make your return reservations as soon as you arrive; the ticket office is conveniently located on the mole. Even if you've already purchased your tickets, they must be stamped at the Catalina office with your return date and time.

IN AVALON

Hotels

With kids, there are several things to keep in mind when choosing a hotel. Some have outside areas where you can wash the sand off before entering. Some also have lockers where you can store beach toys so you won't have to take them to your room; others have outside clothes lines to hang up wet suits and towels. If all these things are important to you, ask when you make reservations. Be sure to find out if there's a hotel courtesy car waiting at the mole. With children and luggage it can be a big help, especially if your hotel is at the top of one of the many hills. If the service is not provided, the tram (50¢ pp) will take you to the central Island Plaza; several taxis also meet the boat. If none is in sight, use the public phone on the mole to call Avalon Taxi (510-0705/510-0025); $3-4 will usually get you and your luggage to the hotel.

Beaches

Avalon is small, a one-square-mile community, and children quickly learn the lay of the land. The biggest attraction for kids is the beach and the water. Avalon is on the lee (protected) side of the Island, so the surf is calm. Although it's a very safe area for children to swim and play in, a Los Angeles County lifeguard is on duty every day until dusk. Small children should be supervised at all times. The beaches in the center of town are sandy, and drop off to deep water very quickly—sooner than most Mainland beaches. **Middle Beach** and **South Beach** each have a diving float with a slide, anchored some 50 feet offshore during the summer months.

North Beach (a very small sandy area) has a retaining wall with steps down to the water's edge. It gets deep quickly when the tide is in and can be quite surgy. This beach is not recommended for small children or any child that cannot swim. A walk along the shoreline from the mole past Abalone Point will bring you to **Lovers Cove**. This rocky beach (without lifeguard) becomes very deep very quickly, so it's not a good play area for toddlers or young children who can't swim. However, because it's a fish preserve, it's a good place to introduce the older *swimming* child to snorkeling.

AVALON RECREATION DEPARTMENT

The following is a brief list of supervised activities for kids offered by the Avalon Recreation Department. Unless otherwise noted, the number to call for information and schedules is (213) 510-0220.

Day Camp

Monday, Wednesday, and Friday from 9:30 a.m. to 1:30 p.m., children (four to 12 years) can attend, with reservations only, a day camp at the City Park. They must bring a bag lunch and a drink that will not spoil (no refrigeration). A fun-filled half-day of various activities includes field trips, games, arts and crafts. Shoes necessary, $4 daily fee. For reservations call 510-0928/510-1987.

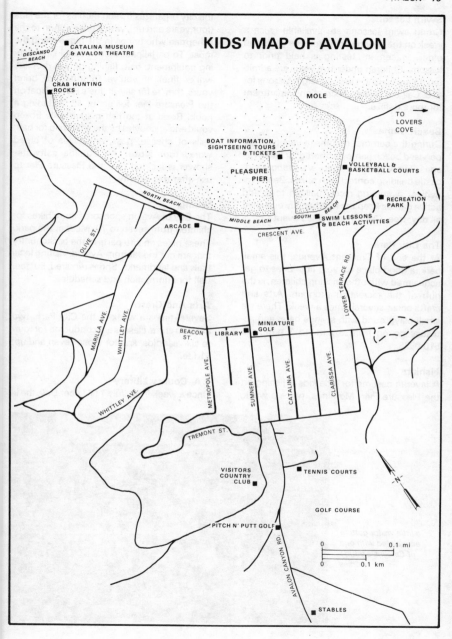

KIDS' MAP OF AVALON

DESCANSO BEACH

CATALINA MUSEUM & AVALON THEATRE

CRAB HUNTING ROCKS

MOLE

TO LOVERS COVE

BOAT INFORMATION, SIGHTSEEING TOURS & TICKETS

PLEASURE PIER

VOLLEYBALL & BASKETBALL COURTS

RECREATION PARK

NORTH BEACH

OLIVE ST.

ARCADE

MIDDLE BEACH

SOUTH BEACH

SWIM LESSONS & BEACH ACTIVITIES

CRESCENT AVE.

LOWER TERRACE RD.

MARILLA AVE.

WHITTLY AVE.

BEACON ST.

LIBRARY

MINIATURE GOLF

CATALINA AVE.

CLARISSA AVE.

WHITTLEY AVE.

METROPOLE AVE.

SUMNER AVE.

TREMONT ST.

VISITORS COUNTRY CLUB

TENNIS COURTS

N

GOLF COURSE

PITCH N' PUTT GOLF

AVALON CANYON RD.

0   0.1 mi
0   0.1 km

STABLES

Swim Lessons

Group swim lessons are available twice a week on the beach to children five years and older. Placement testing is held prior to lessons. Children under five years are admitted if they can pass the test. Eight lessons for $10. Call the Avalon Recreation Department for more details.

Beach Games

During the summer months, a variety of supervised beach games is offered for kids of all ages. Every summer there's a grand sandcastle building contest with prizes. Beach activities, swimming races, balloon toss, and active games keep the kids happily occupied all day, free. Call for scheduled events.

The City Park

At the end of Crescent Avenue, this small park, a good place for your little ones to get acquainted with other visiting children, is the hub of the recreation program. Arts and crafts occur several times a week. There's a small playground with swings here, and activities go on from 9 a.m. to 3 p.m., tel. 510-0928.

Fishing

A favorite pastime for little kids is fishing off the Pleasure Pier. Mornings, twice a week, the city organizes fishing derbies for the kids (four years and up), with a prize ribbon to the fisherman who brings in the biggest and the most. To participate they need minimal fishing equipment: bait, fishing pole (a dropline works fine). If you've forgotten to bring yours, they're for sale at Joe's Rent-a-Boat on the Pleasure Pier for about $2, including a hook. Rosie at the fish market sells frozen squid and anchovies by the small bag for bait; balls of cheese, peas, and wads of bread work, too. **Note:** An outside saltwater shower is located near the Pleasure Pier to use after this activity.

Hiking

The City of Avalon sponsors nature hikes for children from seven to 70. Meet at the park. These hikes go into parts of the backcountry that are not too far from Avalon, visiting local trails and landmarks. Shoes required; 50¢ fee. Call for information and schedule.

Arts And Crafts

Several times a week at the City Park, two arts and crafts classes are conducted for four- to six-year-olds, and for those seven and up; $1 fee.

L.A. County Library

Once a week from July 1 till Labor Day, the li-

a little visitor getting acquainted with one of Catalina's young horses

Catalina giant ice cream cones are enjoyed by kids of all ages.

brary offers a special story time for children pre-school and up. Librarian Donna Eisenhut welcomes children with an up-to-date selection of children's books. The library is at 215 Sumner Avenue. For information, tel. 510-1050.

Special Events
On Wednesday of each week at the City Park, there is a surprise activity (five years and up); scavenger hunt, bingo, art show, and who knows what else. 50¢ fee.

Beach Bingo
All ages meet at South Beach once a week at 6 p.m. for beach bingo. Lots of great prizes.

Mini Golf Tournament
At the Golf Gardens on Thursday at 8:45 a.m., take part in a mini tournament (eight years to teens). Tee-off time is 9:00 a.m. sharp, prizes; $3 fee.

Softball
Bring mitt and shoes (no bare feet or thongs allowed in the game) for an hour of softball fun at the Avalon Ballfield. First group age five to eight; second group nine and up, all coed. Free.

Teen Volleyball
Bring a group or come to make friends at the volleyball court parallel to South Beach, Thursdays at 3-4 p.m. Basketballs and volleyballs available Monday through Friday; deposit required.

Community Sing-along
On Wednesdays at 7 p.m., all ages are invited to Wrigley Plaza Stage for lots of fun singing oldies and goodies; summer only.

Lip Sync Contest
Come to the Wrigley Plaza Stage on Fridays at 7 p.m. with your tape ready to play. Individual or group acts welcome—bring your best costumes, showmanship, props, whatever it takes. Yes, there are prizes! First-place winners will be invited back for the final competition for a grand prize on Labor Day weekend.

BEACH BUMMING

Rock Crabs And Tidepools

Little children seem to wake up at the crack of dawn, vacation or not, so it's wise to have a couple of surprises up your sleeve to keep them occupied. One morning, surprise them by taking them crab hunting. Six- to nine-year-olds seem to enjoy this the most; younger kids might not be sure-footed enough. You'll be clambering around some big rocks by the ocean, and all involved will probably get wet, so dress for the beach—swim suits and tennis shoes. This activity is best done at low tide; on the night before check the tide timetable on the end of the pier at the Harbormaster's office. Crabs love raw hamburger. If you're out before the grocery stores are open (Fred and Sally's Market: 8 a.m.), most restaurants will sell you a raw hamburger patty. Give each child a small plastic bag of meat and one with cracker crumbs for the tidepools if it's really a low tide. One burger patty should do for two children for about half an hour. Walk along the boardwalk toward Casino Point past the Tuna Club. Below the rails are large rocks along the edge of the water. Look to see if you spot any of these small crabs out scavenging a meal. If you have a sharp eye, you'll see lots of them about one to three inches in size, even though they're almost the color of the rocks. Put the tiniest pinch of raw meat on the top of a rock (not in the water), and these awkward little creatures will rush sidelong to grab the meat in their great claws with delight. If you have a very curious child who wants to examine a crab up close, have them pick it up carefully from behind; it will pinch if given a chance. Have your childen treat them kindly

limpet

periwinkle

and return them gently back to the rocks. Meander toward the Casino along the rocks. If it's really low tide, investigate the small tidepools; the sea is alive with little creatures, wispy grasses, kelp, and sea urchins. The water is clear enough to watch the fish scrambling for the cracker crumbs (crunched up very fine). This is a pleasant, relaxing way to show your children some of the wonders of sealife and work up an appetite for breakfast.

shore crab

Bird And Fish Feeding

All small children love to feed animals, and Avalon has a large resident family of pigeons that strut around town, especially near the Busy Bee Cafe. The pigeons love cracker or bread crumbs and they'll practically do a jig for stale popcorn. The end of the Pleasure Pier is a good place to feed the fish. They'll gather in groups close to the surface for cracker crumbs; however, sometimes a clownish seagull will get there before the fish do. The seagull is such a glutton that it'll try eating just about anything, even if it's not edible. Most animals, fish and gulls included, are just like us: they seem the hungriest early in the morning and at dusk.

Boating For Kids

If your kids are 11 or older, renting a rowboat is always an adventure. Rowing around the harbor gives them plenty of exercise and they can even fish if they like. The cost is $5 per hour at Joe's Rent-A-Boat on the Pleasure Pier, and they must know how to swim. Joe also rents paddleboards for $3 per hour ($2 deposit).

Beachcombing

Another early-morning activity is beach-combing. Priceless treasures can be found on any of the beaches on Catalina before the crowds arrive. Most children enjoy searching for shells along the waterline. Be sure to bring a plastic bag to hold them. One of the favorites is a small purple shell called the purple olive shell. At one time they were used for money (called *wampum)* by the Catalina Indians, who also used them for making necklaces and ornaments. Other Indians on the Mainland who didn't live close to the ocean would trade precious goods to the Catalina Indians for these shells. Look for tiny mussel shells and baby clam shells. Perhaps you'll be lucky enough to find a rare, delicate chambered nautilus. Another bit of booty found on the beach are tiny bits of colored glass, "ocean jewels" that have been smoothed and polished by the constant movement of the surf and friction with the sand and rocks. Collect these to sparkle in a pretty glass jar full of water set on a sunny windowsill. Seahewn driftwood can be found in intriguing shapes, and who knows what else you'll find. The best part of beachcombing is the sur-

prise you have each day when you look to see what fascinating bits of flotsam and jetsam the sea has carried in on the last tide.

sea star

Older Kids

Volleyball lessons and tournaments are given through the Avalon Recreation Department. The volleyball court is on the road to the mole. A basketball league gets underway in the summer months. Biking on the Island is great fun for the whole family. Pack a picnic and bike up to the Wrigley Memorial and Botanical Garden, out to Pebbly Beach, or the road leading to the Casino. See "Getting Around in Avalon" for more details about bicycles.

OUTDOOR RECREATION

DIVING

Diving Catalina is a unique experience due to the crystal-clear water and fascinating marinelife. Excellent diving locations within 30 feet of the shoreline eliminate tedious walks with heavy equipment over long beaches or rocky shores. Campsites for beach dives are conveniently located on both sides of the Island. Most of the coves along the lee (protected) side offer kelp forests as well as steep cliffs and caves thrust into the foundation of the Island millions of years ago and now alive with sealife. There are wrecks to be explored which, with the caves, are reachable by rental boats available on the Pleasure Pier. Catalina's nearly transparent waters offer visibility ranging from 40 to 80 feet depending on the time of year. Summer blooms of plankton lessen minimum visibility to 30 feet; in the winter visibility can be as much as 100 feet. Bring your underwater camera! Summer water temperature averages 67-70 degrees, winter 56-59 degrees. Call the Avalon Harbor Department to check on weather conditions, tel. (213) 510-0535.

Dive School

If your fantasy is learning to use scuba equipment and roaming the seven seas, you can combine a vacation on Catalina Island with an intensive certification course. Catalina is an ideal place to learn to dive. On the lee side, the water is very clear, the steep drops make for short surface swims, there's only a little surf to contend with, and the marinelife is abundant. The Argo Diving Service offers a certification program as well as a variety of underwater adventures. Certification instruction for beginners costs $200 for about 24 hours of diving. If you're already certified and would like an introduction to the territory, Argo also offers guided tours, private or semi-private, for almost any adventure you dream up: observing, handling, and feeding

Catalina Divers Supply on the Pleasure Pier in Avalon Bay.

fish; underwater photography; night diving; exploring kelp beds and wrecks; taking game such as abalone, scallops, and lobster. Private fees range from $30 hourly, including boat transportation in Catalina waters. For a free packet loaded with good diving information, write to Argo Diving Services, Box 1201, Avalon, CA 90704, tel. (213) 510-2208.

Dive Truck
Catalina Divers Supply parks its equipment truck on Casino Point on weekends year-round—fill your air tanks for $2.50. Their booth is at the Pleasure Pier, open daily from 8:00 a.m. till dark during the summer months; winter hours are shorter. Prerequisites for renting diving supplies are a valid diver's Certification Card and a driver's license. Full line of rental gear is available. For more information, call (213) 510-0320 or write Box 126, Avalon, CA 90704.

DIVE LOCATIONS

The First Underwater Park
Set aside in 1965 by the Avalon City Council, this is a unique underwater park on the lee side, directly off Casino Point. It's the only place within city limits where snorkeling or scuba diving is permitted. Several wrecks have been placed in the park near some of the finest kelp forests in the world, and artificial reef areas have been established to provide additional fish habitats. In this same area are deep underwater cliffs and pinnacles waiting to be explored by the adventurous. The park is often used as the underwater backdrop for Hollywood films.
Note: Removal of game and specimens from the underwater park is prohibited, as well as salvaging artifacts placed there to serve as subject matter for photography. Spearfishing is also illegal.

The *Valiant*
A short distance from Avalon, in Descanso Bay, is the wreck of the *Valiant,* a deep dive site (90-100 feet) on the outer edge of the

On most summer days Casino Point is lined with diving equipment brought by diving students from the Mainland.

Descanso Bay Moorings. The *Catalina Islander* newspaper covered the sinking in 1930:

> The *Valiant* burned for three days and then sank. Divers still occasionally find a small coin-like token that says "good for one drink MV Valiant," an inside joke among guests who sailed during Prohibition days. One of the most costly shipwrecks in Catalina waters, the valuable metals were salvaged long ago. But it's reported that an excess of $75,000 in cash and gems went to the bottom, and no one has ever claimed to have found it! It's necessary to obtain a (free) permit from the Harbor Department to dive the *Valiant* or any other spot within city limits, with the exception of the underwater park off Casino Point.

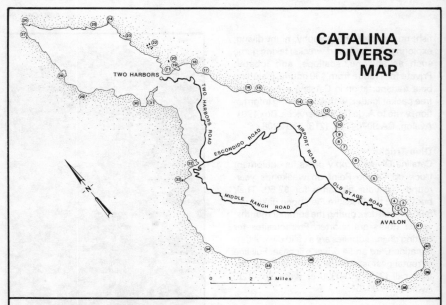

CATALINA DIVERS' MAP

TWO HARBORS

TWO HARBORS ROAD

ESCONDIDO ROAD

AIRPORT ROAD

MIDDLE RANCH ROAD

OLD STAGE ROAD

AVALON

N

0   1   2   3 Miles

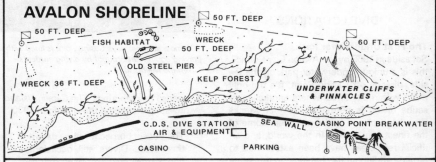

AVALON SHORELINE

50 FT. DEEP

50 FT. DEEP

FISH HABITAT

WRECK
50 FT. DEEP

60 FT. DEEP

OLD STEEL PIER

WRECK 36 FT. DEEP

KELP FOREST

*UNDERWATER CLIFFS
& PINNACLES*

C.D.S. DIVE STATION
AIR & EQUIPMENT

SEA WALL

CASINO POINT BREAKWATER

CASINO

PARKING

CATALINA UNDERWATER PARK

WRECK OF VALIANT
80-120 FT. DEEP

CATALINA UNDERWATER PARK

SEAPLANE LANDING AREA

HAMILTON
BEACH

LOVERS COVE

GAME PRESERVE

SNORKEL
AREA

30 YDS.

SCUBA AREA

CASINO POINT

CABRILLO MOLE

SNORKEL
AREA

W-52   W-51

AVALON BAY

BALBOA BAY
ISLAND BEACH CLUB
&
C.D.S. AQUATIC
SPORTS CENTER

C.D.S.
DIVE STATION

CASINO

CATALINA
DIVERS SUPPLY

AVALON

AVALON

CATALINA DIVER'S MAP KEY

1. Game Preserve. Open to snorkel divers and glass-bottom sightseeing boats only. Look—but don't touch!

2. Permit from Harbor Master required to scuba dive within city limits except in Catalina Underwater Park.

3. Catalina Underwater Park, the first on West Coast. Excellent scuba or snorkel area. Explore, photo. No taking of game or salvage. Dive Station provides air and rentals.

4. Fine snorkel areas flank Descanso Beach Club. Dive, dine and drink in the relaxed atmosphere of a private club.

5 to 6. Rocks and kelp to 40 feet deep. Explore, photo.

7. Large kelp bed to 60 feet deep. Lobster, bass, yellowtail.

8. Moorings, sand bottom, best area for halibut.

9. Fine snorkel and scuba. Abalone, all fish, explore photo.

10. Very clear cove at point; sand, rock and kelp, fine for photos.

11. Deep water, vertical cliffs to 130 feet deep. Caution: strong current and boat traffic.

12. Fine snorkel and scuba. Lobster.

13. Rocks, kelp and sand to 100 feet deep. Lobster, yellowtail.

14. Fair anchorage and snorkel area. Halibut and abalone east.

15. Many small scenic coves, fine photo, exploring.

16 to 17. Steep dropoff at rock quarry. Green abalone shallow, kelp.

18. Small coves, caves, clear water. Excellent photo, explore, lobster.

19. Marine Lab. Good snorkel area. Caution: boat traffic.

20. Kelp bed, abalone, bass, lobster; buoyed reef south, best.

21. Moorings, yacht services and air, in season. Landing permit required.

22. Buoyed reef 20-80 feet deep; kelp, rocks. Explore, photo. Lobster, bass, yellowtail. Caution: occasional heavy current.

23. Moorings, white sand 20-40 feet deep. Fine visibility. Photo and beginners.

24. East and west, explore, photo, abalone, lobster. Caution: strong current on point.

25. Many scenic coves west, photo, explore, abalone.

26. Steep dropoff to 140 feet deep. Caution: strong current and swell.

27. Kelp beds to 60 feet deep. Explore, abalone, lobster, exposed to westerlies.

28. Fair exposed anchorage, kelp to 40 feet deep. Photo, explore, lobster.

29. Cliffs to 140 feet deep. Photo, lobster, scallops.

30. Deep water, photo, lobster, scallops. Caution: current and swell.

31. Shallow inside, moorings, wreck of *Ning Po* awash east. West shore outside, kelp and rocks to 40 feet deep. Explore, lobster, halibut.

32. Protected anchorage, reef awash west, photo, explore, abalone, lobster. Coast northwest, kelp and large rocks, fine explore, abalone, lobster.

33. Coast south, kelp rocks to 80 feet deep. Explore, lobster, abalone, scallops.

34. Kelp beds to 80 feet deep. Lobster, abalone, scallops.

35. Kelp bed 100 yards off point; explore, lobster, abalone, halibut.

36. Beach looks inviting, but shorebreak treacherous. Good offshore kelp beds east; lobster, often poor visibility.

37 to 38. Kelp beds, huge rocks and caves to 60 feet deep. Explore, abalone, lobster. Caution: current and boat traffic off Church Rock.

39. Seal colony, seasonal. Area southeast, abalone, lobster when calm.

40. Deep water, explore, photo, abalone. Caution: boat traffic.

*Catalina's Under-
water Park*

Sue-Jac

A more recent shipwreck (1980) still shrouded in mystery is the *Sue-Jac.* This modern 70-
foot schooner went down during a severe
northeaster while bystanders watched Los
Angeles County's Bay Watch crew rescue all
aboard—three crew members and one dog.
The *Sue-Jac* sank gently and came to rest
on a 90-foot-deep slope, bow down, almost
in one piece. An experienced diver can
swim through an entrance into the cabin
and then out the skylight—an exciting dive
destination.

Other Wrecks

Many believe that in 1598 a Spanish galleon
struck a rock and sank with a reported $2 mil-
lion in bullion and artifacts. In 1602, some of
the goods from the wreckage were found on
Catalina shores, and in 1850 what may have
been part of its hull was found off Ship Rock
in six-plus fathoms. In 1852, a Spanish frigate
sank near the Island with a $1.2 million cargo.
In 1920, the *North Star* sank; in 1924 the
Taurus, a 551-ton U.S. schooner, went down.
1926 took the *William G. Irwin* to the bottom
and in 1929 the *Charles F. Crocker,* an
860-ton U.S. barkentine, foundered. The list
continues with the USS *Koka* sinking in 1937.
Ten years later, in 1947, the *Rossino II* hit bottom off Catalina Head. Basic NOAA charts
show some spots by wreck symbol, with
"PA" (position approximate).

SPECIAL DIVERS'
ACCOMMODATIONS

A few hotels encourage diving clientele by
providing facilities for storing and cleaning
equipment. It's smart to mention your equipment when making reservations.

Bay View Hotel

An older hotel, with men's and women's
showers and toilets on each floor. Washdown facilities for dive gear, outdoor shower,
barbecue pits, jacuzzi, accommodates
groups up to 150. Courtesy car on request.
$55 and up single or double, winter rates
available; 124 Whittley, Box 1017, Avalon,
CA 90704, tel. (213) 510-0600.

Westbrook Motel

Another older hotel, private baths, some
kitchens, center of town, 217 Sumner Ave.,
Box 105, Avalon, CA 90704, tel. (213)
510-0091. From $50, winter and group rates
available.

Blue Dolphin House

Ideal for groups, families, or clubs. Three
units, one- and two- bedroom apartments
with fully equipped kitchens. Saturday to
Saturday weekly summer rental, $650. Win-
ter rate, $600; sleeps six to eight persons. On

a single night basis the fee is $135. Facilities for washing and drying diving gear, outdoor shower, rental equipment for divers. Open-water training and NAUI Certification through NAUI Student Referral Program. Located at 603 Beacon; mailing address Box 2605, Avalon, CA 90704, tel. (213) 510-1811.

La Paloma Cottages
Located in the heart of Avalon (one and a half blocks to beach). Housekeeping cottages and apartments, some with view, peaceful and quiet, wisteria-covered walkways and gardens, kitchens and private baths, TV, radio, heat, barbecue, patios, luggage storage, courtesy car, coffee. Seasonal rates, $85 and up, closed January. Box 1505, Avalon, CA 90704, tel. (213) 510-0737.

Seaport Village Inn
Views, beach one half block away, color TV, spa, sundeck, complimentary coffee, one- and two-bedroom family suites with kitchen, studio suites, view rooms, transportation from boat. Group and package rates, from $74 double. Avalon tel. 510-0344, in San

Diego (619) 571-0663, Southern California (800) 2-CATALINA.

OTHER SPORTS

Horseback Riding
Catalina Stables and Kennel is located on Avalon Canyon Road just past the golf links on the left side of the street. You can ride the picturesque mountain and valley trails on a western saddle. A pony ring is used daily by an active group of Catalina riders. Rentals are available by the hour or day. For information, call (213) 510-0478.

riding through Avalon Canyon

hitting a long ball from number one tee that sits on a small bluff overlooking the road

Golf

The nine-hole, 32-par Catalina Golf Course offers a challenge to all golfers, duffers and experts alike. The course, with its narrow fairways hugged by rugged hills, is considered tricky. Tall eucalyptus trees spill welcome shade across the grass while thick groups of scattered fig trees provide a juicy fruit snack in late summer, yours for the taking. Out of bounds is tall dry grass and brambles. Be prepared for an up-and-down climb. The course is kept in good condition—though occasionally a wild boar makes his way onto the green and digs in the tender grass, but the patient attendants make quick repairs. There's a small putting green, but no driving range. In years past, this was the scene of the Bobby Jones Tournament, Bobby himself participating. Since 1968, the Catalina Golf Course has been the site of the prestigious Catalina Junior Golf Tournament. Held the weekend following Easter Sunday, talented juniors from all over California compete. Several young adults on the pro circuit today began

their careers playing in this tournament— Amy Alcott and Craig Stadler to name two. A pro shop sells the basics: clubs, balls, gloves, hats, and tees. Rentals include clubs and motorized carts. Pro Silky Reyes gives lessons, either group or private. Also fun for the golfer is the nine-hole Pitch and Putt course, a good place to practice your short game or to play if you don't have a lot of time. Located on the Pitch and Putt course is the Sand Trap, a great outdoor sandwich shop that also serves breakfast. To reach the Country Club, walk to the end of Sumner Avenue and on up the small hill (well marked with a sign that says CATALINA VISITORS COUNTRY CLUB). This is where you pay your fees for both courses; call (213) 510-1530 for more information. Green fees: $5 weekdays, $6 weekends for nine holes; Pitch and Putt nine holes, adult $1.50, child 12 and under $1.

Tennis

Laykold tennis courts are available (free) throughout the summer at the Avalon School Grounds in Falls Canyon. From mid-September to mid-June, the courts are available before 11:00 a.m. and after 2:30 p.m. Bring your own equipment. The Las Casitas Bungalows (see "Accommodations") also rent their Laykold 60 x 120 courts, and you need not be a guest to play. Equipment not available; fees: $6 an hour per court.

At the Catalina Visitor's Country Club you'll find Pacific Pave tennis courts. Rackets and balls can be rented. The courts are lit for night use. (For directions to the Country Club see "Golf.") Fees: summer $6 hourly, winter $5, racket rental $1.

Water-skiing

Avalon's lee side has calm ocean water where the water-skiing is ideal. You must bring your own equipment and boat; as of this printing, no rentals are available. Avalon Harbor is well marked and the speed limit for all boats and dinghies is five mph or "wakeless speed," whichever is less.

A favorite fishing spot is close to Avalon along the Seal Rock Coast.

FISHING

Where there's an ocean and a boat, you'll find fishermen. The water along the Southern California coast is noted for being rich with sealife of all varieties. Visiting sportsmen revel in the knowledge that they have a good to excellent chance of catching a trophy in Southern California waters. The biggest question is deciding what variety to go for.

Catalina is renowned for its excellent fishing, notably for marlin. The roar of the Avalon cannon alerts you that another marlin has been brought into the Pleasure Pier at Rosie's Fish Market. Amidst crowds of visitors and fishing buffs, an Avalon ceremony follows: the big fish is hung on the pier's scale, a bottle of champagne is presented to the angler, and a photo is taken to record the exciting moment. Sea bass, rock cod, sand dabs, button perch, and sheepshead are some of the more delicious fish also brought in. If you're a lucky diver, you can find lobster and abalone. Tackle rentals from Joe's (on the Pleasure Pier): still-fishing rods one to four hours, $3; trolling rods complete with lures and hooks one to four hours, $5; rock cod rods one to four hours, $6. Bait available. **Note:** Please respect the nonfishing areas, Lovers Cove and the underwater park off Casino Point,

and be aware of the fishing seasons. If in doubt, ask the Harbormaster at the end of the Pleasure Pier. A valid California fishing license is required, available at Joe's Rent-A-Boat and Island Marine, 124 Catalina Street.

The cannon booms and beachers rush to the pier to see a marlin brought in to Avalon.

Tackle

What kind of fishing tackle to use! Choice of equipment grows every year. Quiz 10 fishermen and get 10 answers to a simple question, like what's the best tackle for catching a yellowtail. Are you one that uses the same tackle whether fishing surf, pier, or live bait? Is your favorite a conventional reel or the spinning type; brass, plastic, or chrome plate? How about the line? Is it 20 pound, 50, or maybe 12? And then there's the rod, which can be eight feet or six feet. What's a beginner to do!? One thing is to get a fellow fisherman to recommend a good tackle shop, find a salesperson who instills confidence, and start handling the options. As for price, you usually get what you pay for.

Tuna Family

The variety of fish in Southern California waters is enormous. The tuna family includes among others albacore, yellowfin, big eye, and blue-fin tuna. These are all good eating fish, and many fishermen put up sensational canned (or jarred) tuna from these big babies; wahoo is also a taste treat for tuna lovers. In the late 1940s and '50s commercial fishermen made a killing for several years with huge schools of albacore running between Catalina and the Mainland.

Flat Fish

Sole, sand dabs, and turbot are all flat fish. Sand dabs are particularly popular with local fishermen in Catalina, usually caught in water 300 feet deep or more. The sand dabs are small fish, up to about a pound, and great eating (once filleted); sole grow to about six pounds and turbot to about two pounds. All are good table fare.

Sheepshead

This toothy fish can be a 30-pound catch. It dines regularly on shellfish in kelp and rock beds and is part of the wrasse family. The young female is generally an all-over pink color, and the male is more colorful with a white lower jar, black head, and red and black striped body; this is one of the fish that changes sex during their development. As the small pink females grow, they begin to change color and sex. Other fish also change sex: giant black seabass and marlin are two. Trimmings of mussels, squid, abalone, and shrimp make good bait for the sheepshead and can be found in 60 to several hundred feet of water when fishing for rock cod. It can sometimes be caught while surf-fishing.

Sculpin

Look out for this fish. Although it's great eating, the sculpin is the only venemous fish common to Southern California. Rather an ugly creature, it has a high, spiky dorsal fin. Rust and white colored, this bottom-dweller seldom grows to more than three pounds and has a large mouth. The only safe way to handle this fellow is by grabbing the lower jaw with the thumb and forefinger. Though without teeth, the fish has spiny fins and rays that carry a toxic substance that when introduced into a person will produce severe pain, shock, and nausea; the only remedy seems to be time. They are good eating fish with fine white flesh, but catching them is better left to the experienced fishermen. The roe is also poisonous, but fillets of the fish bought in the market are perfectly safe.

Barracuda

At one time this was a very common fish locally; however, overfishing and pollution have thinned out the numbers. A 28-inch limit is helping the barracuda to make a comeback. This fish strikes both lures and bait, especially anchovies, and puts up a good fight. They show up around Southern California in late January, into February and March and can be big: from seven to nine pounds, though the average size is four to six pounds.

Bonito

Bonito is an inshore fish that's found almost year-round. This is a good fighting fish and can weigh from two to over 12 pounds.

Sometimes called the poor man's tuna, the fish is attracted to surface commotion, like splashing, and tackle shops even sell "bonito splashers." They strike at free-swimming anchovy bait as well as lures. This fish is good eating when smoked.

Halibut

Halibut is a bottom fish that eats anything that passes him by, dead or alive. It's a lethargic fish with bulging eyes that hides on the bottom after flipping sand over its body; it just hangs around waiting for its prey. Another victim of overfishing in local waters, they were large in the past, up to 50 pounds. Nowadays a 10-pounder is a good catch. There's a size limit of 22 inches as well as a bag limit of five fish. According to Charlie Davis, fishing guru of the Pacific Coast, the halibut got its name in England where in the early days all flat fish were called "butts." All butts were saved for priests, or "holy" men, thus *holybutts,* now halibut.

Kelp Or Calico Bass

Found around reefs, rock jetties, breakwaters, and kelp beds, this bass grows to over 10 pounds, and will take most live baits and a variety of lures, but it especially likes anchovy, squid, and jack mackerel. It has a large mouth and a three- or four-pound bass can easily consume a bait that weighs half a pound. Favorite times to fish from a local breakwater are about an hour before and several hours after dark. Best fishing is when there's a full moon just a few hours after sundown. This is a great eating fish, and cannot be sold; a protected species, its size limit is 12 inches.

Black Sea Bass

This is great trophy material! The black sea bass is the largest of the bass family along the California coast. Very slow growing, it can attain weights of 500 pounds, and since it's estimated that a 300-pounder is 20 years old, the 500-pounder is really a granddaddy. A bottom feeder, it takes most bait, but favors

bonito, mackerel, squid, barracuda, and whitefish—heavy tackle is in order. A night feeder that usually schools, good catches are made after sundown. When young (under 50 pounds), they're silvery with large purple spots that disappear as the fish dies. The older bass is brownish/black with a bronze blush. These are caught in rocky areas and kelp beds in depths of 60 to 200 feet. Look for these near Anacapa, Santa Barbara, and San Nicolas islands. Good eating!

White Sea Bass

Another favorite eating fish is the white sea bass. It grows to about 70 pounds, but a fish weighing 50 pounds is considered a prize catch. Though they're seen year-round, the best time to catch them is from January through June. Live squid is a desired bait, and fishing after dark can be most effective, but sardines and Pacific green mackerel also

This giant black bass was caught at the turn of the century.

do the job. **Note:** Don't put your bare hand into the very sharp gills of this fish.

Marlin

Most fishermen feel that once they've caught the big trophy—the marlin—they've made it to the big time. Marlin were first caught around Catalina Island at the beginning of the century. At that time they were almost exclusively caught with trolled flying fish. Though not considered a deluxe food fish in the States, the marlin has been fished by the ton by the Japanese, who make a very popular wiener-like sausage in Japan. Over-fishing has diminished the size of the fish. Marlin arrive in Southern California about July and stay as long as the water temperatures and food are to their liking, sometime as long as December. Marlin make exciting fishing. They spend most of their time close to the surface, and can be seen jumping if they're in the area. It's not unusual to see a marlin "sleeping" or "sunning" with its tail and the hump of the shoulders out of the water. The marlin can take hours to land—all part of the fun.

Non-fishing Supplies

There are many more varieties of fish that make great sport and/or terrific eating in Southern California. Fishing is not only great for the fisherman, but a relaxing way to spend a day on the ocean for a non-fishing companion. But do make sure you bring a few things to stay comfortable: sunscreen, sun hat, lots of water or other beverages, ice, an extra shirt (a hot sun can burn right through a white T-shirt), motion sickness medication if it's a problem, first-aid kit, waterproof poncho, binoculars, and don't forget the camera and lots of film. Birdwatchers, bring along your favorite birding book.

Southern California Landing Locations

Fishermen can bring their catches into the following Southern California cities and will find good facilities and/or supplies:

Gaviota
Goleta
Santa Barbara
Ventura
Oxnard
Port Hueneme
Paradise Cove
Malibu
Santa Monica
Venice
Marina del Rey
Manhattan Beach
Hermosa Beach
Redondo Beach
Long Beach
Seal Beach
Huntington Beach
Newport Beach
Balboa
Laguna Beach
Dana Point
San Clemente
Oceanside
Mission Bay
San Diego
Avalon, Catalina Island

BOAT RENTALS

A variety of boats can be rented at **Joe's Rent-A-Boat** on the Pleasure Pier (see chart). They can be taken to any one of the many coves along the Catalina coast for fishing, picnicking, skin diving, or just sightseeing. If you don't bring your own fishing tackle you can rent or buy most of the equipment needed here at Joe's (see "Fishing"). Take a bright flashlight with you if you're planning to be out after sunset on a boat without running lights. Joe's is open Easter week through October. For reservations, call (213) 510-0455. **Note:** Coast Guard regulations limit these small boats to six passengers. **Island Marine and Sports**, 124 Catalina Ave., tel. (213) 510-0238, also rents and sells fishing

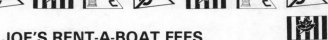

JOE'S RENT-A-BOAT FEES

Type of Boat	Deposit	Hourly	Half day	Day
Paddleboard	$2.00	$3.00	Inquire	Inquire
Rowboat	$10.00	$5.00	$15.00	$25.00
14 ft. 6 hp	yes	$16.00	$48.00	$80.00
16 ft. 10 hp	yes	$18.00	$54.00	$90.00
Sportster 15 hp	yes	$20.00	$60.00	$100.00
Pedal boats (2 passenger)	$10.00			
Pedal boats (4 passenger)	$15.00			

gear, bait, and diving and boating supplies. If you need outboard or inboard parts, they carry Evinrude and Mercury.

Charter Boats

If you'd like to try for big fish and/or want to indulge in a little luxury, this is the way to go. Charters generally come with a skipper and, in some cases, a deck hand. Some provide you with lunch and drinks for the day. They all have a different set of rules and prices; most are negotiable.

Paddleboards

Avalon's calm, clear, surf-free waters are perfect for exploring the bay on a board. Rent

Joe's Rent-A-Boat stand on the Pleasure Pier rents boats and fishing equipment.

one on the Pleasure Pier at Joe's Rent-A-Boat; $3 per hour plus $2 deposit.

Flyer

A 46-foot, fully equipped sport fisher, winner of the 1982 Catalina Gold Cup Marlin Tournament. Also available for around-the-island and evening cruises. For prices and reservations, tel. (213) 510-1352.

Argonaut

Basically a diver's charter boat, but will charter for other activities also. Costs $50/hour including drinks and lunch. For further information, call Jon Hardy at (213) 510-2208.

HUNTING

The Catalina hills are rich with wild goat, boar, deer, quail, and turkey. Each year the hunts are determined by the "hatch." The historical old Banning house has been used as the Hunting Lodge for some years. All hunting is directed by Doug Bombard of the Catalina Hunting Program. A package deal is offered that includes all food, lodging, transportation while on Catalina Island, guide fees, and game cleaning for return shipment to the Mainland. It does not include deer tags or transportation to and from the Island. All hunters must have deer tags and a valid California hunting license in their possession on arrival at the Hunting Lodge. There's always a waiting list of hunters for the Island hunts; applications are taken and then names are drawn. Call (213) 510-0303 for detailed information.

Getting There

All hunters are requested to use the same means of transportation—the *Catalina Express.* It departs from the San Pedro terminal, at the foot of the Harbor Freeway and across Harbor Boulevard. This minimizes confusion for picking up and delivering hunters, allowing more time for hunting (see p. 29).

Clothes And Equipment

No rifles or shotguns are available at the Hunting Lodge. Pistols or handguns may not be used for hunting on Conservancy lands. Bring a set of field glasses, and a good deer rifle with scope and ammunition. Also bring a warm jacket and good hiking boots.

HUNTING FEES

Antlerless Season	$200 pp per day
Buck Season	$400 pp per day
Boar & Goat Season	$200 pp per day
Non-hunter	$85 pp per day (observer only)
Boar Tag	$50 (limit one per day)
Goat Tag: Trophy	$40 (limit one per day)
Goat Tag: Non-trophy	$25 (limit one per day)

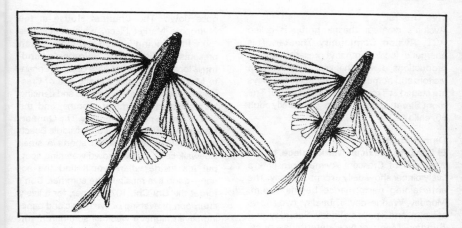

AFTER DARK

It's perfectly safe and highly recommended to walk Avalon's streets after dark. This is a magic time of dancing lights, shimmering sights, and the moon rising dramatically from behind Mt. Ada. Take a romantic walk along Pebbly Beach Road to Abalone Point (aptly named Lovers Cove) for a glimpse of Avalon after dark. Stroll along the serpentine wall of the waterfront; follow the front street, Crescent Avenue, past the Tuna Club and the Yacht Club to the Casino. Be sure to take a boat ride over the black silky water for a glimpse of flying fish, or stargaze on a harbor cruise.

ENTERTAINMENT

Movies

The **Casino Theater** presents first-run movies, which change every two to three days. Two showings—7:15 and 9:15 p.m.; adult $5, child $2.50 The usual theater snacks are sold in the lobby. Get there when the box office opens at 7 p.m. (or earlier if it's a popular film—there'll be a line); this will give you a few minutes to inspect the monumental art-deco murals painted 50 years ago by John Beckman. When the movie is over, stroll around the theater to the edge of the sea wall for another impressive view of the bay and glimmering Avalon town.

Dances

About 10 times a year the big band sound comes to the world-famous **Casino ballroom**. These events generally begin at 8:30 p.m. and last until 1 a.m. Reservations are necessary; get your tickets and information, from the Chamber of Commerce office on the Pleasure Pier, tel. (213) 510-1520 or (213) 510-2000, or from Ticketron offices in Southern California. The 20,000-square-foot ballroom, which can accommodate 3,000 dancers, is veneered with seven hardwoods laid over cork for an ideal dancing surface. The open balcony encircling the ballroom presents a breathtaking view of stars, moon, and sea. Liquor is served at the bar and food is available. For special dances such as on New Year's Eve and other special dates, excellent food is catered by the Villa Portofino. Prices vary according to the event. Drinks average $3. Call the Avalon Chamber of Commerce, tel. (213) 510-1520 or (213) 510-2000, or your local Ticketron office for scheduled bands and ticket information.

Live Theater

Avalon's amateur theater group is called ACT, **Avalon Community Theater**. This energetic local company presents several productions during the year. Popular with visitors and home-town audiences, the plays are staged at Tremont Hall (at the end of Tremont Street) and admission is generally adult $6, child $2.50.

Dinner Theater

El Encanto Mexican Marketplace, on the west end of Crescent Avenue, presents a lively dinner show daily except Tuesday. The entertaining performance begins 7 p.m. Monday, Wednesday, Thursday; two shows at 5 p.m. and 8 p.m. on Friday, Saturday, and Sunday. Menu choice determines price, $19-32 for complete dinners. The performance and dinner at "Solomon's Street Fare" take place in the patio of the El Encanto, a good fun-filled way to spend an evening in Avalon.

Night Clubs

Avalon's night spots come alive after the sun goes down. The **Channel House** at the Metropole Market Place, which advertises "sky-lit dancing" each evening, often presents good jazz bands. **Solomon's Landing** is located on the top floor of the El Encanto Mexican Marketplace at the end of Crescent Avenue. There's live music and dancing here during the summer months, and the view from the patio is fabulous. The **Galleon** restaurant and bar across from Middle Beach (also on Crescent Avenue) sports a small sidewalk cafe, a great crowd-watching spot, but it's inside where you'll find the action—good live music in the summer. Don't forget the **Chi-Chi**, 107 Sumner, for a lively afternoon or evening of live music and dancing seven nights a week all summer. If you just want a quiet spot to share a late evening espresso with a special person, drop by the **Ristorante Villa Portofino** at 101 Crescent Avenue.

Arcades

Avalon's two game arcades are located on either end of Crescent Avenue. **Avalon Arcade** is at 601 Crescent, tel. 510-0291; a**Mar-**

Stroll through the El Encanto Marketplace where a variety of stores make evening shopping an event.

di Gras Arcade is at 225 Crescent, 510-0967. Like most arcades everywhere, they have all the latest electronic games, are well lit, and generally crowded with young kids.

Catalina Museum
If you didn't get around to visiting the museum during the day (1-4 p.m.), it also has night hours, 7-9 p.m. Admission is free. Call 510-2414 for the winter schedule; lower level of the Casino building.

Miniature Golf
The miniature golf course is open every day from April to October and weekends during the winter months. This 18-hole park is on a one-acre garden set back one block from the beach. Enter from the Island Plaza. Open from 9 a.m. till midnight, tel. 510-1200.

Avalon Shops
Evening is a favorite time for a stroll through the shops. The new **Metropole Market Place** offers an antique shop, several clothing stores, gift shops with unique Catalina souvenirs, and an art/gift shop where you can find original drawings and paintings of Catalina. For an after-dinner treat the **Catalina Cookie Company** sells home-style cookies and luscious old-fashioned handmade chocolate turtles and fudge. Or for ice cream go to **Catalina Ice Cream** parlor. You might prefer to walk up a flight of stairs to the **Buoy 205**, with an outdoor patio for a drink or dinner and enjoy the view over the harbor. After leaving the Metropole Market Place, wander up Crescent to the El Encanto Mexican Marketplace, with its bubbling water fountain and Latin atmosphere. Shops include **Carlotta's**, which specializes in imported Mexican clothing.

EVENING CRUISES

Sunset Cruise
At dusk, the **Phoenix,** a large paddle-wheel glass-bottom boat, is converted into a floating buffet supper boat. Cruising leisurely to

Cruising the coast is great fun on a Twilight Dining trip.

the rhythm of a live band, it travels north to Long Point. Dancing on the gently rocking deck is a challenge. Leave your wallet at home; all drinks and a sumptuous buffet supper served during the cruise are included in the $27.50 pp fare. It's an unforgettable way to watch the sun set behind the golden Catalina hills. Reservations are a must. Tickets are available in the Island Plaza ticket office and Catalina Visitor's Center on Crescent Avenue or call 510-2000 in Avalon. Operates May to mid-October.

Twilight Dining

The five-and-a-half-hour trip begins with a 14-mile sightseeing cruise along Catalina's stunning coastline on a comfortable 90-passenger motor vessel to Two Harbors at The Isthmus. This is a special evening of romantic cruising under the stars, good food, dancing, and a chance to see the fauna that makes Catalina unique. On the outgoing passage you'll enjoy the birds, the mountains, maybe the goats, the setting sun, the conviviality of fellow passengers, and of course the comic crew. Take a walk along Two Harbors' palm-lined beach before your complimentary cocktail and delightful buffet dinner at **Doug's Harbor Reef Restaurant.** Then it's time for music and dancing.

There's more. On your cruise back to Avalon, scan the seas for flying fish, aided by the *Blanche W's* 40-million-candlepower searchlight. Be sure to bring a warm jacket for the return trip. If you still get cold, tell one of the crew; they always carry a good supply of blankets since late evening on the ocean is usually chilly. Get full information and make your reservations for this trip at the Catalina Visitor's Information Center across from the green Pleasure Pier or call 510-2000. Summer only, beginning June 15; $27.50 pp.

Shore Boat
An important service for the boating community is the shore boat. The several shore boats which dock at the Pleasure Pier run every hour, shuttling passengers to and from their boats. This is also a fun way to spend an hour sightseeing on the bay if you don't have your own boat; you'll get a close-up view of the many vessels that visit Avalon Harbor--from the small fishing boat to the super-deluxe powerboats docked in the outer harbor to the sleek-lined sailboats. Fare: $1.50 pp inner harbor, $2 outer harbor.

Harbor Cruise
At the ticket counter of the SS *Seaview,* ask about the Coastal Cruise. It travels to White's Landing four times a day for $6 RT, with the last departure at midnight. For those mooring their boats at White's Landing, it's an opportunity for a night out on the town. A Harbor Cruise around Avalon Bay is also offered for $3.75 adults, $2 children, $2.75 seniors for as long as you care to cruise.

Flying Fish
A boat trip on the *Blanche W* to see the flying fish leaves the Pleasure Pier every evening at dark. This trip starts up in April and continues into September when the warm Pacific lures the four-winged fish to the waters surrounding Catalina. The boat is an open launch equipped with a 40-million-candlepower searchlight. When the light is broadcast on the sea, it attracts this unusual fish into gliding as much as 50 feet along the water. These fish often fly over the boat and have even been known to land in a viewer's lap. The species found in Catalina waters grows

Keith Sheets is just one of the narrator/guides that make the Flying Fish trip fun.

19 to 24 inches in length and can weigh one and a half to two pounds, goliaths compared to the tiny flying fish common in the South Pacific. They have a blue back and silver belly, with practically transparent fins that serve as wings. When the wings dry out the fish plummets back into the water. The *Blanche W* motors north along the coast of the Island, the powerful light playing up and down the steep cliffs that edge the water. It's quite common to see wild goats scattered along the hillside, eyes glowing silver in the light. Be sure to bring a sweater or light jacket because the ocean air after dark can be chilly—even in summer. The trip lasts one hour; fare: adult $5, child $2. Tickets and reservations are available from the Catalina Visitor's Information Center on Crescent Avenue. For more information and schedules, call 510-2000 in Avalon.

The *Seaview* is a glass-bottom boat equipped with a powerful quartz light that shines down around its three glass walls. A powerful 30-foot diesel-driven craft, its four sheets of laminated quarter-inch glass allow an unusually clear view of the marine environment. The boat operates year-round, with night trips April to September. On this evening trip you may see a hungry seal swimming gracefully through the water chasing after the flying fish that are attracted to the brilliant underwater light. Here's a good opportunity to see certain species of marinelife that hide or sleep during the day, such as the Catalina lobster. Tickets are sold on the Pleasure Pier and reservations should be made ahead of time. Fare: adult $4, child $2.

SPECIAL DINING

Top-Of-The-Island Dinner Tour

A ride along the inland roads to the top of the Island at the Airport-In-The-Sky brings you within touching distance of the stars and the brilliant lights on the Mainland coast. A delicious buffet dinner is served at the airport dining room, along with a chance to see the Island's night creatures, especially the small Island fox. Buy tickets at the Catalina Visitor's Information Center on Crescent Avenue. The bus leaves from the Island Plaza Terminal and reservations are necessary.

Barbecue It Yourself

Every evening, except Monday, the **Descanso Beach Club** fires up its giant barbecue and invites the public to bring their own steaks, fish, or whatever to roast over the hot charcoal. The cost is $5.95 for salad, a baked potato with all the trimmings, bread and butter, and table service. A bar provides alcoholic and non-alcoholic drinks. With all the tropical splendor of a beach open to the sea and sky, you'll truly enjoy this repast under the stars. To get to the Descanso Beach Club follow the palm trees past the Casino. For reservations call 510-0484 in Avalon. Summer only. Thursday is barbecue night at the **Sand Trap**. From 5:30 p.m. to 9 p.m., bring your entree to grill over the mesquite coals and then help yourself to a salad bar, baked potato, and garlic bread; adult $5.95, child $3.

cruising on the Blanche W's *Flying Fish Trip*

GETTING AROUND IN AVALON

Avalon town is small, just one square mile. It boasts clean, fresh air, broad walkways along the ocean with spectacular coastal views, and narrow, scenic streets up Mediterranean-like hillsides. Visitors cannot bring an auto to the Island, and Islanders can ship them over only with a special permit. But there's plenty of public and private transportation, car and bike rentals, and always the best—your own two feet.

Walking

By far the most popular way to get around this small town is to walk. Many Islanders remember when autos were used only for business and deliveries. In those days the city fathers didn't think twice about barricading a street for a roller skating party, since there wasn't enough traffic to hinder and no one ever complained. During WW II part of Crescent Avenue was routinely closed off for Saturday night dances for the servicemen stationed on the Island. Most Avalon streets were built before cars were common transportation, so streets and sidewalks are narrow. Walking these delightful winding streets or alongside the clear blue water surrounding this smog-free island community remains a favorite pastime of visitors and residents alike.

Foot Traffic

A section of Crescent Avenue, the main street which fronts the bay, is reserved for foot traffic. One side of the street is lined with shops, restaurants, and small hotels, while the other parallels the beach and Pleasure Pier. Bikes are not allowed, and your dog must be on a leash. Keep a pooper-scooper and plastic bag with you for your dog.

Interior Shuttle

From the Plaza in Avalon there's a shuttle bus that takes backpackers and campers to: Bird Park Campground, $1; Airport-In-The-Sky, $4; Black Jack, $4; Little Harbor, $7; Two Harbors, $9. For other routes and a comprehensive schedule, go to the Catalina Shuttle Bus office at 213 Catalina Street in the Island Plaza (shown on the Avalon city map, p. 56), or write to Catalina Shuttle Bus, Box 1037, Avalon, CA 90704.

Bike Rentals

At Cartopia, 615 Crescent, the rental fee for most bikes is $4 hourly; $12 for a full day (10 a.m. to 4 p.m.), no weekly rental, $10 deposit. These bikes may not be taken out of the city limits. Brown's Bikes, at 107 Pebbly Beach Road, tel. 510-0986, charges about the same hourly rate; ask about special group rentals. They also rent tandem bikes at $8 an hour or $25 a day, and baby seats. U-drive Auto Car Rental rents bikes and tandems for the same rates.

Bring Your Own Bike

Each boat company handles bicycle portage in its own way. See "Getting There" in the "Introduction." Bikes are not allowed on the roads of the interior. Trips to the Botanical Garden, Pebbly Beach, and the Casino make good bike rides for youngsters and adults.

Taxi

There is one taxi company operating within Avalon city limits: Avalon Taxi. It runs year-round, with a stand on Crescent Avenue across from the Metropole Marketplace and is easy to find. Several taxis meet each boat; $3-4 will get you up most of the Avalon hills.

Car Rentals

Catalina Auto and Bike Rentals, on the corner of Metropole and Crescent, rents manual-shift "towncar" compacts by the hour for $12, or the day for $35 (10 a.m. to 4 p.m.) with a $20 refundable deposit. Four passengers fit comfortably; five is a squeeze. An eight-passenger car is available for $24 an hour with a $50 deposit. A map of Avalon comes with all rentals. You can drive within

While there are more autos in Avalon than ever, most people get around in golf carts; they're for rent at several places in Avalon.

the city limits only, and this includes the Botanical Garden and Pebbly Beach; tel. (213) 510-0111. **U-drive Auto Car Rental** charges $20 an hour with a $20 deposit, $15 for the second hour. **Island Rentals,** 125 Pebbly Beach Road, tel. 510-1456, wants $20 hour with a $20 deposit. **Cartopia Car Rental,** 615 Crescent Avenue, rents electric golf-type carts for $20 per hour with a $20 deposit.

WALKING TOURS OF AVALON

In Avalon strike out on foot. Avalon is a small town with narrow streets to explore and many architecturally unusual houses to view, some constructed on the original 20-foot-wide lots laid out by George Shatto, who developed Avalon in the late 1800s. Land is scarce in Avalon and property values have skyrocketed over the years so landowners have used remodeling techniques to garner every possible inch of living space. About half the homes are built on the level streets just up from the Pleasure Pier called the "flats" by the Islanders, while the other half climb the hills, giving Avalon a sunny Mediterranean-island appearance. On these walking tours you'll discover homes built before there were many roads in Avalon; a few still can only be reached by a flight of stairs up a hill to the front door.

Take your camera, your *Guide to Catalina*, and bring a hat and sunscreen if you're prone to sunburn. Be prepared for a few steep climbs.

Whittley Walk

From Crescent Avenue on the shoreline start up Whittley. Turn left at East Whittley, the first street you come to, and follow its steep curve up and around to the right. As you walk up East Whittley you pass several small houses; the second from the corner on the right was built in 1903 for $500 and is still occupied by the Trout family, descendants of the 1911 owners. Originally the little house was built on one of the small lots leased from Banning's SCI Company. When Whittley Street was widened the house next door on the corner of Whittley and East Whittley was moved eight feet and pushed right up under the eaves of the Trout house. After Wrigley purchased the Island, the Trouts were able to buy the land beneath their house. Farther on your right you come to the Christian Science Church and a Spanish-style house with a red-

tile roof. Both were built by a devout Christian Scientist, Count Mankowski, an avid fisherman who loved Catalina. The count was married to an American woman named Morris; though of Polish descent the count was a British citizen who enjoyed summers on Catalina. The church next door was built at the same time and in the same Spanish style as his classic home; he kept his horses across the street in a stable that overlooked the bay. The stable has been replaced by a modern apartment building. Present owner of the count's home, now a bed and breakfast, is Guy Sanders, who calls his home a castle: the Sand Castle Bed and Breakfast.

Continue on up to the top of the hill bearing to your right (this is a steep climb, but not impossible) where you'll see a pergola. The white wooden latticework structure sits on a small knoll up a short dirt path. Benches here provide a good resting place with a spectacular panoramic view of Avalon and the bay. From here East Whittley curves to your right and then left over to Marilla Avenue and back down toward town. Follow Marilla a short distance to Hiawatha Avenue on the left and up another short street where you come to the Barlow House with its wide circular porch.

Barlow House

In the early 1900s a circus act called the Travillo Brothers came to Catalina Island on a talent hunt for a new member for their team. The search took them to Seal Rocks off the east end of the Island where the California sea lion rookery was mobbed with potential ball-bouncing circus stars. While on the Island the family quickly decided that this was where they wanted to settle. In 1906, the charming circular house became a reality for the Travillo family and their seals trained in the yard overlooking Avalon town. Mrs. Travillo had a gift shop on Crescent Avenue

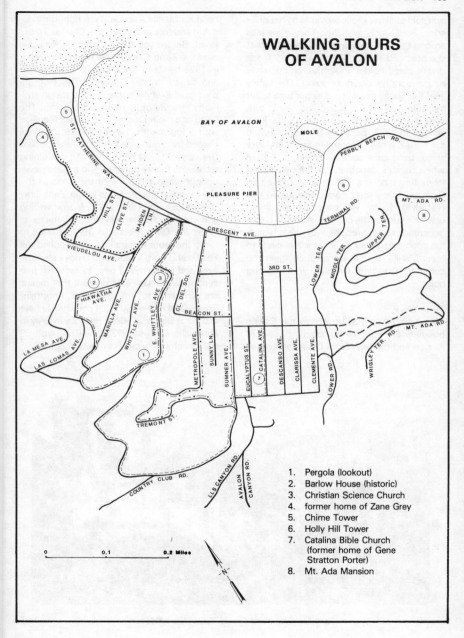

WALKING TOURS OF AVALON

BAY OF AVALON

MOLE

PEBBLY BEACH RD.

ST. CATHERINE WAY

PLEASURE PIER

MT. ADA RD.

HILL ST.
OLIVE ST.
MAIDEN LN.
VIEUDELOU AVE.
CRESCENT AVE.
TERMINAL RD.
LOWER TER.
MIDDLE TER.
UPPER TER.

3RD ST.

HIAWATHA AVE.
MARILLA AVE.
WHITTLEY AVE.
E. WHITTLEY AVE.
CL. DEL SOL
BEACON ST.
MT. ADA RD.

LA MESA AVE.
LAS LOMAS AVE.
METROPOLE AVE.
SUNNY LN.
SUMNER AVE.
EUCALYPTUS ST.
CATALINA AVE.
DESCANSO AVE.
CLARISSA AVE.
CLEMENTE AVE.
LOWER RD.
WRIGLEY TER. RD.

TREMONT ST.

COUNTRY CLUB RD.
LLS CANYON RD.
AVALON CANYON RD.

0   0.1   0.2 Miles

N

1. Pergola (lookout)
2. Barlow House (historic)
3. Christian Science Church
4. former home of Zane Grey
5. Chime Tower
6. Holly Hill Tower
7. Catalina Bible Church
   (former home of Gene
   Stratton Porter)
8. Mt. Ada Mansion

and sold abalone shells provided by her diver sons, Ford, Jack, and Guy. They were also among the avid coin divers that would meet the boat and shout, "Throw a coin!" These divers could hold a mouthful, and actually had a lucrative business going. The family sold the house to an opera singer who spent her summers on the Island and she in turn sold it to Mr. Feek, principal of the local school. In 1923, Sarah C. Smith purchased the house. It has remained in her family ever since, used as a summer home until 1973 when Sarah's daughter, Liz Barlow, retired from her teaching career and moved to Catalina. This elegant home, designated as a Historical House, will be preserved in its gracious turn-of-the-century style for future generations to appreciate. From here Hiawatha soon completes its angular half circle to meet Marilla Avenue where once again you come to Crescent Avenue, your starting point.

Zane Grey

This walk takes you up above the Casino building for another spectacular view of Avalon and the bay. From Crescent Avenue head up Marilla Avenue. Turn right on Vieudelou and follow the curve to Chimes Tower Road. Before you arrive at the Chimes you pass the **Zane Grey Hotel** to your left, built in 1926 by Zane Grey, big-game fisherman and famed Western novelist. This Hopi Indian pueblo-style home fit the rough-and-ready lifestyle of its remarkable owner. The living and dining room, graced by a fireplace with a log mantle, has open-beam ceilings shaped from teak brought from Tahiti aboard Grey's yacht, *The Fisherman*. An oak dining table with heavy benches and a hand-hewn upright piano are some of the massive furnishings that still grace the home. Zane Grey spent most of his later life in Avalon writing and fishing. As he said about Catalina in *What the Open Means to Me* "...I used to climb the mountain trail that overlooked the Pacific and here a thousand times I shut my eyes and gave myself over to sensorial perceptions.... It is an environment that means enchantment to me. Sea and mountain! Breeze and roar of Surf!... I could write here and be at peace...." Born Pearl Zane Grey in Zanesville, Ohio, in 1872, Zane Grey wrote 89 books before his death in 1939 at age 67.

Zane Grey Home and Chimes Tower, late 1930s

Chimes Tower

Farther up and across Zane Grey Road is the Chimes Tower. Manufactured by the Deagan Company in Chicago at a cost of $25,000, these chimes have been tolling the time every 15 minutes since 1925, when they were presented as a gift to the town of Avalon by Mrs. Ada Wrigley. On holidays and special occasions the electric console is played manually, the resonance blending in with the surrounding harbor sounds to create a cadence unique to Catalina. From this spot looking across the bay you'll have a good view of the Holly Hill House on the southeast tip of Avalon Bay. Its conical-shaped roof can't be missed.

Holly Hill House

In 1888, a remarkable man named Peter Gano bought what some consider to be the choicest parcel of land in Avalon from George Shatto for $500. An engineer with extensive experience in water works, Gano generously offered to design Avalon's first freshwater system, laying pipe from Avalon Canyon Springs to the only large building at that time, the Metropole Hotel. He shipped building supplies from the Mainland to Avalon aboard his boat, the *Osprey*. On the project, his only helper was Mercury, a former circus horse that performed the heavy labor of this monumental task. Gano designed an ingenious cable car system to carry his equipment up the steep incline to the top of the hill. Mercury, on whistle command, walked down the hill pulling ropes wound around pulleys to power the loaded cable car up the hill to the building site. Gano also laid water pipes directly to his home site, and designed a three-cistern system to catch rainfall. Building the house to last with strong, durable materials, he was a craftsman who took great pride in his work. The open-air circular cupola patio with the cone-shaped roof captures the attention of everyone that visits the Island. And living in the house must be an even greater pleasure with beautiful vistas of the sea and Avalon town from every window.

Holly Hill House

This remarkable man has a bittersweet legend associated with his name. Fable tells us that he labored on the house for the love of a lady. But, when it was completed, she couldn't bring herself to give up Mainland society for life in a small seaside village — even in a fabulous house built for entertaining. She told Gano it was either her or the house. Convinced she would change her mind he chose the house — naming it Look Out Cottage. The battle of wills ended when ultimately she married another, leaving Gano to live alone in his hand-built masterpiece until very old age. Old-timers who were children during Gano's time tell of signs posted around his house that stated bluntly, NO WOMEN ALLOWED.

The house has had four owners since it was completed in 1890. The Giddings family bought it from Gano in 1921 and renamed it Holly Hill House (for the abundant holly that grew on the hill) and for the next 40 years spent their summers in Avalon. In 1971, the Smiths (along with the Richard Land Company) bought it with the intention of developing the property below the house into condominiums. Excavation began, destabilizing the foundation of the house. To make the hill safe again extensive steel, concrete, and Gunite repairs were made, but the condos were never built. Then soon after the repairs were completed a fire destroyed the cupola roof. In 1971, Holly Hill House was bought by Victor and Shari Kreis, frequent visitors to Catalina and long-time admirers of this Victorian house on the hill. The Kreises' first project was to rebuild the cupola; since then the family has been involved in an energetic restoration program. In an ongoing project, old photos are studied, and every detail is painstakingly approached with the original Gano house in mind. Modern improvements from earlier renovations were replaced with antique or old-style carpentry and appliances. Woods were stripped and brought back to their original luster; furniture of the era has been brought in—the family uses a 1907 gas stove in their 1890s kitchen. Visiting this house is a trip into the past. Contact the Catalina Museum, Box 366, Avalon, CA 90704, tel. (213) 510-2414, for information about special group tours.

DAY HIKES OUTSIDE THE CITY OF AVALON

These trails take you short distances out of town and in some cases you must backtrack on the same trails; in others a circular route will be given. Hike with a companion and bring water since it's not available on the trail. See "Vicinity of Avalon" map.

Catalina Stable To Botanical Garden

From downtown continue up Sumner Avenue and follow it to the left of Country Club Road. Pass the golf course on the left, and take the left V when you come to the Sand Trap Restaurant and Pitch and Putt Golf Course. Continue past the Catalina Stables and just beyond the picnic grounds is the graded dirt road to the Botanical Garden. This easy hike takes about an hour each way.

Hermit Gulch Trail/Canyon Road/ Divide Road

These steep slopes on undeveloped pathways combine for a strenuous hike, five hours for a good hiker, with little shade along the way.

Renton Mine Road/Mount Ada Road To East Mountain

Expect moderate to steep slopes along a graded dirt road, strenuous hike; plan about three hours for the hardy hiker.

Jail Road/Indian Trail To Stage Road

Along fire roads, most involving steep slopes. At 1,460 feet this is a spectacular vantage point. From here you can see the Island's rugged coastline and (when Mainland smog doesn't interfere) the San Gabriel Mountains across the channel. Strenuous hike. For more hikes on Catalina, see p. 131.

Mount Ada Walk

This is a good early-morning breakfast stroll. Walk toward the mole and continue on Pebbly Beach Road along the ocean boardwalk where you'll meet other early risers—fishermen, walkers, and joggers. The sun rises over this part of the ocean, and it's a sparkling, invigorating walk past Lovers Cove Beach, a nice place to stop and watch the fish splashing out of the water looking for breakfast.

At Pebbly Beach is a small airport, with a cement ramp for landing amphibious planes and a helicopter pad. Lots of traffic flies in and out of this little airport. Freight is brought in on a special amphibian, and another passenger amphib makes daily flights back and forth to the Mainland, with a bus to meet each plane. This is a fine place to stop for breakfast (or lunch or dinner) at the Buffalo Nickel. If you're a plane buff, the rooftop patio offers a great vantage point from which to watch the amphibs and helicopters come and go. The restaurant also serves meals inside (you can get buffalo burgers here).

The Southern California Edison Company

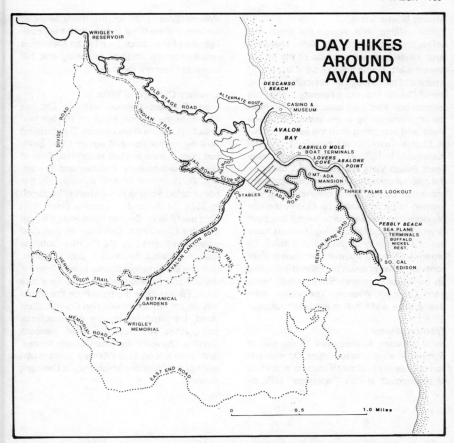

DAY HIKES AROUND AVALON

maintains its utility plant in Pebbly Beach and about a dozen families live across the road. Past the houses the road turns up the hill, and goes by the former home of William Wrigley Jr. In 1919, after the Wrigleys purchased the Island, they chose Mt. Ada, 350 feet above the bay, for their future home. It's said that Mrs. Wrigley (Ada) determined that from here she could see the sun rise and set with the purple hills of Avalon as a backdrop. The house was built in 1921 with only the immediate area around the structure landscaped. Now at night well-positioned floodlights turn the building into a floating white mansion against the black hillside. In 1978,

the estate was donated to the University of Southern California for use as an academic and cultural center. Managed by the university's Institute for Marine and Coastal Studies, seminars and workshops were held here year-round, hosting such groups as the U.S. Geological Survey, the U.S. Office of Naval Research, and other organizations from many parts of the world. For the lazies that don't hike, the Avalon Scenic Drive takes you past Mt. Ada (see "Guided Tours"). Today, Wrigley's home is a fabulous bed and breakfast called The Inn On Mt. Ada (see p. 67).

Mount Buena Vista

While walking, look across the street and below the entrance to Mt. Ada. There's a large white cross on the side of the hill. At one time Mt. Buena Vista was the location of a park and terminus of an old incline railway, called "Island Mountain Railway." The little railroad operated two cars: one going from the amphitheater up to the summit at Buena Vista, and one going from the summit down to Lovers Cove. It was built in 1904, and dismantled in 1920. For over 60 consecutive years Buena Vista has been the location of the colorful costumed Easter sunrise pageant presented by the Island community. If you happen to be in Avalon on Easter, the city provides free bus service to the hill site from downtown on Easter morning (ask the Chamber of Commerce for time and details). To return to Crescent Avenue from Buena Vista continue walking down the hill and you'll end up on lower Clemente Street a half block from Crescent Avenue. The views from Buena Vista and Mt. Ada are breathtaking.

Tremont Street

From Crescent Avenue walk to the end of Sumner Avenue and turn right. On your left you pass newly built rental condos, and a few of the original stucco "ranchitos" built by William Wrigley Jr. for the many Mexican families that he hired to help with the development of the Island. Turn left on Metropole (another steep incline) following the hill down to Crescent Avenue.

Country Club Road Walk

From Crescent Avenue walk up Catalina Street. In the second block on the left you pass the Catalina Bible Church. This building was the former home of author Gene Stratton Porter, born in 1868 in Indiana. Two of her best-sellers were *Freckles* and *Laddie*. Ms. Porter spent several summers in her home called Singing Waters before her death in 1924. At the end of Catalina Street turn right past Avalon Canyon Road and go left up Country Club Road. Continue on this road where it wanders past the Country Club, the exclusive Palms Restaurant, putting green, golf pro shop, tennis courts, tee-off area for the golf course, and a place to stop for a cool drink. Farther on is the turnoff for the cemetery on the left. Continuing on Country Club Road, bordered by dozens of eucalyptus trees, takes you past the large, pleasant Catalina Canyon Hotel and Canyon Restaurant. Turn left on East Whittley going down and right on Whittley which ends at Crescent Avenue.

GUIDED TOURS

Catalina Sightseeing Tours offers a variety of guided tours for the visitor who wants to see as much of the Island as possible in a short amount of time. Although you can wander the hills and interior on your own feet, it's a big island — 76 square miles. For most visitors these tours are the only opportunity to see the Island's interior and its distant coves. The roomy motorstage is comfortable, the boats are fun, and the guides witty, well versed, and pleasant. Ask about a money-saving combination ticket for three of the described trips at the Catalina Visitor's Center on Crescent Ave., tel. 510-2500.

Scenic Terrace Drive
This 50-minute trip is especially gratifying for the one-day visitor. The bus leaves from the Sumner Avenue side of Island Plaza and passes Avalon's major points of interest. You first travel along Avalon's beaches and into the hills that surround its sparkling bay. The bus takes you by the Inn On Mt. Ada (today a

bed and breakfast, but originally the residence of Mr. and Mrs. William Wrigley Jr.), along the waterfront, through the residential section of Avalon, and to vistas that are perfect for picture taking — the views are fabulous. Fare: adult $3.75, senior $3, child $2.

Skyline Drive
A two-hour tour, this is a good way to see part of the interior, if you only have a day. It takes you 10 miles inside the Santa Catalina Island Conservancy's nature preserve to the Airport-In-The-Sky. Along Catalina's skyline you see mountain scenery on one side, and deep canyons and hidden coves indenting the coastline on the other. Flora here can only be seen on Catalina, such as the Catalina ironwood tree. Ironwood trees, once common in the western United States, have been extinct there for over 20,000 years. This rugged country is also the home of Catalina's wild animals: buffalo, deer, goat, boar, and fox. The tour departs from the bus terminal in the

Island Plaza; reservations required. Part of the fare goes to the Santa Catalina Island Conservancy and is a tax-deductible contribution; adult $7.50, senior $6.50, child $4.

Inland Motor Tour
If you plan on spending several days in Catalina, take the four-hour Inland Tour. Though more expensive than some of the other trips, this half-day trip is well worth your time and money. The tour goes to the heart of the 66 square miles of rugged wildlands owned by the Conservancy. You travel along a high ridge with vistas of rolling hills on one side and the vast Pacific on the other. You'll see Middle Ranch, nestled in a valley with growing crops and farm houses. Refreshments are served at Rancho Escondido, where you're a guest at a mini-rodeo with performances by purebred Arabian horses raised and trained here. Wander the grounds of the ranch and visit the tack room where the Wrigley family stable gear is stored, including remarkable silver riding equipment, ornate bridles, carved saddles, and old photos of the family in equestrian gear. In another part of the ranch are old stagecoaches that at one time carried tourists along the dirt roads of Catalina. Today's modern buses were designed to somewhat resemble the old stages of yesteryear.

Returning, you circle back by way of the Airport-In-The-Sky and along the high ridge overlooking hidden coves along the Catalina coast. Bus leaves from the Island Plaza daily at 9 a.m.; adult $13.50, senior $11.50, child $6.50. Reservations required.

Casino Tour
Take this 45-minute walking tour for a complete circuit of the Casino. A tram ride from the Island Plaza brings you to Casino Point, and from there the group is escorted by a guide through the landmark building. You're taken into the theater on the bottom floor to view the heroic-sized murals and see the colossal Page pipe organ (though not advertised, once in a while there's a demonstration of its many sound effects when an organist is around). From here you'll walk the ramp to the mezzanine and the large ballroom. The balcony surrounding the dance floor is a perfect vantage point from which to photograph Avalon Bay. (For more Casino information see p. 57). A tram ride back into Avalon concludes the tour; adult $3.75, senior $3, child $1.75.

Coastal Cruise
The 55-minute Coastal Cruise goes to the eastern tip of Catalina—the "working" side
(continued on p. 110)

*Catalina Visitor's
Information Center*

RANCHO ESCONDIDO

Within 10 years after William Wrigley Jr. had acquired Catalina and the Santa Catalina Island Co., his son Philip began making plans for the development of the interior. After many months of traveling through the beautiful countryside, he came upon a setting called Cottonwood Canyon that he thought would make an ideal site for a horse ranch. He and the rest of his scouting group set up camp to get acquainted with the area for a few days. It was a good move; the wind howled through the canyon and it turned out to be a cold place. As Wrigley put it, "We quickly found out from bitter experience that it was the wrong spot except during the middle of the day." As it turned out, Cottonwood led them to the location that would prove to be just right, only a short distance away. The setting was lovely, but as they discovered, it was not easy to locate the second time. Undoubtedly that's why the ranch was ultimately called *El Rancho Escondido* ("The Hidden Ranch"). Even now, surrounded with tall eucalyptus, the ranch remains hidden from sight until you're just a few hundred yards away.

As the first set of buildings was begun, plans were in the making to breed a Catalina Arabian horse. Helen and Philip Wrigley were the owners of two Arabians and were much impressed by their beauty and stamina. They then had to find a horseman to take charge of this frontier location and develop it into a ranch. The choice was Jack White, a longtime cattleman. In 1931, this lanky, leathery-faced Westerner who felt more at home on a horse than anyplace else tackled the job. It was at about this time that the first gray stallion, called Kaaba, was transported to the Island. The horse and White did a good job; Jack didn't even mind sleeping in a tent for the first months while the ranch took shape. The breeding program was initiated under the experienced eye of Millard Johnson, who said he'd try it out for a "few months." Jack White eventually took over the SCI Co. cattle ranch and Johnson ended up running the

continued

ranch—for the next 16 years. During World War II, the breeding program was put on hold, but by 1949 Escondido had grown to include over 75 horses and was the largest purebred Arabian breeding ranch in Southern California.

Millard Johnson's young assistant, Joe Dawkins, took over in 1951. He knew horses and he liked people, and it was at about this time that the SCI Co. began its new bus tour called the "Inland Motor Tour." Tourists were taken on a good bus tour of the interior with a donut-and-rodeo stop at Rancho Escondido. It continues to be a favorite attraction on Catalina. Every visitor to the Island should make a point of taking the Inland Tour, not only to see Catalina's rugged interior, but to have the opportunity to see what

showing a working horse (Inland Tour)

Catalina Arabian horses are all about. Escondido's Arabians have garnered hundreds of awards over the years, and have started a dynasty of Catalina Arabians. The number of Arabians on the ranch varies between 16 and 20. The Wrigley family visits the ranch several times a year, and needless to say they are all avid riders.

Since Dawkins retired in 1972, several ranchers have managed El Rancho Escondido. The newest resident ranch manager (since June 1986) is enjoying the extra glory of being unique on Catalina. Not only is she an extraordinary manager, but Dixie Johnson is the first woman in the ranch's 50-year history to accept the challenge of running El Rancho Escondido. Dixie is a former San Diegan who rode with the Search and Rescue division of the San Diego Sheriff's Department for nine years. Her husband, Dr. Louis Johnson, is a retired veterinarian who spent over 30 years caring for animals in California. They're a good team to look after the ranch.

Dixie currying a Catalina Arabian.

The Spanish-style ranch buildings are graceful and built mostly from Catalina materials, right up to the red tiles on the roof (from Catalina's old tile factory). Shaggy eucalyptus trees surround the buildings, giving welcome shade on hot,

sunny days. The grounds are spotless and well kept (you can definitely see a woman's touch). Visit the tack room, with its hundreds of ribbons, awards, interesting saddles, and pictures of the Wrigley family and their horses. Also, take a look at some of the original stagecoaches that rolled along the dirt roads in the early days of Catalina's development. The most exciting part of the visit is the show put on each day (twice daily during summer months) for visitors. Dixie and her equine assistant explain the history of the ranch as well as the history of the Arabian horse. In an arena with bleacher seats for guests, they put the horses through actual exercises that show what the breed is capable of doing as a working ranch animal. Don't miss this great show, even if you aren't a horse person.

Dixie's expertise is really as a horse trainer. She says it gives her great pleasure to take a young horse on the trail for the first time and help accustom it to new sounds, sights, and smells along the way. Dixie's husband is a welcome addition to the island. This is the first time the Island has boasted a resident veterinarian. Not only does he maintain the general health of the horses and other animals on the ranch, but he's ready and willing to help whenever needed. He often works with Terry Martin at the Santa Catalina Island Conservancy. He's taken on an interesting variety of jobs since moving to the rugged frontier of an island where the main concern is to protect and preserve the wildlife. He has conducted TB tests on buffalo that were being shipped to the Mainland to start other herds, sutured dogs that have gotten too friendly with wild boar, and nursed a sick raven back to health. Asked if they liked living in their country home surrounded by the Pacific Ocean, the Johnsons gave a definite yes, and added that in the last year and a half they'd been off the Island only four times. That tells the story.

(continued from p. 112)
of the Island. This is where the Edison Company runs its electric plant, from this area the barge hauls freight back and forth to the Mainland, and the boat yard operates here. The cruise boat passes the small seaplane airport and helipad, and farther down is the rock quarry where millions of tons of rocks and boulders have been removed from the Island and shipped to the Mainland to be used in most of the sea walls and breakwaters around Los Angeles Harbor and the west coast of Southern California.

When the seals are "at home," it's a wonderful opportunity to see them in their natural habitat. Since seals (in this case California sea lions) are migratory animals, viewing them depends on the season. During the mating season, beginning as early as June, the males take their harems to a private cove; in July and August they return to Seal Rocks in larger numbers to sun themselves, swim, and dive for fish. The tour departs from the Pleasure Pier; adult $3.75, senior $3, child $2.

GLASS-BOTTOM BOATS

In addition to its many other unusual "firsts," Catalina holds the distinction of being the place where a glass-bottom boat was first used. Inspired by the glass-bottomed box that fishermen used for a better view under the surface for untangling lines or to spot abalone on the rocks below, Charles Feige created the first practical glass-bottom rowboat in 1896. In 1897, a glass-bottom sternwheeler was built of boiler iron by P.J. Waller; it was operated with wheels, bicycle fashion. After more study it was found that a power-driven boat didn't disturb the water and its inhabitants as had been originally believed.

Phoenix
Today, one of the ships, operated daily by Santa Catalina Sightseeing is the MV *Phoenix,* built in Wilmington, California, in 1931. The *Phoenix* leisurely cruises Catalina's marine gardens around Lovers Cove, Pebbly Beach, and west toward White's Landing. Many radiantly colored fish thrive in Lovers Cove, the most vivid resident being the golden garibaldi, a species of perch. Others you may see are the silver perch, button perch, and the toothy sheepshead. Occasionally, a transparent jellyfish will float by. Adding grandeur to the scene is the iodine kelp forest, with its amber tendrils and leaves reaching up 100 feet and more to the surface, supported by air bulbs. Daylight trips depart from the Pleasure Pier frequently during the summer months. This 40-minute trip costs adult $4, senior $3.75, child $2. By the time this book hits your bookstore the new glass-bottom *Moonstone* will be completed and floating through the marine gardens of Catalina.

Seaview
This glass-bottom boat embarks on 45-minute night trips as well as daytime cruises. The *Seaview* is equipped with a brilliant light that attracts a variety of sealife and makes it possible to view bottom dwellers not ordinarily seen by day. It departs from the Pleasure Pier daily and each evening during the summer months; ask about a combination day-and-night ticket. Fare: adult $3.50, child $2.

Others
For the Flying Fish Tour, Sunset Buffet Cruise, Twilight Dining at Two Harbors, and Top-of-the-Island Dinner Tour, see "After Dark."

WRIGLEY MEMORIAL
AND BOTANICAL GARDEN

William Wrigley Jr. maintained his enthusiasm for Catalina Island from his first visit in 1919 until his death in 1932. He generously spent millions for the development of the Island, and put his energies into many projects that are still an important part of the Island's culture today. After his death, the Santa Catalina Island Company built an imposing memorial for him at the head of Avalon Canyon. The Wrigley Memorial and Botanical Garden, including the site of the memorial, covers almost 40 acres.

Getting There

It's a 1.7-mile walk up a gentle incline from downtown Avalon to the Botanical Garden. The road leads you past the golf course and Bird Park Campground. A year-round bus service leaves from the Island Plaza every half hour, $2 RT pp. Admission into the Botanical Garden is free for children under 12 and for anyone who belongs to the Wrigley

Memorial Foundation. For all other visitors the charge is 50¢. If you're interested in joining the Wrigley Memorial Foundation, write Box 88, 1400 Avalon Canyon Road, Avalon, CA 90704, tel. (213) 510-2288.

The Monument

Wrigley's memorial was constructed mostly from native Catalina materials. A graceful lookout tower, it stands 232 feet wide, 180 feet deep, and 130 feet high from the bottom of its wide circular stairway to the top of its main 80-foot tower. Climb the stairs for a stunning view of the Botanical Garden that spreads across the canyon floor below. From the now-defunct Catalina tile production plant initiated by Wrigley, red roof tiles and colorful handmade glazed tiles were used for the interior. Blue flagstones from Little Harbor surface the ramp and both terraces of the tower. Pink and green marble was brought from Georgia only because it had the coloration to provide the desired finishing effects. At one time Wrigley's body was entombed here, but it has since been moved.

The Garden

It was originally Mrs. Wrigley's idea to begin planting a garden of cactus and succulents in picturesque Avalon Canyon shortly after 1919. In 1969, the Wrigley Memorial Garden Foundation undertook a plan of expansion and revitalization, and this garden has since grown into a comprehensive botanical showcase attracting visitors, researchers, students, and teachers. It's a living laboratory for the study of plants endemic to Catalina. It also provides a thriving natural habitat for further study of specimens of particular interest and value—learning how they may be used

a walker's first view of the Wrigley Memorial from the road

to ecological advantage. There are hundreds of species of plants available for your inspection.

Botanical Studies

All eight known plants endemic to Catalina are included in the garden's collection. In addition, a number of special plants from Santa Rosa, San Clemente, and other Santa Barbara Channel islands, many of them extremely rare, have recently been planted. The garden includes an herbarium and an area for students to study the herbarium specimens. There is an excellent library of botanical publications, also containing the garden's pressed-plant collection. Due to limited staff, please call (213) 510-2288 for an appointment if you wish to use these facilities for study.

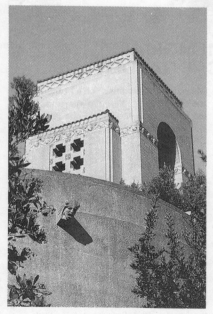

another view of the tower

Catalina dinghy dock (Oz Mallan)

1. Catalina Boaters (Oz Mallan); **2.** Catalina interior (Oz Mallan); **3.** Avalon Golf Course (Oz Mallan); **4.** Avalon Harbor (Oz Mallan); **5.** Eric's on the pier (Oz Mallan); **6.** Catalina diver (Jon Hardy)

1. Casino balcony (Oz Mallan); **2.** Wrigley Memorial (Oz Mallan); **3.** Gabriel Beckman tilework on Catalina Casino (Oz Mallan); **4.** dowtown Avalon, Catalina I. (Oz Mallan)

1. Arch Rock, Anacapa Island (Channel Islands National Park); **2.** Lovers Cove, Catalina I. (Oz Mallan)

CATALINA ENDEMIC PLANTS

CATALINA MAHOGANY
(Cercocarpus traskiae)
Catalina mahogany is a large
evergreen shrub or small tree
which grows to about 15 feet.
The young shoots are reddish brown.
The grayish-green leaves are thick and
leathery; the lower surface covered with dense
fur-like hair. The small whitish flowers usually grow
in clusters, and are produced in great abundance.
Following flowering, the seed, or fruit, grows a long,
hairy, twisted tail which gives the plant a
most unusual appearance.

ST. CATHERINE'S LACE
(Eriogonum giganteum giganteum)
St. Catherine's lace is usually
broader than it is tall and is
generally thought of as an evergreen shrub. The flowers on this
beautiful plant are borne on long
stems well above its silvery gray-
green leaves, and grow in
clusters which form a flat, lacy canopy. The plant is soft grayish-white
in May and June, then turns to ivory, beige, and light brown, and finally
in autumn it turns a rich russet color.

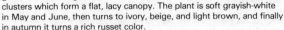

CATALINA MANZANITA
(Arctostaphylos catalinae)
Catalina manzanita is a
spreading evergreen shrub or
small tree which stands as much as
eight feet tall with smooth, dark red
bark and bright green hairy leaves.
The leaves are oblong or elliptical
and have a leathery texture. The
flowers bloom from January to March in large spreading
clusters at the tips of the branches and individual flowers
are urn-shaped, white, fragrant and about one-half inch
long. The fruit is about three-eighths inch thick and is
pinkish-yellow when forming and usually turns golden
brown to dark brown when mature.

CATALINA LIVE-FOREVER
(Dudleya hassei)
This low-growing succulent
rosette type perennial has
numerous slender, pencil-shaped
leaves, which are bluish to light
green. The yellow-white, star-shaped
flowers are borne on fleshy pink
stalks which are five to fifteen
inches long. It blooms in May and June.

ENDEMIC PLANTS (CONT.)

CATALINA IRONWOOD
(Lyonothamnus floribundus floribundus)
Catalina ironwood is a handsome
slender-crowned evergreen
tree which grows 50 to 70 feet
tall with a single trunk or with
a number of stems arising from
the ground. The dark green leaves are three to
six inches long and are generally entire
or whole with an occasional tendency toward a
fern-like dissection. It has reddish-brown
stringy bark. The small white flowers, borne in
large flat-topped clusters four to eight inches across,
mature in June and July.

YERBA SANTA
(Eriodictyon traskiae traskiae)
This evergreen shrub (not pictured) has shredding bark and a pungent
fragrance. It has an open, sprawling growth habit. The leaves are
grayish-white and wooly, usually toothed and mostly crowded toward the
ends of branches. The whitish-purple flowers cluster on the branch
tips, and bloom in May and June.

CATALINA BEDSTRAW
(Galium catalinense)
This plant (not pictured) is a perennial herb with four-angled slender woody
stems and branches. This dense, low-growing under-shrub with
inconspicuous whitish flowers blooms from April through July.

CATALINA'S INTERIOR

TWO HARBORS

In 1602, when Vizcaino's ship approached the mountains of Catalina rising out of the Pacific, he was certain he had reached two islands. From a distance, the bulk of land on the east end of Catalina appears to taper to a low point, which is separated by the sea from the small nub on the west end. In fact, there is no separation, only a low-lying neck, a half-mile-wide isthmus just 50 feet at its summit, comprising the narrowest section of Catalina Island. The ocean side of this isthmus is Catalina Harbor, the most protected harbor on the Island; the channel side is Isthmus Cove. This area is now called Two Harbors. It lies 26 miles by ocean and 14 miles by road from Avalon.

HISTORY

Two Harbors, at one time called Union Harbor, was also referred to as the "Isthmus" for many years, and many long-time visitors still do. It is the site of some of the most intriguing history of the Island. Allegedly, this is where one of the largest groups of Indians was located, along with the still-sought "temple" or *yuv'r* observed by the Vizcaino expedition. Their description fits the worship of the religious cult of Chingichnich that was the custom of most of the Gabrielinos at the time. You can still see the sink holes of the gold mines that flourished at the Isthmus,

Catalina Harbor in the early 1900s. Today the harbor is usually filled with pleasure boats.

Cherry Valley, and Fourth of July Cove in the 1860s. The Civil War barracks, built in 1863, are still in use by the Isthmus Yacht Club. Most of the roughnecks of the gold rush were driven out after the arrival of the Union volunteers. (See "History" in the main "Introduction" for details.)

Fact Or Fiction?

The history of Catalina abounds with legends. In most cases there is a minutia of truth, but as time passes and the stories are repeated they take on the embellishments of each storyteller. Most pirates and smugglers did not keep diaries, or if they did, none has ever been found. Still, some stories persist; but accept them for what they are, legends that may or may not be historically accurate.

Buried Treasure

The brig *Danube,* out of New York, was wrecked in 1824 on the rocks near San Pedro. Samuel Prentiss and other survivors made their way to the San Gabriel Mission. There Prentiss found an old Gabrielino Indian called Turie, alleged to be a chieftain from Catalina Island. The 70-year-old Indian, close to death, welcomed Prentiss' friendship.

Before he died, Turie told grand stories of rich treasure buried by the Island Indians beneath a tree on Catalina. He sketched a crude map, which launched the legendary treasure hunt of Sam Prentiss. He first returned to the site of the wreck in San Pedro, and from the salvage of the *Danube* built himself a small vessel and set sail for Catalina. In the middle of the channel he was caught in a severe storm. Everything he owned was washed overboard and it was all he could do to keep himself alive in the small boat. The treasure map was buried at the bottom of the sea but the dream was not forgotten. Prentiss made it to the Island, remembering only that the treasure was buried at the base of a tree. He built a small cabin overlooking Emerald Bay. For the next 30 years he hunted sea otter, fished, and spent every extra moment searching for his treasure. Gripped by the dream of riches, he sold firewood from the trees that he cut down and dug up in his relentless quest for the mysterious treasure. Purported to be the first white man to die on Catalina Island, today near where his cabin stood you can see the wind-grazed tombstone erected by Joseph Banning, one of the early owners of Catalina:

In memory of
Samuel Prentiss
A native of Massachusetts
Came to California in 1824
Died on Catalina 1854 — Age 72.

Apparently he never found the treasure. Keeping his secret to himself almost until the day he died, he ultimately shared it with Santos Louis Bouchette, giving rise to yet another bit of Island lore.

Bouchette

Santos Louis Bouchette was the son of one of the survivors of the *Danube* shipwreck. When Prentiss shared his secret with this young man it stimulated within Bouchette's heart the same desires about the treasure that had consumed Prentiss for 30 years. Bouchette also began the search, but he was luckier than Prentiss — or maybe wilier. In the midst of his treasure hunt he stumbled across rich veins of silver, lead, and gold. There are those who tell the story a little differently, saying that Bouchette "salted" the mine to encourage heavy financial backing from outsiders. Whether this is true or not, his mine was incorporated under the name of Mineral Hills Mines Company, and it became his real treasure. Bouchette operated the mine for some years, and on one of his many cross-channel trips to the pueblo of Los Angeles, after a whirlwind romance he came back to the Island married to a French dance-hall girl. The story goes that she didn't like the rough life the miners led, so Bouchette built her an elaborate house one and a half miles from Johnson's Landing, furnishing it with English mahogany furniture and a plate-glass mirror from France that cost him $1,000. He kept borrowing money to keep his mining venture solvent, and continued to prospect around every tree even remotely likely to be the one that guarded the treasure of Turie, the old Indian chief. Apparently, after some time his wife was still dissatisfied — or could he have finally found Samuel Prentiss' long-coveted Indian treasure? For one day in the spring of 1876 Bouchette and his wife were seen loading silver ore and a few provisions into their sailboat, and they were never seen again.

Gold

Francisco Lopez, a Mexican youth, has been credited with discovering the first gold in California near Newhall in 1842. While digging up a wild onion he found a gold nugget entangled in its roots. However, according to Catalina legend, Captain George Yount, a friend and associate of Samuel Prentiss, discovered an outcropping of gold-bearing quartz in a canyon near Two Harbors in 1830, a full 12 years before the strike at Sutter's Mill on the American River that started the California gold rush. Yount was deeply involved in otter hunting, and the bit of quartz he chipped off and stuffed into his pocket in Cherry Valley was forgotten until the Sutter's Mill find. He returned to the Island three times over the years trying to rediscover, without success, the location of the gold quartz he had first seen. In a fit of depression the sea captain shared his frustrating story with gold miners on the Mainland, which began the gold stampede on Catalina Island. There are various stories concerning the amount of gold found. Some say there was a lot, but the cost of mining was prohibitive. Others say the quality of the ore was not high. An English syndicate in 1873 forfeited its dreams and a $40,000 down payment on a mining deal to George Shatto after discovering the difficulties involved in getting the ore out of Silver Canyon with burro power.

The First Tourists

The Banning brothers, who owned the Island from 1892 to 1919, made one of the first changes to the landscape of the Isthmus. They could see its potential as a fishing paradise, so to encourage tourists a fishing bungalow (still being used by employees of the Catalina Camp and Cove Agency) was built on the hill between the two harbors in 1893. As the Bannings and then the Wrigleys developed the Island, the Isthmus, now

Hesperia, *the ship used in making the film version of Robert Louis Stevenson's* Treasure Island. *This classic children's adventure story, directed by Victor Fleming for MGM and starring Wallace Beery and Jackie Cooper, was filmed at the isthmus of*

Catalina in 1935. For the past 63 years, Two Harbors *and other Catalina coves have served as venues for such films as* MacArthur *and* The Sea Witch, *and more recently as the backdrop for TV dramas.*

called Two Harbors, also grew—but not in the same way as Avalon.

It remained a harbor only for those who could indulge in the luxury of yachting. This limited traffic in the 1920s and '30s to the elite. Christian's Hut, a Polynesian-style resort with a tropical-beach atmosphere, was a gathering spot for the affluent, glamorous film celebrities of that era. The Isthmus was a place where they could get away from autograph seekers and socialize with others who shared their status. The "star" status is far less important now, though just a few short years ago everyone was thrilled when the late John Wayne brought his large yacht, the *Wild Goose,* to Two Harbors.

Today, Two Harbors quietly bustles with campers, boaters, and vacationers who enjoy the serenity of low rolling hills and the fresh

breeze that skips across the narrow strip of land from the Pacific side of the Island.

Movies
Many films were shot at Two Harbors, especially in the days of the silents when the noise of the elements was unimportant. The shaggy palm trees on the sandy beach and the clear blue water met on the horizon by a smog-free sky were the backdrop for Clark Gable in *Mutiny on The Bounty,* for *Treasure Island, The Sea Witch, McHale's Navy,* and in 1976 Gregory Peck's landing on Corregidor in *MacArthur.* For many years the *Ning Po,* a nefarious junk built in China in 1773, was an attraction at Catalina Harbor. With an unsavory history including piracy, smuggling, and destruction at sea, it was rebuilt by an enterprising businessman for use as a Chinese cafe at the Isthmus, where it

was also a prop in several movies. Built of camphor and ironwood, no nails were used in its construction, but each joint was carefully fitted. The *Ning Po* stood as a monument to the genius of the Chinese shipbuilding industry. It was ultimately destroyed by the sea and lies buried beneath the mud in Catalina Harbor.

GETTING THERE

Day Trips

A day trip from Avalon on the shuttle bus leaves you plenty of time to explore Two Harbors, take a swim in exceptionally clear water, hike, fish, camp, or just relax away from the madding crowds. While at Two Harbors, enjoy a leisurely lunch at Doug's Harbor Reef Restaurant and Saloon or at the Snack Bar. Another alternative is to bring a lunch and picnic either at the beach or at Catalina Harbor. This is a short, easy hike across the narrowest part of the Island (a quarter mile past the old Union Army barracks) to the windward side of the Island where there are wooden tables, barbecue facilities, water, and restrooms. Coin-operated showers are included at public restrooms. The bandstand area (where there are tables, benches, and barbecue pits) on Isthmus Beach can be

reserved for private groups by calling (213) 510-0303.

Another good day trip for those interested in sightseeing, but not necessarily in hiking, is a trip to the Airport-In-The-Sky. Transportation is available in the Island Plaza (make reservations in advance) on one of the shuttle buses, and the ride up takes about a half hour. You have your choice of three buses, the Airport Bus, tel. 510-0143; Safari Bus, tel. 510-0303; or the Catalina Island Shuttle, tel. 510-2078. The Runway Cafe is open for breakfast and lunch, the views are lovely, and the Conservancy has a small natural history museum with samples of many types of cactus that grow on the Island. Be sure you make return reservations.

From Avalon

Shuttle buses leave several times a day from Avalon Island Plaza, 213 Catalina Street, for Two Harbors. The drive through the reserve gives you a view of the undeveloped lands of the Catalina Conservancy and the stunning wildlife of the Island, including herds of roaming buffalo.

From The Mainland

Two Harbors is becoming more and more accessible. There are two express boats: the speedy (90 minutes) *Catalina Express* and

Catalina Island shuttle buses make several trips daily to the interior.

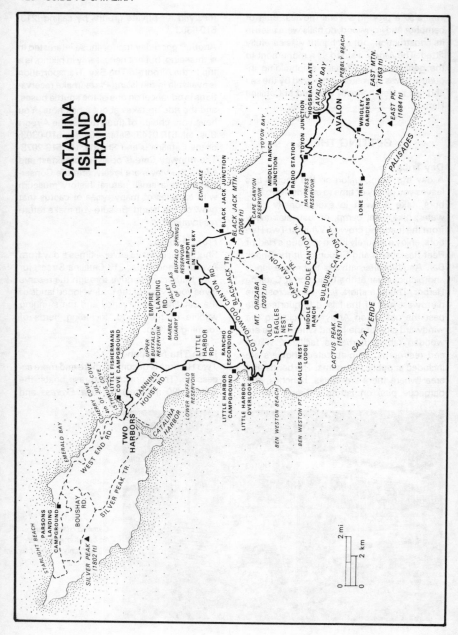

CATALINA ISLAND TRAILS

Avalon Express leave the San Pedro Terminal on a regular schedule every day year-round. These boats have stabilizers, airline-type seats, and a stewardess to serve you snacks and drinks. For reservations and schedules, call (213) 519-1212; $25 adult RT, child $15. Catalina Cruises runs a large boat to Two Harbors on a regular schedule throughout the year. During the summer they make two trips daily to Two Harbors. Call (213) 832-4521; $21.90 adult RT, child $11.70.

Health And Help

There are no medical facilities at Two Harbors. However, Los Angeles County has a group of highly trained paramedics and a fast boat, the *Bay Watch Isthmus,* equipped with all the high tech of an ambulance stationed year-round at Isthmus Cove. The *Bay Watch I* is stationed in Avalon. Between these two medical evacuation boats and the Avalon Municipal Hospital, Catalina possesses a highly effective emergency system for both land or sea accidents.

ACCOMMODATIONS

Banning House Lodge

The history-rich Banning House, built as a summer house for the Banning family in the late 1800s, is now operated as a lodge available with reservations only. It is used by hunters during the appropriate seasons. Doug's Harbor Reef Restaurant and Saloon is close by and open for dinner, and the Snack Bar is open for breakfast and lunch, all in walking distance. For overnight lodging information write to Box 5044, Two Harbors, Santa Catalina Island, CA 90704, tel. (213) 510-0303.

Camping

Make reservations with the Camp and Cove Agency for a campsite in the improved Little Fisherman site. Two Harbors to Little Fisherman's Cove is a quarter-mile walk on a narrow bumpy path, so carrying too much could be a problem. The campsites are located on a

hillside that slopes down to the blue water. On site are barbecues, picnic tables, toilets, cold showers, sun shades, and fire rings. Fires are a real danger; please restrict all fires and smoking to the barbecue and fire ring area only. Water is provided at each site; family and group campsites are available.

Restrictions

All groups must be accompanied by an adult at least 18 years old, who will assume full responsibility for the group at all times. Campers must stay in an assigned camping area. Plant collecting, wood cutting, or removing any natural feature is strictly prohibited. Please use the trash cans that are provided. Motorcycles, archery equipment, fireworks, and firearms are prohibited anywhere outside the city of Avalon. No pets are allowed in the campgrounds. Keep it quiet between 10 p.m. and 7 a.m.

The Coast Guard prohibits passengers on board the cross-channel vessels to carry propane, charcoal, gas stoves, and lanterns. Stoves and lanterns are available to rent from

Banning House

the campground ranger at Two Harbors; all rentals include fuel. Bring a flashlight and a water canteen if you plan on hiking.

RECREATION

Nature Hikes

At Two Harbors, several exploration trips are offered. Nature hikes are led by a naturalist who points out nature's unique exhibits, explains the colorful history, and helps you explore the plant and animal life surrounding the Two Harbors area. Hikes are conducted regularly, and walking tours last about two to four hours; wear good walking shoes and bring water. Cost begins at $4 pp. For information and reservations call 510-0303.

Island Safari

A van takes you into the rugged interior accompanied by a naturalist. You'll have a chance to see the spectacular views of the rugged cliffs and rolling sea as well as a close-up look at Catalina wildlife, including buffalo that wander the hills of the Island. Three- and four-hour tours available; tours start at $12.50 pp. Check with Two Harbors Camp and Cove, tel. 510-0303.

On Your Own

For independent exploration, scheduled bus service is available between Avalon and Two Harbors, leaving from Island Plaza in Avalon. Some runs stop at the airport and Little Harbor. Reservations necessary, call the Camp and Cove office at (213) 510-0303.

Diving

If you've come to Two Harbors for diving you won't be disappointed; about 75 percent of all boat-diving off Catalina is done on the west end. Snorkeling is excellent in any of the remote coves or kelp beds at the west end of Isthmus Cove. Near the mouth of the Isthmus is Bird Rock, kept white by flocks of seagulls, cormorants, brown pelicans, and other passing seafowl that pause during their migrations. The submarine terrain in this area

loading scuba tanks aboard for a day of diving in the clear waters around Two Harbors

is well worth exploring. The shallows, which range from 15-40 feet, are interspersed with giant kelp fronds and patches of eel grass which hide the small, colorful fish and strange sea creatures that feed on it. From here the bottom suddenly drops to a depth of about 100 feet, creating steep walls covered with gorgonia, sea urchins, and sea stars.

Tricky currents can be a hazard here as well as at some of the other popular dive spots, including Ship Rock and Eagle Reef. Blue Cavern Point offers several short underwater passageways that have been tunneled by wave action over the millennia. Probably the most attractive and treacherous dive spot on the windward side of the Island is Farnsworth Bank, three miles southwest of Ben Weston Beach. An ecological reserve, it has the only known purple coral on the Island; no souvenirs may be taken. Farnsworth has built-in hazards of strong currents and sheer sides that can plummet 35 fathoms. The Isthmus Dive Shop has air for tanks, and fins, masks, and snorkels can be rented. The selection is limited; they have no underwater lights or cameras, for example.

Snorkeling Safari
For the snorkeler or would-be snorkeler who didn't bring his own equipment but would like to see offshore marine fantasies, a snorkel trip is offered by the Camp and Cove Agency at Two Harbors. A snorkeling guide who knows the best places in the kelp forest takes you by boat to sunny coves and sandy beaches to snorkel Catalina's marine world. Equipment included in fee; $12 pp.

Fishing
Many fine eating fish swarm around the Two Harbors area. Although not the easiest to capture, lobster and abalone are two big favorites (check out fishing seasons and limits).

West End Cruising Club
Operated by Doug Bombard Enterprises, which also directs the Camp and Cove Agency. Most of the coves on the west end of Catalina are private and a landing fee is required. For a simple one- to two-day visit the landing fee is $4 per day. If, however, you are a boater and visit Two Harbors regularly, a yearly membership of $45 entitles you to year-round landing fees for up to six persons, plus many events. There are beach parties with big bands, theme parties, and fish and steak barbecues. Planned activities include dinghy races, volleyball tournaments, and wildlife seminars. Once a year members get together and have an underwater and shoreline clean-up in the Isthmus harbor. Doug's Harbor Reef Restaurant and Saloon is available for cocktail parties and catered events on the beach. The 4th of July is a special time with a flamboyant firework display over the bay jointly sponsored by the West End Cruising Club, Fourth of July Cove, and others. If you've never watched fireworks on an Island it's an experience you won't soon forget— brilliant lights over black water, the smell of explosives mixed with fresh sea air, and a cacophony of sounds from the boats as they blast their horns in thanks when the display is over. For information about the West End Cruising Club, call (213) 510-0303 or write Box 1566-F, Two Harbors, Santa Catalina Island, CA 90704.

PRACTICALITIES

General Store
Two Harbors General Store stocks a little of everything: most of the essential grocery items along with sundries, liquor, a few items

The Two Harbors pier

of clothing, even marine supplies. For large-group grocery orders call at least two weeks in advance and they'll be waiting for you when you arrive, tel. (213) 510-0303, ext. 217.

Marine Science Center

If you're staying at Two Harbors for several days visit the Marine Science Center. Operated by the University of Southern California's Institute for Marine and Coastal Studies, it offers courses in the marine sciences both at undergraduate and graduate levels. The center was established in 1968 through a Santa Catalina Island Company gift and lease of 45 land acres and 360 acres of sea floor. Buildings include laboratories, a hyperbaric chamber for emergency treatment of the bends (open to anyone along the Southern California coast who needs it), and dormitories for students. A guided tour of the facility with an illustrated lecture about the research at Catalina Marine Science Center, a viewing of the award-winning documentary about the kelp forests of Catalina, a visit to the touch tank, and a walking tour of the laboratory and the hyperbaric chamber takes two hours, every Sunday from July 5 through Labor Day weekend; $5 pp. A pleasant 2.2-mile hike from Two Harbors, or a shoreboat leaves the Two Harbors dock at 2:45 p.m. and returns from the Science Center dock at 5:15 p.m. Reservations needed; call (213) 510-0811 or 743-6792. For information about the program offered to marine-science students write: Resident Director Catalina Marine Science Center, P.O. Box 398, Avalon, CA 90704, tel. (213) 743-6792.

HIKING

Backpacking is a real adventure in the rugged hills of Catalina. Be aware of the interior's mountainous terrain and allow enough daylight to reach your destination. The network of undeveloped trails running across Catalina vary in type from goat trails and footpaths to jeep trails and fire roads. However, Los Angeles County Parks and Recreation asks that you keep to designated trails. There are no streams with potable water so take an ample supply; there's safe drinking water at all the improved campsites. Be prepared for very few commercial contacts like stores (general store at Two Harbors), and only a few phones are found along the way (phones are noted on hiking map). Hikers should carry a first-aid kit. Remember, you'll be sharing this outback with wild animals: bison, wild boar, goats, deer, and rattlesnakes. Expect to encounter poison oak — even in winter when the branches are bare. A brush against them will cause a reaction if you're allergy sensitive. A hiking permit (free) is necessary before you begin your trek into the interior. These are available at the Department of Parks and Recreation located in the Island Plaza, 213 Catalina Street, tel. (213) 510-0688, at Two Harbors, and at Airport-In-The-Sky.

A few tips to first-time hikers on Catalina: good hiking shoes are important, and the weather can differ from the interior to the coastal sections of the Island, varying as much as 30 degrees. Wearing layers is recommended. The days may be hot and wearing shorts and a T-shirt is comfortable, but the evenings (even in summer) usually always cool down, and long pants and a heavy sweatshirt feel good. If traveling around the Island during the rest of the year, a waterproof poncho is suggested. Don't forget to bring sun protection, a hat, and sunblock lotion.

HIKING TRAILS

Route Out Of Avalon

You can start your trip in Avalon—trails and roads lead from there to within one mile of the west end of the Island. To hike out of Avalon, go toward the Casino on Crescent Street, turn left on Marilla Street, right on Vieudelou Street, and then take a last left on-to Stage Road. A paved street, it's the main road out of Avalon into the interior; expect lots of vehicular traffic. This first part of your trip is a hilly climb from the first turn on Marilla.

Silver Peak Trail To Parson's Landing

(10.1 miles—strenuous.) A backcountry trail for the experienced hiker. Use a compass. On this hike, you'll get sensational views of the mountains meeting the sea. Campsites are available at Parson's Landing, but reservations are necessary through Camp and Cove; tel. 510-0303.

Two Harbors To Parson's Landing

(6.8 miles, 0-5% grade.) This is all dirt, fairly level, a comfortable walk with beautiful views of the ocean. The trail takes you past the scout camps.

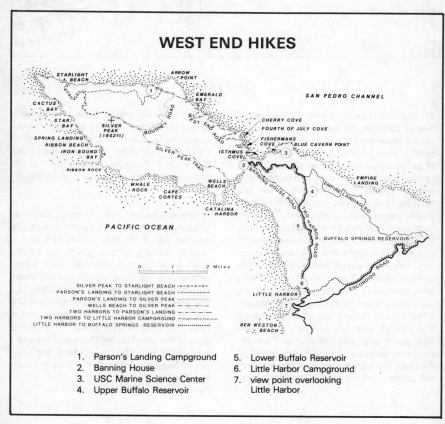

WEST END HIKES

SILVER PEAK TO STARLIGHT BEACH —·—·—·—·—
PARSON'S LANDING TO STARLIGHT BEACH ——————
PARSON'S LANDING TO SILVER PEAK ————————
WELLS BEACH TO SILVER PEAK ——————
TWO HARBORS TO PARSON'S LANDING ——·——·——
TWO HARBORS TO LITTLE HARBOR CAMPGROUND ————
LITTLE HARBOR TO BUFFALO SPRINGS RESERVOIR ·············

1. Parson's Landing Campground
2. Banning House
3. USC Marine Science Center
4. Upper Buffalo Reservoir
5. Lower Buffalo Reservoir
6. Little Harbor Campground
7. view point overlooking Little Harbor

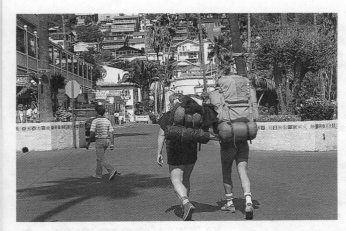

backpackers heading
into the interior from
Avalon

Little Harbor To West Summit
(4.3 miles, 5-10% grade.) This is a gradual uphill dirt trail, moderately difficult: you travel uphill for two miles.

West Summit To Two Harbors
(2.5 miles, 10%-plus grade.) This dirt trail is mostly downhill from West Summit to Two Harbors. It takes you past the turnoff to Fisherman's Cove, USC Marine Center, and Little Fisherman's Campground. While at Two Harbors notice the Isthmus Yacht Club, formerly the old Civil War barracks.

Avalon To East Summit
(3.2 miles, 10% grade.) This is all uphill. The road is slurry and lined with eucalyptus trees. You'll enjoy great views, though it gets quite steep in places. When you reach the summit stop to admire more superior views.

Empire Landing Road From Two Harbors
(6.2 miles—moderate.) Leave Two Harbors on the surfaced main road to Avalon, and break off to an abandoned dirt road which leads to Airport-In-The-Sky.

Boushey Road
(2.1 miles—strenuous.) The connecting dirt road between Silver Peak Trail and Parson's Landing. For only the hardy hiker.

West Summit To The Airport Via Empire
(7.0 miles, 5-10%-plus grade.) This is an undeveloped dirt trail. Half the time it goes up and half down. This takes you past the old Empire Landing rock quarry where you can get water. It's uphill to the airport, a moderately difficult hike.

Airport To Little Harbor Overlook
(5.8 miles, 10%-plus grade.) This road is all dirt and downhill. It goes through the Wrigley family's Rancho Escondido. The trail parallels Cottonwood Canyon. If you want to make a detour through Cottonwood, make a left at the airport to hit Cottonwood Canyon. Water is available at Little Harbor. Be aware of wild pigs in the area.

Little Harbor Overlook To Little Harbor
(1.2 miles, 5-10% grade.) An all downhill dirt trail. Be aware of vehicle traffic through here, including tour buses.

Ben Weston Junction To Little Harbor Overlook
(2.3 miles, 10%-plus grade.) This trail is mostly uphill—about two miles of it. You'll see the location of a World War II gunnery station at the top. From here the view of the coast and Little Harbor is breathtaking.

Old Eagles Nest Trail

(2.6 miles, 5-10% grade.) This is an undeveloped loop trail that begins at the old Eagles Nest stagecoach stop and meets the main road into Little Harbor. Hill climbing involved, moderately difficult.

Cottonwood Trail

(5.5 miles, 5-10%-plus grade.) Moderately difficult undeveloped trail.

Black Jack Junction To Black Jack

(1.5 miles, 5-10% grade.) Dirt trail, gradual upgrade. The turnoff to the campground is marked. Black Jack is the island's second highest peak, at 2,010 feet. Old mine shafts dot the area. There's a telephone at the junction.

Black Jack Junction To Airport

(2.5 miles, 5-10% grade.) There are some lovely views on this hike. Runway Cafe and water available at the airport. Lots of buffalo roam the area. This is a moderately easy hike.

Middle Ranch To Black Jack Via Cape Canyon

(2.7 miles, 0-5% grade.) Fairly level walking along Catalina's China Wall.

Middle Ranch To Black Jack Via Cape Canyon

(4.4 miles, 5-10% grade.) This dirt trail is all uphill. The last mile and a half is very steep. Cape Canyon is a pleasant hike, giving you a good look at the farming activities of Catalina. Note: the Conservancy asks that you do

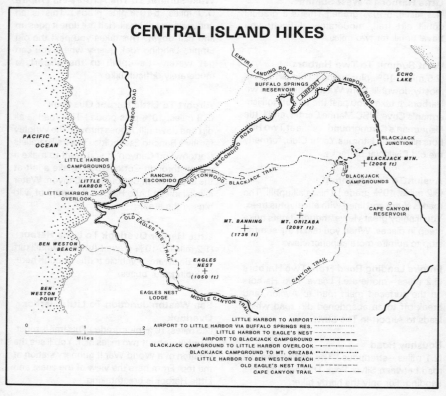

CENTRAL ISLAND HIKES

LITTLE HARBOR TO AIRPORT ················
AIRPORT TO LITTLE HARBOR VIA BUFFALO SPRINGS RES. ················
LITTLE HARBOR TO EAGLE'S NEST ——————
AIRPORT TO BLACKJACK CAMPGROUND ————
BLACKJACK CAMPGROUND TO LITTLE HARBOR OVERLOOK — ■ — ■ —
BLACKJACK CAMPGROUND TO MT. ORIZABA ————
LITTLE HARBOR TO BEN WESTON BEACH ———————
OLD EAGLE'S NEST TRAIL ————
CAPE CANYON TRAIL ————

Hiking in Catalina's interior was only made possible since the formation of the Catalina Conservancy in 1972.

not cut through crops. The second bump gate is the trail marker turnoff. Difficult.

Middle Ranch To Ben Weston Junction
(2.4 miles 10%-plus grade.) Moderate. The dirt road passes the Camp Cactus turnoff (old Army camp). Turn at the Ben Weston Junction for the beach.

Middle Ranch Junction To Middle Ranch
(4.8 miles, 0-10%-plus grade.) All dirt road and downhill. Lots of buffalo and maybe deer. Stay to the side of road due to traffic — tour buses and other vehicles.

Bullrush Canyon Trail
(7.5 miles, 5-10% grade.) Undeveloped dirt trail, hardy trekkers call this the best hike on the Island. Lots of scrub oak and wildlife. Downhill, level.

Summit To Middle Ranch Junction
(2.0 miles, 0-5% grade.) This is a slurry road, and it's fairly level. Behind Haypress Lake are two others called Hidden Lakes, gateway to Silver Canyon — lots of poison oak. Taking a left at the third lake takes you to Silver Canyon. Moderate hike.

**Hiking To Little Harbor
From Two Harbors**
From Doug's Harbor Reef Restaurant and Saloon, walk to the main road towards Avalon and follow it up and over the hills past upper Buffalo Reservoir and into Little Harbor. For the highly experienced hiker in excellent physical condition there's another strenuous trail to Little Harbor by way of the old Banning House Road that cuts off about a mile from the Banning House. Follow the Banning House Road for 3.2 miles, until you run into the surfaced Little Harbor Road, where you turn right. Following that for another 1.9 miles brings you to Little Harbor Campgrounds. Beware of rattlesnakes.

Organized Nature Hikes
These treks offer you the opportunity to explore the plant and animal life surrounding the Two Harbors area. Nature hikes are conducted upon request during the summer months only. Contact the L.A. County or Two Harbors ranger. Slide lectures are also given at various times on the beach at Two Harbors.

CAMPING

On Catalina you'll find two types of campgrounds: primitive and improved. Primitive camps have no facilities whatsoever; improved sites include toilets, fire rings, and barbecue pits. Some have showers, most have phones, some are accessible only by boat (B), some by shuttle (S), some hike-in (H), and a few by shore boat (SB) from Isthmus Cove at Two Harbors.

The five improved campgrounds are all accessible by road; three shuttle bus companies offer daily summer service to all of them; check with L.A. County and Camp and Cove for winter schedules. Of the six primitive sites, five are accessible by boat only on a first-come first-served basis (see "Hiking Maps"). Little Fisherman, Parson's Landing, and Emerald Bay, at the west end near Two Harbors, require landing permits (obtained at the Camp and Cove office at Two Harbors for $4). For a map of the areas described, send a stamped, self-addressed envelope to the Los Angeles County Parks, Box 1133, Avalon, CA 90704. **Note:** Fires are permitted at improved campsites *only.*

Getting There
In Avalon, at 213 Catalina Street in the Island Plaza, catch the shuttle bus to the Bird Park Campground, Airport-In-The-Sky, and to all the improved campsites in the interior. Reservations to the interior are required. For more information and seasonal schedule call (213) 510-2078, 510-0143, or 510-0303.

IMPROVED CAMPGROUNDS

Bird Park Campground
This was the former location of the famous Wrigley Bird Park. Its large garden setting was the backdrop for thousands of exotic birds until it was removed. Bird Park Campground is the closest campground to Avalon, and is within walking distance of all the town attractions. It can be easily reached by walking up Sumner Avenue through Avalon Canyon. Follow the sign that says "Avalon Canyon Road." From the sign it's one mile inland, located across from the picnic grounds. Operated by the SCI Co., facilities include 75

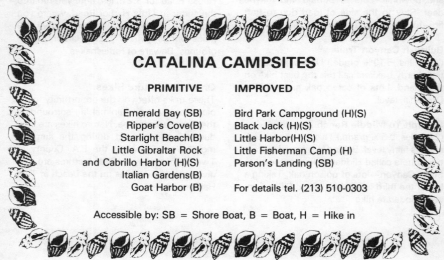

CATALINA CAMPSITES

PRIMITIVE	IMPROVED
Emerald Bay (SB)	Bird Park Campground (H)(S)
Ripper's Cove(B)	Black Jack (H)(S)
Starlight Beach(B)	Little Harbor(H)(S)
Little Gibraltar Rock	Little Fisherman Camp (H)
and Cabrillo Harbor (H)(S)	Parson's Landing (SB)
Italian Gardens(B)	
Goat Harbor (B)	For details tel. (213) 510-0303

Accessible by: SB = Shore Boat, B = Boat, H = Hike in

Camping in Catalina's coves is a time to enjoy the sea, stars, and fauna.

campsites with water, cold showers, toilets, picnic tables, fire rings, barbecue pits, and a public phone. Fees: adult $5, child under 15 free; for reservations call (213) 510-0688.

Black Jack

Mount Black Jack, at 2,006 feet, is the second highest peak on Catalina (the first, at 2,097 feet, is Mt. Orizaba). It's the site of old Black Jack Mine (lead, zinc, and silver). Black Jack Camp, 10 miles from Avalon and 15 miles from Two Harbors, is located at a 1,500-foot elevation. It is the principal inland camping area on Catalina, set in a lovely, protected pine forest. Some vantage points in the camp overlook the channel side of the Island and toward the Mainland. Operated by Los Angeles County Department of Parks and Recreation, the camp offers accommodations for 75 campers. Facilities include water, toilets, fire rings, barbecue pits, public phone (at Black Jack junction), and shuttle bus service. Fees: adult $5, child 14 and under 50 cents. For reservations call (213) 510-0688.

Little Harbor

The primary campground on the Pacific side of Catalina, Little Harbor is also considered by some to be the most picturesque and historic. Bring your camera for spectacular views from Indian Head Point above Little Harbor. Much of the history of the Catalina Indians has been brought to light in a deeply stratified archeological site overlooking the twin bays of Little Harbor (see "History"). In 1894 Dr. O.T. Fellows built an inn here as a stopover for stagecoach passengers visiting the Island. The inn has long since gone, but the old stage road, still used today, meets the sea at its twin harbors: the smaller one, Little Harbor, is a placid anchorage, while the larger Shark Harbor is a surf-pounded strand that offers exciting beachcombing possibilities (especially after a storm) and excellent bodysurfing. Little Harbor campground is on the site of an ancient Indian village. A good base for day hiking to a variety of destinations, it's seven miles from Two Harbors and six miles from Black Jack. Though on the windward side of the Island, the camp is located in a protected patch of flat land close to the road and the ocean. Operated by the Los Angeles County Department of Parks and Recreation, it can accommodate 150 campers, with toilets, cold showers, barbecue pits, fire rings, picnic tables, phone, and shuttle bus service. It offers excellent swimming, diving, and fishing. Fees: adult $5, child 14 and under 50 cents; call (213) 510-0688 for reservations.

CAMPING SUPPLIES

As a camper you know what food and clothes will fit your lifestyle. The following is a checklist of other things to consider taking on your camping trip to Catalina Island.

- ✓ flashlight
- ✓ extra batteries
- ✓ sunglasses
- ✓ pen/paper/cards/book
- ✓ knife
- ✓ extra pair of broken-in shoes
- ✓ lightweight tent
- ✓ lightweight sleeping bag
- ✓ something to anchor a windbreak
- ✓ camera/film
- ✓ waterproof matches
- ✓ water supply
- ✓ canteen
- ✓ extra pair of glasses
- ✓ toilet paper
- ✓ Chapstick
- ✓ water purification tablets
- ✓ towel
- ✓ Calmitol ointment (good for
  burns, bites, and rashes)
- ✓ snake-bite kit

Little Fisherman Camp

This privately owned campground is a half mile from Two Harbors on a bluff overlooking the rocky beach and crystal-clear waters of the cove. From here you can see right down to the bottom and watch the variegated hues of blue and green continue for some way out to sea. It's a good base from which to explore the many trails and coves of the west end. There's a general store, dive shop, restaurant, bar, and many other activities available thanks to the close proximity of the West End Cruising Club (see "Two Harbors"). Facilities accommodate 250 campers, with toilets, cold showers, fire rings, barbecues, picnic tables, phone, swimming, fishing, and diving. Since it is illegal to carry combustible materials on public transport, be prepared to buy charcoal and lighter fluid from the park ranger. Fees: $5 pp, payable at the Camp and Cove office at the foot of the pier at Two Harbors. For reservations, call (213) 510-0303.

Parson's Landing

The easiest way to get there is to travel from Two Harbors by shoreboat (seasonal schedule). The boat ride offers spectacular coastal views. By trail, Parson's Landing is seven miles west of Two Harbors. This undeveloped campground adjacent to the beach can be a quiet spot, but very crowded on a holiday weekend. Facilities can accommodate 150 campers, with latrines, fire rings, barbecue pits, limited water, firewood, charcoal, and lighter fluid available from the campground ranger. Fees: $5 pp, payable at the Camp and Cove office. For reservations call (213) 510-0303.

PRIMITIVE CAMPSITES

Camping is permitted at six different coves on the lee coast of the Island. These completely undeveloped sites are not maintained by any agency, and provide little more than a flat area to lay out your sleeping bag. Fees ($3 pp per day) are paid to Conservancy rangers who will find you. First come, first served.

Emerald Bay/Sandy Beach

The cove of Emerald Bay is leased to the Corsair Yacht Club, and a portion of the beach and surrounding area is leased to the Boy Scouts of America for use as a summer camp. However, public camping is available in a primitive campsite on Sandy Beach. Accessible by boat or by road from Two Harbors. Emerald Bay, too, has exceptionally clear water and its share of Catalina's colorful past. Samuel Prentiss was the first white man to build a house on Catalina, here at Emerald

Bay. He is buried on the hill overlooking what almost became the mining town of "Queen City" during the gold frenzy of 1863-64. Today this out-of-the-way area continues to provide tranquil retreat for the explorer who prefers the peace of a grassy hillside sloping down to a spacious Robinson Crusoe-style beach.

Rippers Cove
An excellent primitive campsite, accessible only by boat. There's good anchorage on the sandy bottom, and the sloping grassland behind the beach provides vigorous safe and scenic hiking.

Starlight Beach
A small beach one mile short of Land's End, the westernmost tip of Catalina Island. Access by boat only. The diving is excellent in the transparent waters of this cove.

Little Gibraltar Rock And Cabrillo Harbor
The small leased camp at Cabrillo Harbor is operated by the Long Beach Council of Boy Scouts as a summer camp. The harbor also contains a primitive campsite for public use. Access to the interior from the beach is very difficult due to rough terrain. Boat-in only.

Italian Gardens
Named for the many San Pedro fishermen that successfully fished here some years back, this is a long beach with access by boat only for primitive camping and terrific diving. There is no hiking into the interior from the beach.

Little Harbor

Goat Harbor

This is a rugged geological area. Access by boat to a sandy beach offers primitive camping. The cliffs are dangerous. Access to the interior from the beach is very difficult due to rough terrain.

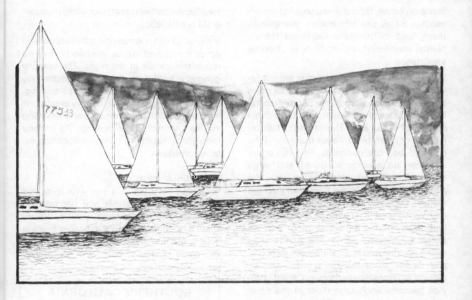

BOATING

CRUISING CALIFORNIA'S SOUTHERN COAST

The Channel Islands are unquestionably the most popular destination for boaters along the Southern California coast. An island is an obvious draw for boaters, and at least one is close enough to Santa Barbara, Ventura, Los Angeles, Orange County, and San Diego to be accessible—even to smaller craft. For boaters who're looking for an active nightlife and other shore activities, Avalon is the harbor for your visit. On the other hand, if it's the quiet life you're seeking, escape to one of the other Channel Islands; or head to one of Catalina's many small isolated coves, where the loudest thing you'll hear—aside from other boaters—is the slap of the water on your bow, and maybe a squawking seagull. Most

of these isolated coves show no sign of man's intrusion. Day hikes will bring you into direct contact with the natural phenomena of the islands, and diving is unparalleled along the entire California coast.

PRACTICALITIES

Weather Information
Every seaman has a big responsibility—not only for his own personal safety and that of his crew, but (as most would concede) for a large financial investment as well. Weather plays an important part in boating, and a lot of tragedies could be averted with the use of

common sense. Boat owners should take advantage of all the information available to them, and in Southern California there's plenty; monitoring the weather is of prime importance.

Even though some of the islands are not far from the Mainland (Catalina is only 22 miles from Long Beach Harbor) the Santa Barbara/ Catalina Channel is known as a formidable stretch of open sea. The crossing can be smooth or it can pitch waves that pound the hull and leap the gunwales. Fog can occur any time, but in winter it's denser and hangs in there longer. Fog seldom forms when the air is at least five degrees F warmer than the water, so visibility improves with fresh southerly winds and a steady or slowly falling barometer. During the winter months in the Catalina Channel, Santa Ana winds (also called northeasters) can shift swell direction and render an anchorage unsafe. And although all coves and harbors in Catalina provide peaceful anchorage most of the time, pay heed to the forecasts. When an advisory is in effect or storm warning is up, don't go out unless you happen to be a highly qualified sailor and have experience in the prevailing sea conditions — and it's an emergency trip! If you're already at sea, go home or to the nearest harbor that will give you protection from the predicted wind and sea direction. Check the flags and lights on the mole in Avalon and at Two Harbors Office.

Note: One red pennant or red-over-white lights mean forecast is an 18- to 33-knot wind and/or sea, dangerous for small boats. Two red pennants or white-over-red lights mean a 34- to 47-knot gale. One square red flag with black center, or red-over-red lights mean a 48- to 63-knot storm. For marine weather information from Los Angeles 24 hours, call (213) 477-1463; for aircraft weather from FAA, call (213) 776-1640 or 787-4911. By radio, 24 hours from the National Weather Service, use VHF Channel Wx-1 to about 97 miles from Mt. Wilson. Or from FAA Los Angeles, use beacon band 332 kHz. Southern California harbormasters are always on call

for a local weather report; the Avalon number is (213) 510-0535.

It's wise to know where the safe harbors and coves are located in case you need to make a run in the middle of the night. The seasons generally hold true, but to eliminate any unpleasant surprises, know what's coming. One of the biggest aids in stormy conditions is to stay calm and remember everything you've learned about sailing. As in any emergency situation, panic compounds existing problems.

Radio Equipment

For about $400 you can buy a receiver that will pick up the weather and not take up much space. Undoubtedly, you've already spent a great deal of money on your boating hobby, but it's false economy to do without this piece of equipment. For more money

---

SOUTHERN CALIFORNIA COASTAL STORM WARNING DISPLAY LOCATIONS

San Diego: Ballast Point, B Street Pier, Coronado Yacht Club, Shelter Island, Mission Bay Aquatic Headquarters, Oceanside Harbor

Dana Point Harbor

Catalina Island: Avalon Pleasure Pier, Isthmus Cove

Sunset Beach

Newport Beach Harbor: Channel Entrance

Long Beach Marina: Administration Building

San Pedro: Marine Exchange Building

Redondo Beach: King Harbor on the Breakwater

Marina del Rey: Administration Building

Port Hueneme Naval Station, Oxnard: Channel Islands Harbor

Ventura Marina

Santa Barbara: Weather Signal Station

CALIFORNIA COASTAL STORM WARNING FLAGS AND LIGHTS

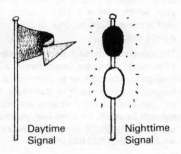

Daytime Signal   **Nighttime Signal**

Small Craft Advisories

One red pennant displayed by day and a red light over a white light at night indicate winds as high as 33 knots (38 mph) and/or sea conditions considered dangerous to small craft. operations are forecast for the area.

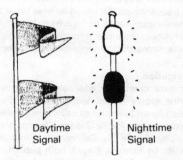

Daytime Signal   **Nighttime Signal**

Gale Warning

Two red pennants displayed by day and a white light above a red light at night indicate that winds 34-47 knots (39-54 mph) are forecast for the area.

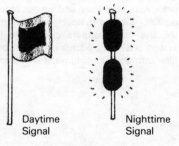

Daytime Signal   **Nighttime Signal**

Storm Warning

A single square red flag with a black center displayed during daytime and two red lights at night indicate that winds 48 knots (55 mph) and above are forecast for the area. If the winds are associated with a tropical cyclone (hurricane), the storm warning displays indicate that winds 48-63 knots (55-73 mph) are forecast.

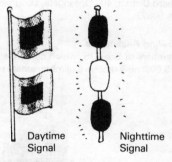

Daytime Signal   **Nighttime Signal**

Hurricane Warning

Displayed only in connection with a tropical cyclone (hurricane). Two square red flags with black centers displayed by day and a white light between two red lights at night indicate that winds 64 knots (74 mph) and above are forecast for the area.

(about $1,000) you can buy a ham radio rig. You must have a license to broadcast, but not to listen. Other boaters talk to each other and give good information about the weather in different areas. Anyone interested in sailing frequently and far would be wise to get a general-class license (or higher) to have full capability to broadcast through the ham networks, especially in an emergency situation.

Navigation

Accurate charts are available from most marine supply stores. Valuable books that should be on board for all sailors that cruise the channel are *Pacific Boating Almanac* and *Cruising Guide To California's Channel Islands,* by Brian M. Fagan, both published by Western Marine Enterprises, Inc. The Chart Guide for Catalina is also handy to tuck away. For maximum convenience and safety ask to have your name put on a free mailing list for the "Local Notice to Mariners," which provides weekly NOAA chart editions that indicate shoreline and depth changes. For this service write to: Commander, 11th Coast Guard District, 400 Oceangate, Long Beach, CA 90822.

Towing Assistance

Members of Boat/US (which number about 215,000) now receive a reimbursement up to $50 for boat-towing service. Membership in the non-profit organization is $17 and entitles each to up to $1,500 per year insurance coverage. Broader towing coverage is available from Boat/US for an additional $5.50 per year, which covers a $150 incident, $11 a year to cover a $350 incident, or $15 a year for a $500 incident.

The association made this service available in 1984, when the Coast Guard turned all non-emergency towing over to commercial firms (except in foul weather or darkness). Other services and marine insurance are available through Boat/US; for more information contact Boat/US, 880 S. Pickett St., Alexandria, VA 22304, tel. (703) 823-9550.

Boat Gadgets

There are many gadgets that you can buy for a boat that make it pretty, practical, efficient, easier, or just fun. One that could be a health saver is a water-filter system. There are several on the market, one of which is the Brita Filter System from West Germany. It's designed to remove chlorine and chlorine compounds, lead and copper, organic pollutants, rust, chemicals, and various other impurities—without removing valuable minerals, the manufacturers claim. The basic system is a plastic pitcher and a replaceable filter cartridge. Drinking water is poured into

Don't let this happen to you.

the top section of the pitcher and filtered into the bottom for pouring or storage. Also available is a Travel Pack, which removes impurities unsafe for drinking. This includes germicidal disinfectant tablets to help destroy parasites, plus the Brita cartridge to filter out the chemical taste of the tablets. Including the Travel Pack, the price is about $50. For more information contact Brita America Marketing West, 444 Castro St., Suite 426, Mountain View, CA 94041; in Southern California call (800) 672-3470 ext. 825; out of state call (800) 538-8157.

Underwater Repair Service
If you need an emergency underwater repair, or your line gets wrapped around the prop, or you've dropped your only prescription glasses overboard, don't panic. In Avalon, Gary's Mooring & Diving Service, tel. 510-0779, is available for any diving jobs you need to have done. Argo Diving, tel. 510-2208, is also available for even the most creative of diving needs.

CATALINA COVES AND HARBORS

AVALON MARINAS

Mooring Information
Moorings are assigned on a first-come first-served basis. There are 400 moorings in Avalon and on a busy weekend, rafting (two boats tied together to one mooring) increases the boat population to as much as 500. Upon arrival please stand by at the harbor entrance until a patrol boat assigns a mooring. Mooring fees are payable to the patrol boat or at the Harbormaster's office. Departing without paying incurs double charges. On your day of departure, moorings must be vacated by 9 a.m. If you arrive in Avalon on a busy weekend and find all moorings occupied, you can anchor free of charge in specified areas at the discretion of the Harbormaster. The Harbor Patrol maintains a 24-hour service year-round; there is no landing fee at Avalon, Descanso Bay, Hamilton Beach, or any Conservancy property.

Besides Avalon, 17 other coves have moorings, and many others provide anchorage. For more detailed information about the numerous coves on the Island, call the Camp and Cove Agency at (213) 510-0303. They can tell you where to moor, what the prices are, the hazards, and if anchorage is available.

Note: Do not bring firearms, bow-hunting gear, or motorcycles to shore—all are prohibited. Fires are a real danger, not allowed except in designated camping and picnic areas. Make charcoal fires only (charcoal is available on the Island). Do not cut trees or shrubs or remove any artifacts you might find on shore or underwater.

Note: Between October 15 and two weeks before Easter, two nights' fees buy five additional consecutive nights if the moorings are available.

Avalon's Harbormaster, John Phelps

AVALON MOORING FEES

Boats 39' and under	$12 per night
40' to 49'	$16 per night
50' to 59'	$20 per night
60' to 69'	$25 per night
70' to 79'	$30 per night
80' to 89'	$35 per night
90' to 99'	$40 per night
100' and over	$45 per night

Services

Complete cooperation is necessary to keep the harbor and beaches clean. Harbor Department service boats pick up trash daily, free of charge, at approximately 10 a.m. and 2 p.m. Plastic trash bags can be obtained from the patrol boats or at the Harbormaster's office. Leave the trash bag on the stern of your boat, making sure there's nothing around it that might be mistaken for trash and hauled away. A holding-tank pump-out station is located on Float No. 5 in the southeast corner of Avalon Bay. All generators and other noisy motors must be shut off by 10 p.m. Shoreboats and fueling service are available year-round. Shoreboat fees to the Pleasure Pier are $1.50 pp for the inner harbor and $2 for the outer harbor. Some summers, enterprising Island kids operate a boat-to-boat shopping service from a small outboard. You can order almost anything and it'll be delivered to your boat for a price. Please anticipate your water needs because Avalon has a water shortage. Fresh water is available at the Chevron fuel dock.

Gas Dock

The Chevron Oil gas dock is located on Casino Pier in Avalon for all your boat fuel needs,

Avalon Harbor

Hamilton Cove

tel. 510-0046. Diesel fuel and regular gasoline and oil are also available at Two Harbors, tel. 510-0303.

Descanso Bay
There are 47 moorings and anchorage in Descanso Bay; you are requested to keep dinghies out of the swim area and no beach landings are permitted. For your convenience a dinghy dock is located on the gas dock at Casino Point, another between the Tuna Club and the Yacht Club, and one at the Pleasure Pier. Dinghies up to 13 feet may be tied to any of these docks for up to 72 hours. Don't leave removable motors or anything else loose, and be aware that even an entire dinghy can be a victim of theft. Stopping at any dock other than the dinghy docks men-

tioned is permitted only long enough to transfer people.

Hamilton Beach
There are 52 moorings and uncomfortable anchorage. This cove was once the location of the prewar seaplane terminal. Today, the cove is the home of a beautiful Mediterranean village of condos that graciously climb the hillside, all with fantastic views. The architecture and design of these condos really make a lovely vista from a boat as well.

Lovers Cove
To encourage the growth of marinelife in this underwater preserve, there are no moorings; anchorage is prohibited. Lovers Cove is used for swimming, snorkeling, and glass-bottom boat cruising only.

MOORINGS AND ANCHORAGES
AROUND THE ISLAND

Cruising around the Island gives you a glimpse into each of the coves that circle Catalina. The following information touches on each cove, the number of possible anchorages and how many moorings are at each location, as well as other miscellaneous information.

Seal Rocks
Past Lovers Cove toward the east end is Pebbly Beach. Here the amphibian airport and ramp share the shoreline with the helicopter pad, boat yard, freight dock, Southern California Edison plant, Buffalo Nickel Restaurant, and the only gas station serving Avalon town. There are no moorings and no anchoring is allowed. Continuing past Pebbly Beach you'll see one of Catalina's two rock quarries. This and the quarry at Empire landing (in operation since before the turn of the century) have provided millions of tons of rock for Mainland sea walls and breakwaters. The Los Angeles Light breakwater is 90 percent Catalina rock, Pier J next to the *Queen Mary*

contains three million tons, Redondo Beach and Port Hueneme breakwaters each contain one and a half million tons, and Playa del Rey breakwater three-quarters of a million tons. None of this seems to make a dent in the Catalina shoreline. On past Jewfish Point is a rookery for the California sea lions. Boaters: watch for submerged rocks in this area.

To China Point
As you round the east end of the Island you'll pass Church Rock before coming to the Palisades area, so named because of the steep

mountains that drop to the sea. From the water you can see the web-like paths of the goats that roam these hills. This is good anchorage during Santa Ana storm conditions. Going on, Silver Canyon Landing has no moorings, but it does have anchorage with some westerly protection. Going ashore is risky due to the surf, but if you plan to attempt a landing you'll find the fewest breakers on the southwest corner. Continuing on past Bulldog Rock and Salta Verde Point with its "painted cliffs" will bring you to China Point. In the 1800s, this was the location of one of the camps where illegal Chinese immigrants, supposedly being returned to China by government order, were dropped off by unscrupulous sea captains before being smuggled back to the California Mainland. Between China Point and Ben Weston Point you may spot seals. There are no moorings at Ben Weston beach and anchorage is considered unsafe.

Little Harbor

West, beyond Indian Head Rock, you'll come to one of the most picturesque harbors on the Island, which is really two individual harbors, Little Harbor and Shark Harbor. Little Harbor has no moorings, but excellent anchorage for 10-15 boats. Shark Harbor, the larger, has no moorings; anchorage is considered unsafe. Surfing, however, is good. Little Harbor offers improved camping facilities for 150 persons. From here, you can hike to the tops of the surrounding hills for spectacular coastal vistas, see wildlife, and explore the ancient location of one of the main communities of the Catalina Indians.

WEST END AND TWO HARBORS

Catalina Harbor

"Cat" Harbor has 85 moorings (mostly leased to the California Yacht Club) and anchorage for 235. Following the coast past Pin Rock you'll sail into Catalina Harbor. This is the isthmus of the Island, the narrowest point (one-half mile wide). Unless you have a membership card, a $4 adult, $1.50 child per-day fee is charged by the West End Cruising Club for coming ashore at Catalina Harbor. Pay at the foot of the pier at Isthmus Cove or to one of the employees who keeps track of the area. You'll find firepits, good picnic facilities, and toilets, but camping is not allowed. The wreck of the nefarious Chinese pirate ship *Ning Po* is buried under the mud here. Ballast Point (see map) is said to have been formed by Yankee clippers who dropped ballast here to scrape the bottoms of their ships.

In the days before these waters were charted, this nub of land separated by Two Harbors fooled sailors into thinking that this was another island. Continuing on around Catalina Head, you come to Lobster Bay, which, according to legend, was a pirate hideout. At Whale Rock, what looks like a whale's water spout is only a "blow hole" caused by the tide hitting the rock and forcing a column of water along it and up into the air. Ribbon Rock attracts attention with its striated layers of quartz against the high dark face of the cliff. It was here, according to Frederick Holder's story "Adventure of Torqua" (see "Blue Cavern Point" in this section), that white settlers forever trapped a band of Indians in an underground cave by sealing the exit. Iron Bound Cove has no moorings; although the anchorage is exposed, it's considered fair. From here legend has it that the Chinese immigrants would leave their temporary camps and hike over to Catalina Harbor to gamble.

From Eagle Rock To Land's End

Eagle Rock is almost at Land's End, on the western tip of Catalina. Until 1952, the American bald eagle used this isolated area to breed. Today, although there are no eagles here, you can see brown pelicans in sizeable numbers. As you cruise around Land's End you'll see the West End Light; expect strong currents and swell.

Parson's Landing

Here you'll find two moorings and anchorage for 10. This is a good beach for camping, with fire rings, toilets, and barbecue pits. Call Camp and Cove at (213) 510-0303 for reservations. In all but very dry years, there's a freshwater spring up canyon. At one time the home of miners and pioneers, the area was named for the twin brothers Nathaniel and Theoples Parsons who lived here in the middle 1800s. Beyond Arrow Point are Johnson's Landing and Emerald Bay. Samuel Prentiss lived in a small stone house here at Johnson's Landing while he searched the Island for his elusive treasure. During the mining years of 1863-64, grandiose plans for Queen City were begun by the rough and tumble miners who'd set up a temporary community in the flush of the gold frenzy on Catalina. The arrival of the Union Army to survey the Island for a possible Indian reservation ended these plans and the miners' dreams of riches when the military ordered them to leave.

Emerald Bay

Emerald Bay, with its isolation and natural beauty, is a favorite anchorage for boaters. With 97 moorings and anchorage for 5-10 boats. Shore land is leased to the Great Western Council of Boy Scouts. Sandy Beach is used for day camping only.

Howland's

Just around from Sandy Beach is another favorite boat harbor, Howland's Landing, with 39 moorings. High up in the canyon is the windblown stone marker of Samuel Prentiss keeping a lonely vigil as the only marked grave outside of Avalon. Land ashore is leased to Island Boys Camp.

Big Geiger Cove

Anchorage for 10, shore leased to the Blue Water Cruising Club. Little Geiger Cove has

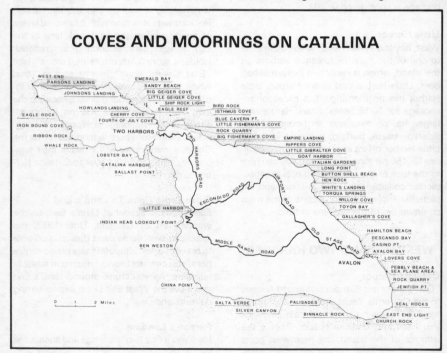

COVES AND MOORINGS ON CATALINA

WEST END
PARSONS LANDING
JOHNSONS LANDING
EMERALD BAY
SANDY BEACH
BIG GEIGER COVE
LITTLE GEIGER COVE
SHIP ROCK LIGHT
HOWLANDS LANDING
CHERRY COVE
FOURTH OF JULY COVE
EAGLE REEF
BIRD ROCK
ISTHMUS COVE
EAGLE ROCK
IRON BOUND COVE
RIBBON ROCK
WHALE ROCK
TWO HARBORS
BLUE CAVERN PT.
LITTLE FISHERMAN'S COVE
ROCK QUARRY
BIG FISHERMAN'S COVE
EMPIRE LANDING
RIPPERS COVE
LITTLE GIBRALTER COVE
GOAT HARBOR
ITALIAN GARDENS
LONG POINT
BUTTON SHELL BEACH
HEN ROCK
WHITE'S LANDING
TORQUA SPRINGS
WILLOW COVE
TOYON BAY
GALLAGHER'S COVE
LOBSTER BAY
CATALINA HARBOR
BALLAST POINT
LITTLE HARBOR
INDIAN HEAD LOOKOUT POINT
BEN WESTON
TWO HARBORS ROAD
ESCONDIDO ROAD
AIRPORT ROAD
OLD STAGE ROAD
MIDDLE RANCH ROAD
CHINA POINT
SALTA VERDE
SILVER CANYON
PALISADES
BINNACLE ROCK
HAMILTON BEACH
DESCANSO BAY
CASINO PT.
AVALON BAY
LOVERS COVE
AVALON
PEBBLY BEACH &
SEA PLANE AREA
ROCK QUARRY
JEWFISH PT.
SEAL ROCKS
EAST END LIGHT
CHURCH ROCK

0   1   2 Miles

1. Cherry Cove (Oz Mallan); **2**. Casino walkway, Avalon (Oz Mallan);
3. Catalina's Airport-In-The-Sky (Oz Mallan)

1. Catalina buffalo (Oz Mallan); **2.** Channel Islands fox (Channel Island National Park);
3. Elephant seal (Channel Island National Park)

1. tuna cactus (Oz Mallan); **2**. Catalina cactus (Oz Mallan); **3**. Catalina cactus (Oz Mallan); **4**. bougainvillea (Oz Mallan)

1. Santa Barbara sailboats (Santa Barbara Conference and Visitors Bureau); **2**. Long Beach coastline (Vicount Hotel); **3**. Long Beach Harbor (Oz Mallan); **4**. San Diego (San Diego Convention and Visitors Bureau)

picnicking on the rocks

one mooring and anchorage for three, land leased to Offshore Cruising Club.

Cherry Cove

Cherry Cove has 103 moorings but no anchorage. The shore is leased to the San Gabriel Valley Boy Scouts. The cove was named for 77 Catalina cherry trees planted up the canyon. See "Flora."

Fourth Of July Cove

Here you'll find 42 moorings, but no anchorage. Named for the holiday celebrations held every July by the Banning family during their era of ownership. Land is leased to Fourth of July Yacht Club.

TWO HARBORS

Home of the West End Cruising Club, a membership card is required to come ashore to Two Harbors from Isthmus Cove or Catalina Harbor. Yearly membership, $45 for the boat owner and six guests, entitles the holder to open access as well as to many other activities sponsored by the club. Membership is open to the general public; applications and cards are available at the office at the foot of the Isthmus Pier. If you're making an occasional visit for a day or two, a guest card good for 24 hours is available—adult $3, child $1.50.

Isthmus Cove

This large cove has 239 moorings available with anchorage for 100. Transient moorings are on a first-come first-served basis. Mooring fees are paid to the Patrol Boat or at the Harbormaster's office at Isthmus Cove. Anchoring is permitted outside of established mooring areas, except under special weather conditions at the discretion of the Harbor Patrol. They will assist you if you have any difficulty anchoring. Rafting of boats in mooring areas is not allowed unless expressly permitted by the Harbor Patrol. Speed limit within all mooring areas is five miles per hour or "wakeless" speed, whichever is slowest; this includes dinghies. Keep your neighbor happy—no generators or other motors before 7 a.m. or after 10 p.m. For your own safety, please carry a bright flashlight when traveling after dark in a dinghy skiff or inflatable raft which does not have navigation lights.

Bird Rock

A large white mound that can be seen by boaters from some distance at sea, this landmark was once bought by Helen Webb with Civil War scrip to build a gambling casino. The casino wasn't built and the SCI Co. now owns the rock.

Little Fisherman's Cove

Moorings are counted as part of those of the Isthmus Cove. The southwest shore is leased to the Channel Cruising Club; the south shore has camping facilities (reservations necessary through Camp and Cove Agency). The southeast shore is leased to King Harbor Yacht Club.

Big Fisherman's Cove

The home of USC Marine Science Center. Do not use the ramp, dock, or two moorings without invitation. Anchorage for five-25 except when divers are working in the area. The diving-bends recompression chamber at the Science Center is open to anyone that needs it. For emergency calls only, tel. 510-1053.

Two Harbors Services

During the summer season, five shoreboats run regularly between Fourth of July, Cherry, Big Fisherman, and Isthmus coves. During the winter, they're "on call"; three blasts of a horn and a wave during the day, three blasts and a flashing light at night will summon a shoreboat. All shoreboats monitor channel 11 on CB and channel nine VHF. When calling, give them your mooring number and cove name. It helps if you use a flashing light at night when you see the boat approaching. Fees are: Isthmus Cove and Fourth of July $1 pp, Big Fisherman and Cherry Cove $1.25 pp.

Floats on the Isthmus pier are for loading and unloading passengers. Dinghy docks are provided at the Isthmus Cove and Catalina Harbor for dinghies up to 16 feet. Tie them with a long bow line.

Trash cans are located at the end of the dinghy dock at Catalina Harbor and on the southwest side of the Cove Agency office at Isthmus Cove. During summer months, a trash collection boat operates in the Two Harbors area. In winter, Harbor Patrol boats will accept your trash for 75 cents. If all else fails, take your trash with you. There is a fine of $500 and/or six months in jail for trash thrown over the side.

FROM BLUE CAVERN POINT TRAVELING SOUTH

Blue Cavern Point

With its clear deep waters, this is a favorite diving spot for taking photos. Caves and small coves invite exploration. This is the site of one of the scenes described in Frederick Holder's "Adventures of Torqua," a tale of Indian raiders who take valuables from the camps of the white man, make their way to Blue Cavern Point, and from there into an underwater opening into a tunnel that passes through to the opposite side of the Island. The Indians then exit at Ribbon Rock to escape with their loot. While the victims are bewildered at first, they eventually work out the puzzle. After discovering the Indians' method of escape, the disgruntled white men cement the exit at Ribbon Rock and wait for another raid. Once again the Indians creep into camp, take what they can carry and make their way to the point, slipping silently into the black water and the even blacker cave. The white men hide and when all the Indians are inside, seal the entrance of the cave, entombing them for eternity. Surely fiction?

Empire Landing

Two moorings and anchorage for 20. Another quarry site with a dock for emergency landing only. Operating intermittently over the last 30 years or more, it has provided Island stone for building sites and breakwaters all along the Southern California coast. One of the largest hills of soapstone on the Island was located at Empire Landing. It was used by the Indians to carve religious artifacts and everyday utensils such as *ollas* (for grinding acorns and other hard grains). Many fascinating artifacts were found, including remnants of half-made *ollas* attached by stems of stone to the outcropping, as though the carver had been interrupted and left his project unexpectedly. During the 1950s, the soapstone rock was blasted and removed in the course of production.

Rippers Cove

No moorings here, anchorage for five-10. Two beaches have crystal-clear water, a fine place for swimming and diving. Look for "velvet-covered" sand dollars spinning along like miniature wheels on the sandy bottom of the bay.

Little Gibraltar

No moorings, but there's anchorage for five to seven boats. Around Little Gibraltar to Cabrillo Beach the shore is leased to the Long Beach Boy Scouts.

Goat Harbor

No moorings, but anchorage for five-10 boats. Good camping and hiking. Supplies for Middle Ranch, a working ranch in the interior, used to be unloaded from boats here and taken inland. In 1966, Explorer Scouts were breaking camp on the beach when they discovered a half-buried chest containing opium wrapped in gold leaf. Who knows how old it was!

Italian Gardens

No moorings, but it's a fair anchorage. A good fishing spot, it was here in this "sea-garden" that the Italian fishermen from San Pedro came regularly to take abundant catches of fish back across the channel.

Long Point

Folklore tells of a cave at Long Point that (still) whistles when the wind approaches from a certain direction, with an eerie sound which struck fear into the hearts of the Indians. Long Point Light warns boaters of the presence of this jutting finger of land.

Buttonshell Beach

Seven moorings, anchorage for 10. The land

TWO HARBOR MOORING FEES

SIZE	DAILY	SATURDAY	WEEKLY	HOLIDAYS (3-day min.)
String line	$8.00	$10.00	$47.00	$30.00
10-30 ft.	$9.00	$12.00	$60.00	$36.00
31-40 ft.	$11.00	$13.00	$65.00	$40.00
41-50 ft.	$14.00	$16.00	$85.00	$48.00
51-60 ft.	$16.00	$19.00	$100.00	$57.00
61-70 ft.	$19.00	$23.00	$120.00	$69.00
Over 71 ft.	$22.00	$27.00	$132.00	$80.00

Day Use Fee: under two hours—free.
No-show Fee: 100% of applicable Day Use Fee, charged to sublessee whose designated guest does not occupy reserved mooring.
Garbage pickup—boatside: 75¢ pickup.

NUMBER OF MOORINGS ALONG CATALINA COAST

Avalon Bay 315
Catalina Harbor 85
Parson's Landing 2
Emerald Bay 97
Howlands 39
Big Geiger Cove 1
Cherry Cove 102
Fourth of July 42
Isthmus Cove 239
Empire Landing 2
Buttonshell Beach 7
Hen Rock Cove 25
White's Landing 17
Moonstone Beach 34
Toyon 9
Hamilton Beach 36
Descanso 4

ashore, called Camp Fox, is leased to the the Glendale YMCA.

Hen Rock Cove
Twenty-five moorings, anchorage for 10. Good snorkeling area. The land is leased to the Balboa Yacht Club.

White's Landing
Seventeen moorings, anchorage for 16. The land is leased to Los Angeles Girl Scouts and part of the beach to the Balboa Yacht Club.

Here you'll see a well and the foundations of a smelter where a conveyor brought silver ore to the landing from Black Jack Mine high on the ridge above this beach. This mine produced more silver ore than any other mine on the Island.

Moonstone Beach
Thirty-four moorings and anchorage for 12. This beach is leased to the Newport Yacht Club. It was named Moonstone because in years past the beach was covered with small shiny rocks.

Torqua Springs
From descriptions in old ships' logs this was probably where the Indians came to get their water. For years, this was also one of Avalon's main water sources. Today, it gets its fame from a 100-foot-deep artificial reef that has been established at Torqua Springs, built from old cars, pipes, machinery, and tanks, creating a good habitat for fish, and is an excellent dive area.

Willow Cove
No moorings, anchorage for four boats. A small quiet cove, beach camping permitted with good swimming in clear water.

Toyon Bay
Nine moorings and anchorage for six boats.

Gallaghers's Beach
No moorings, fair anchorage for three to five boats. Shore leased to "Campus-by-the-Sea" vacation camp.

SOUTHERN CALIFORNIA MARINAS

SANTA BARBARA
COASTAL AREAS

The prehistory of the site of the present city of Santa Barbara includes habitation by the Chumash Indians. Here beneath the Santa Ynez Mountains was the location of some of the largest communities of Chumash Indians. in 1782, Father Junipero Serra and Captain Jose Francisco de Ortega founded a military presidio to defend against Russian explorers. In 1786, Mission Santa Barbara was built, the tenth mission under the Spanish flag. As was the case with all of the Spanish missions, the Europeans, seeking to convert the Indians to Christianity, managed instead to destroy the culture that had existed for thousands of years in the Santa Barbara area. The peaceful

Pacific coast Indians were content with a productive life of fishing in a generous sea. The first Europeans were so amazed at the quantities of sardines, tuna, and swordfish the Indians caught so easily that they felt there was enough seafood to support a rich economy with the fishing industry alone. Santa Barbara's southern neighbor Carpinteria (Spanish for "carpenter's shop") was alive with long beaches filled with the energetic Canalino Indians industriously building their wood-plank canoes called *tomols*. In fact, two explorers (Cabrillo in 1547 and Portola in 1769) were both so impressed with the boat-building abilities of the area that even though

Santa Barbara Harbor

there was more than 200 years between visits, both chose names in remembrance of the Indian canoe building. Cabrillo's name was *Los Pueblos de Canoas* ("City of Canoes"), while Portola chose to honor the carpenter with the name *Carpinteria.*

The Spanish influence in Santa Barbara lingered longer than in other parts of the West Coast. Many historical buildings from the Spanish era can still be seen by taking a walk through "Old California" on Santa Barbara's "Red Tile Tour." You can begin this walk at the courthouse at the 1100 block of Anacapa Street or anywhere along the route designated by red tiles (a brochure is available at the Chamber of Commerce office at 1330 State Street). The self-guided tour takes you to the Hill-Carillo Adobe built in 1826, Casa de la Guerra (1827), center of Santa Barbara's social life, made famous in *Two Years Before The Mast,* and the Casa de Covarrubias (1817), where the last Mexican Assembly met in July of 1846.

Since the early 1920s Santa Barbara has attracted the celebrity class. There are many lovely homes and horse ranches close by—especially in the rolling hills behind town (President Ronald Reagan's included). Along the often rough Santa Barbara coast, a 2,364-foot breakwater was constructed in the 1920s and covers 84 acres, creating a safe harbor for fishing boats and pleasure craft alike. Santa Barbara's Stearns Wharf, established 1872, is touted as the oldest operating wharf on the West Coast. In the

early days the wharf was used for steamers traveling up and down the coast; ships were then the quickest means to get to San Francisco or San Diego. Today it's fun to walk on the restored wharf, eat at one of the restaurants, buy fresh seafood at the fish market, take pictures of town and the coastline, or just watch the gulls screech and dive when a fishing boat docks alongside.

MARINA INFORMATION

Santa Barbara Harbor

The marina and fishing boat anchorage are located in Santa Barbara Harbor. For information and reservations contact City of Santa Barbara, 132 A. Harbor Way, Santa Barbara, CA 93109, tel. (805) 963-1737. Thirty transient slips are available; altogether there are 1,000 slips to accommodate both pleasure craft and fishing boats. Slip fees are 40 cents per foot per day, 14-day limit. Fresh water is available at each slip. A convenience food store is located on the premises; open 8 to 6. The closest supermarket is a two-block walk. Marine supplies are available 8 to 8. Marine services also available. Fuel dock hours are 6 to 6. No laundry facilities at the marina.

Santa Barbara Yacht Club

Visiting members of reciprocal yacht clubs are always welcome to use the facilities of the Santa Barbara Yacht Club. You'll find showers, bar, good food, and active racing programs; 130 Harbor Way, Santa Barbara, CA 93109, tel. (805) 965-8112. **Harbormaster:** Located on the breakwater at the west end of Cabrillo Blvd. at 132 A. Harbor Way, Santa Barbara, CA 93109, tel. (805) 963-1737 or 963-1738. The office is open 8 to 5; a patrol boat operates 24 hours a day. There's a 24-hour radio watch on VHF channel 16. Steve Lewis is the waterfront operations manager and harbormaster.

MARINE SERVICES

Union Marine Station, On-The-Breakwater, tel. (805) 962-7186. The fuel dock is open daily 7 to 6. The **Coast Chandlery,** On-The-Breakwater, Santa Barbara, 93109, tel. (805) 965-4538, offers a variety of marine supplies, clothing, marine repair, and boat sales; open 8 to 6. **Santa Barbara Sail Makers,** Marine Center, Santa Barbara 93109, tel. (805) 962-5155, makes custom cruising sails and repairs. **Pacific Marine Electrical &**

One of Southern California's busiest marinas is in Santa Barbara.

Refrigeration, 31 Breakwater, Santa Barbara 93109, tel. (805) 962-7935, is open 8 to 5. **The Boat Yard,** On-The-Breakwater, Santa Barbara 93109, tel. (805) 965-0887, has a travelift with a capacity of 30 tons, plus a ship yard with do-it-yourself facilities.

Fishing Information

There's a four-lane concrete launching ramp operated by the City of Santa Barbara. Enter through the main harbor entrance. **Carter's Sport Fishing Center,** On-The-Breakwater, Santa Barbara 93109, tel. (805) 962-4720, has everything for the fisherman including bait, rods, tackle, repairs, and guide service. **Santa Barbara Boat Rentals,** 827 Margo, Santa Barbara 93109, tel. (805) 962-2826, is next to the launching ramp; also sail and power rentals.

SANTA BARBARA ATTRACTIONS

Spend some time poking around Santa Barbara, a modern city that carefully preserves its early Spanish beginnings. A stop at the Santa Barbara Visitors Bureau, 1330 State St., tel. (805) 965-3021, will get you good information and maps of the town. If you plan on visiting the Santa Barbara area in August, do stay for the Old Spanish Days Fiesta. This is a city-wide good time of five days of celebrating the city's Spanish heritage and offers parades, dancing, flamenco and concert music, an arts and crafts show, rodeo, barbecues, and theatrical performances; everyone dresses in the Spanish costumes of early California. It's colorful and ongoing for more than 20 years. Boaters, make reservations early; the harbor is packed during this time. Other busy times are during Semana Nautica Regatta (great sailing races) and the Santa Barbara to King Harbor Race, one of the most popular sailing races of Southern California. Take the opportunity to see a polo match in July, and attend free concerts in the park from June 1 to mid-September at Alameda Park Band Stand.

Museums

The **Museum of Natural History** is on Puesta del Sol Rd. (two blocks north of the mission), tel. (805) 682-4711. Along with exhibits featuring mammals, birds, fish, reptiles, plant life, and geology of the Channel Islands, there's a planetarium. Also of interest is a diorama of prehistoric Indian life; free guided tours, admission by donation. The **Historical Society Museum** is on 136 E. De la Guerra St., tel. (805) 966-1601. Here you'll see treasures from Santa Barbara's colorful past: documents, paintings, costumes, and many rare mementos from the Indian, Spanish, Mexican, and American eras. Admission free, call for hours. **Museum of Art,** 1130 State St., tel. (805) 963-4364, is an outstanding small museum. It's bright and airy with permanent exhibits that include ancient sculpture, Oriental art, a collection of American paintings, and always a visiting exhibit. Admission is free, call for hours. **Santa Barbara Mission,** located at the upper end of Laguna St., tel. (805) 682-4713. Called the "Queen of the Missions" because of its graceful beauty, it is still in use as a parish church. Take a self-guided tour of the museum, garden, chapel, cemetery, and to the remnants of the original water system on the hill north of the mission. Open daily 9 to 5; admission $1, children under 16 free.

NATURE TREKS

The **Botanic Garden** is at 1212 Mission Canyon Rd., tel. (805) 682-4726, one and a half miles north of the mission. Wander through 60 acres of native trees, shrubs, wildflowers, and cacti in natural settings, or explore the five miles of easy-to-walk nature trails. Visit the historic dam built in 1806 by Indians under the supervision of the mission padres. Open daily 8 till sunset. A guided tour is offered on Thursdays at 10:30 a.m.; admission is free. The **Andree Clark Bird Refuge** is at 1400 E. Cabrillo Boulevard. A lovely lagoon and garden adjoin the Zoological Gardens with many varieties of freshwater birds to watch.

Santa Barbara Mission

The **Santa Barbara Zoological Gardens** are at 500 Ninos Dr. off Cabrillo Blvd., tel. (805) 962-6310. In a garden setting the zoo has a delightful variety of elephants, monkeys, lions, sea lions, exotic birds, and other animals. Great for children of all ages, with a miniature train ride, playground, farmyard petting area, and botanical gardens. Snack bar and spacious picnic facilities. Open daily 10 to 5, admission $3 adult and junior, $1.50 senior and children under 12. Train ride $1 adults, 50 cents children.

Santa Barbara is home to the Moreton Bay Fig Tree on Chapala St. and Highway 101. The tree, native to Australia, is the largest of its kind in the States. It was planted in 1877 by a pioneer family and it is said that more than 10,000 people could stand in its shade at noon. The branch spread is over 160 feet. If you are suffering from cabin fever, take a stroll along the paved walkway on top of the breakwater. This is a half-mile walk around the harbor with great views of the city and mountains. Anyone interested in tidepools should go to Carpinteria Beach during the daily low-low tide. Visitors can view the constant battle for survival by nature's feisty organisms. Where shore and sea meet, the tidal ebb and flood probably sustains more life per square foot than any other natural ecosystem. Remember, California's aquatic plants and animals are protected by law. Look, but don't take or disturb anything. Tidepooling is a recreation of looking and learning.

Nearby Restaurants

Breakwater Restaurant, On-The-Breakwater, tel. (805) 965-1557. **Char West**, 221 Stearns Wharf, tel. (805) 962-5631. **Azteca Restaurante**, 623½ State St., tel. (805) 965-9059. **John Dory**, On-The-Breakwater, tel. (805) 966-4418. **Moby Dick**, 220 Stearns Wharf, tel. (805) 965-0549. **Lobster House**, 15 E. Cabrillo Blvd., tel. (805) 965-1174. **Suishin Sukiyaki**, 511 State St., tel. (805) 962-1495.

VENTURA COASTAL AREAS

History

The Chumash Indians were much the same all along the Pacific coast; their lifestyle was closely associated with the sea. It was only after the arrival of the Spaniards that the "sameness" began to change. Mission San Buenaventura was founded in 1782 and many of the Indians were enlisted to do the menial work of the padres. As time went by Indian country became white man's country. The few remaining Indians became ranch hands and were gradually assimilated into the population. In the mid-1800s settlers from the East and Midwest began to discover the fertile valleys of Ventura County, and farming became the number one economic activity. Close behind, another activity began. From as early as 1896, oil has been pumped from offshore wells. (Even earlier, the Indians made use of the asphaltum that oozed from the earth in isolated places along shore to seal their *tomols* [canoes] and to waterproof their basketry.) The oil business continued to grow and though the economic rewards of the industry along the California coast are great, ecologists are greatly concerned over the damage that the occasional spill causes the wildlife of the Pacific.

VENTURA COUNTY MARINAS

The harbormaster for Ventura County is located at 1603 Anchors Way Dr., Ventura, CA 93001, tel. (805) 642-8618.

Ventura West Marina

Phase 1 of the marina is located on the northeast portion of Ventura Harbor; Phase 2 is on the west side of harbor. Mailing address for both is 1198 Navigator Dr., Ventura, CA 93001. Transient slips available, number varies. Slip fees are 30 cents per foot per night. There's a deli and small food store on premises, open daily 8:30 to 5:30. Fresh water is available at all slips and there's a pump-out station. Marine supplies available 8:30 to 5:30. On premises, 18 washers and dryers open 24 hours daily.

Harbortown Hotel

1050 Schooner Dr., Ventura, CA 93001, tel. (805) 658-1212. Guest slips and transient accommodations available.

Ventura Isle Marina

Located at the south end of Ventura Harbor; 1363 Spinnaker Dr., Ventura, CA 93001. Slip fees are $12 a day up to 35 feet; $15 a day over 36 feet; average per foot for permanent slip is $7.18. Small food stores in harbor are within walking distance. There's a water hookup at each slip, also showers, ice, electricity, and a pump-out station. No marine service or supplies available. Laundry services available 24 hours with a guest card.

Vintage Marina

Located near Channel Islands Boulevard next to the Harbor Landing with restaurants, shops; parking lot faces Harborwalk condos. Office is directly across from the Pacific Corinthian Marina. Mailing address is 2950 S. Harbor Blvd., Oxnard, CA 93055. The number of transient slips varies. Slip fees are $6.50 per foot for under 36 feet; $6.75 per foot for over 36 feet; $7.25 per foot for catamarans, trimarans, or boats measuring

sea otter

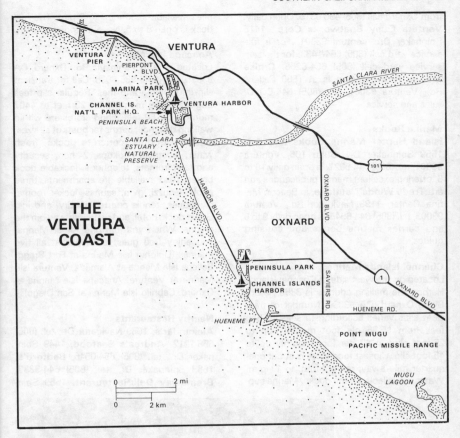

THE
VENTURA
COAST

over 70 feet (N-ties). Nearest food store is less than five miles away, in the Harbor Landing area; open Tuesday through Sunday 9 to 5. Fresh water is located at the dock boxes. No marine services or supplies available. Laundry facilities are available for guests.

MARINE SERVICES

Sylvester Union Fuel Dock, 1431 Spinnaker Dr., Ventura, CA 93001, tel. (805) 644-4845. Open daily 8 to 4; 24-hour service is available with a 100-gallon minimum purchase, both gas and diesel available. **Union**

Fuel Dock, 1404 Anchors Way Dr., Ventura, CA 93001, tel. (805) 644-6776. Open 7 to 6 in summer, early morning and late afternoons in winter. At **Ventura Harbor Village,** 1559 Spinnaker Dr., Ventura, CA 93001, tel. (805) 644-0169, you'll find specialty shops, restaurants, as well as a full-service shipyard, a self-service boat yard, marine fuel dock, commercial fish unloading, processing, and distribution center. Take a stroll along the mile-long bayside walkway; here visitors see yacht activity as well as busy commercial fishing traffic.

Dunne's Marine and Hardware, 2409 E. Harbor, Ventura 93001, tel. (805) 644-8177;

from Oxnard call (805) 485-0315. Open daily. **Ventura Quay Boatworks Corp.,** 1415 Spinnaker Dr., Ventura 93001. For a full-service yard call (805) 654-1433; for the self-service yard call (805) 654-8265. **Cruise Marine Refrigeration** is at 1660 Callens Rd., Ventura 93001, tel. (805) 644-COLD; sales and service.

Marine Books

Island Hunter Marine Books and Art, 1559 Spinnaker Dr., Suite 106, Ventura 93001, tel. (805) 644-5827, is open daily 10 to 6, offering excellent marine publications and art. **Trade Winds Nautique,** in Beacon Marine Center, 1198 Navigator Rd., Ventura 93003, tel. (805) 644-6545, is open daily 9 to 6 and carries marine books and cruising guides.

Channel Islands Marina

Located on the west side of Channel Islands Harbor, the mailing address is 3850 Harbor Blvd., Oxnard, CA 93030. Number of transient slips varies according to season. Slip fees from $5.85 per foot monthly up to 25-foot slip; to $7 per foot monthly up to 48-foot slip. Closest food store is about one-quarter mile away, open 7 a.m. to 11 p.m. Water is available on the docks. Marine sup-

plies available 8:30 a.m. to 9 p.m. The fuel dock is open 8 to 5. No laundromat.

Anacapa Isle Marina

Located at 3001 Peninsula Rd., Oxnard, CA 93035, tel. (805) 985-6035. Call for transient slip information and fees. Regular slip fees begin at $185 monthly for 25 feet to $407 monthly for 50 feet. Food stores are within walking distance; berths for boats of all sizes, clean restrooms, concrete docks, fresh water, electrical hookups, 24-hour security and laundromats, telephone, lockable dock boxes. Also available are apartments, three pools, jacuzzi, gym, saunas, locker rooms, clubhouse, tennis courts, laundry, and ice. Guest dock, hotel, and restaurants adjoin the marina. When you join one Almar Marina, you enjoy free guest privileges at all five marinas (Dolphin Isle Marina at Fort Bragg, Ballena Isle Marina at Alameda, Ventura Isle Marina at Ventura, Anacapa Isle Marina at Oxnard, Cabrillo Isle Marina at San Diego).

Nearby Restaurants

Alexander's, 1080 Navigator Dr., tel. (805) 658-1212. **Andrea's Seafood,** 1449 Spinnaker Dr., tel. (805) 654-0546. **Bedford's,** 1583 Spinnaker Dr., tel. (805) 644-3333. **Bramsway Deli/Restaurant,** 1559 Spin-

naker Dr., tel. (805) 642-3116. **Colony Kitchen**, 2401 E. Harbor Blvd., tel. (805) 642-0261. **Denny's**, 2148 E Harbor Blvd., tel. (805) 643-9192. **Waterfront Deli** (at Ventura West Marina), 1198 Navigator Dr., tel. (805) 644-3354. **First Mate Deli** (next to National Park Visitor Center), 1869 Spinnaker Dr., tel. (805) 654-1300. **Hornblower's**, 1559 Spinnaker Dr., tel. (805) 658-2345. **Hungry Hunter**, 2046 E. Harbor Blvd., tel. (805) 648-5146. **Love's**, 2070 E. Harbor Blvd., tel. (805) 648-3021. **Pierpont Inn**, 550 Sanjon Rd., tel. (805) 643-6144. **Ramon's**, 2401 E. Harbor Blvd., tel. (805) 642-0261. **Scotch & Sirloin**, 1510 Anchors Way Dr., tel. (805) 644-2229. **Seaview On-The-Pier**, Fishing Pier, tel. (805) 643-7030. **Village Inn**, 1591 Spinnaker Dr., tel. (805) 658-0844.

ATTRACTIONS IN VENTURA COUNTY

One of the newest and most important facilities in the area is the **Channel Islands National Park Building**, located across from the ocean at 1901 Spinnaker Dr., Ventura, CA 93001, tel. (805) 644-8262. This is an interesting center with an excellent book store (an extremely good collection of books concerning the area, the Channel Islands, history, and the sea). Exhibits introduce the visitor to the Channel Islands National Marine Sanctuary. Also open to the public are excellent tidepool exhibits and films about the Channel Islands. These precious resources have been misused in the past but now the federal government is ensuring that the islands will be preserved for future generations. They show us what California must have been like at the time of the arrival of the first white man. The Channel Island National Park Center is the best source of information for travelers interested in visiting the Channel

Islands. **Island Packers**, practically next door, offers transportation to and from the Channel Islands on a variety of boats from motor launch to sailing vessels.

Area Museums

The **Albinger Archaeological Museum** is located downtown at 113 E. Main St., tel. (805) 648-5823. The **Olivas Adobe**, 4200 Olivas Park Dr., tel. (805) 644-4346, offers a glimpse into the early days of California living. **Ventura County Museum**, downtown at 100 Main St., tel. (805) 653-0323, is open daily 10 to 5 except Monday.

Nature Treks

For those interested in nature, a visit to the **Santa Clara Estuary Natural Reserve** is well worth the time. It's accessible from Peninsula Beach to the north, or McGrath State Beach to the south. This marshland wildlife preserve is at the mouth of the Santa Clara River. North of the river along Spinnaker Drive the wastewater lagoons are fenced off, making an outstanding habitat for migratory waterfowl. This is a must for serious bird-watchers. Another larger spot (1,800 acres) is the **Mugu Lagoon**, the largest between Morrow Bay and San Diego County. The lagoon is located entirely within the grounds of the Navy's Pacific Missile Test Center. In order to see the lagoon, it's necessary to make reservations at least 30 days in advance, minimum of 15 persons. Public access is limited to weekend interpretive tours. For more information call the Public Affairs Office, (805) 982-8094. **Seaside Wilderness Park** is a small park of palm trees and Monterey pines where the bird watching is good. The only way to get there is a three-quarter-mile walk from **Emma Wood State Beach** to the north. Continue along the beach and sand dunes west of the railroad tracks.

LOS ANGELES COASTAL AREAS

In 1860, Los Angeles had a population of 4,355. By 1870 it had only grown to 5,728. Then in 1876 the transcontinental railroad was completed, and things started to move a *little* faster. However, in 1886 two competing railroad lines had a "fare war"; a ticket from Kansas City to Los Angeles was only a dollar! That did it. By 1890 the population had grown to more than 51,000. It's been growing rapidly ever since. Today the metropolitan population over 10 million and many of those people are boat owners. In 1986, small pleasure boats registered in Southern California alone increased by 14,457—across the state the increase was 23,102. According to an unofficial report from the Department of Motor Vehicles, the pleasure boat registration count in the state is 666,089, making it second in the nation, behind only Michigan.

These totals do not include the really big vessels registered directly with the Coast Guard; minimum size for Coast Guard registration is five tons.

Los Angeles Harbor is one of the largest man-made harbors in the world. It engulfs 7,000 acres of land and water and boasts 28 miles of waterfront. The largest commercial fishing fleet in the U.S. calls Los Angeles Harbor home. Fish canneries thrive and cargo ships from all over the world include L.A. Harbor as a port of call. The pleasure boater has all that he can want—except perhaps isolation. Marinas with thousands of slips, boat yards, hoists, cranes, equipment centers, fishing supplies, boat landings, and terminals for luxury cruise lines can all be found pretty close together. The waterfront has been spruced

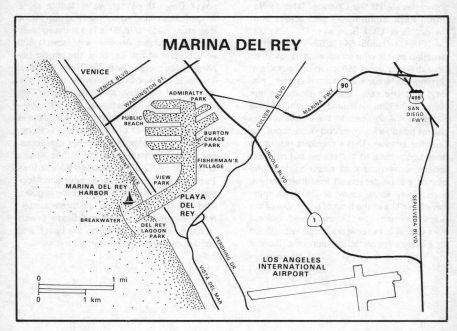

MARINA DEL REY

up in recent years; many of the old ports like San Pedro and Long Beach have undergone complete facelifts. Modern hotels, convention centers, and restaurants have been built next to new state-of-the-art marinas with quaint fishing village-like complexes and shopping centers to attract out-of-town visitors—as well as local boaters.

Part of the greater Los Angeles Harbor, Marina del Rey is the largest artificial small-craft harbor in the world. Built in 1960, it accommodates more than 6,000 pleasure boats and there's a waiting list! This is a busy harbor with every kind of marine service available, including dry storage. Guest berths are located at Basin H; check with the harbormaster. Advance reservations are suggested.

MARINA DEL REY HARBOR

Located at 13650 Mindanao Way, main channel and Basin H. Call or write for information and reservations to Burton Chace Park Transient Docks, 13837 Fiji Way, Marina del Rey, CA 90292, tel. (213) 305-9595. **Harbormaster**, tel. (213) 823-7762. The **Marina Visitor's Information Center** is located at 4701 Admiralty Way, Marina del Rey, CA 90292, tel. (213) 822-0119. Open daily from 9 to 5. There are 36 transient slips available. Slip fees from November 1 through April 30 are 40 cents per foot; May 1 through October 31, 50 cents per foot. Nearest food store is Boys Market, one block away and open 24 hours. Closest laundromat is one mile. Fresh water dockside and marine services and supplies are available at nearby store. Special events at Marina del Rey include the Christmas Boat Parade and the California Cup Race.

Deauville Marina
Located in Basins B and C, Marina del Rey. Mailing address is 13900 Marquesas Way, Marina del Rey, CA 90292, tel. (213) 823-4655. No transient slips available. Slip fees range from $8.34 to $15 per foot for slips

30 to 55 feet. Fresh water is available at each slip and the nearest food store is four blocks away, open 9 to 6. Captain's Wharf Restaurant located on premises.

Special Attractions
Fisherman's Village is a commercial area with trendy shops, art galleries, and good restaurants along with shops that cater to the boater; fishing licenses available here also. Visit the **Burton Chace Park** for a nice change of pace. You'll find an eight-acre park with a great view of the main channel, plus transient docks, fishing dock, picnic area, and watchtower. Free parking on weekdays. **Del Rey Lagoon Park**, 6660 Esplanade, Playa del Rey, is another green park around a lagoon. There's a small boat launching ramp, as well as picnic area, playground, baseball diamond, and basketball courts.

Marine Services
Basin G Boatyard, 4643 Admiralty Way, Marina del Rey 90292, tel. (213) 827-2870. Hoist capacity to 30 feet. Hull and bottom painting, open daily 8 to 5. **Ken Enterprises**, 4039 Lincoln Blvd., Marina del Rey 90292, tel. (213) 827-1808. Offering outboard engine sales, service, parts, marine hardware, electronics, and new boats. Open seven days a week. **Mare Co. Sails**, 4080 Lincoln Blvd., Marina del Rey 90292, tel. (213) 822-9344. A full-service sail loft including sail repairs, custom sewing, wire rope splices, multi-hull nets and trampolines, and marine hardware. Open Monday through Friday 8:30 to 5:30. An all-year fuel dock, **Marine Fuels and Service, Inc.**, is located on the west side of the main channel; 13800 Bora Bora Way, Marina del Rey 90292, tel. (213) 823-2444. Boaters will find fishing supplies, frozen bait, and tackle, as well as ice, marine accessories, and pumpout station. Open summer from 7 to 6, winter 8 to 5. **Wheelhouse Compass**, 766 Washington St., Marina del Rey 90291, tel. (213) 821-5024, has a good selection of clocks, watches, sextants, and navigational instruments along with compass adjusting,

COURSES FROM MARINA DEL REY

To:	Magnetic Course	Reverse Course	Distance Nautical Miles
Pt. Conception	271	091	100
Anacapa Light	260	080	44.0
Santa Cruz Light	254	074	67.0
Santa Rosa Light	252	072	82.0
Begg Rock	225	045	70.5
San Nicolas Island, West End	219	039	68.5
Pt. Vincente	155	335	13.5
Santa Barbara Island	209	029	39.0
Osborn Bank	203	023	45.5
Tanner Bank	189	009	82.0
Bishop Rock	184	004	96.5
Catalina Island, West End	179	359	29.0
Catalina Island Isthmus	166	346	30.0

sales, and repair. **Mariners Unlimited,** 1522 W. Washington Blvd., Marina del Rey 90292, tel. (213) 392-5705, nautical books and magazines. Open daily except Monday.

Nearby Accommodations
Dolphin Marina, Basins C and D, 13900 Panay Way, Marina del Rey 90292, tel. (213) 823-4875. Apartments with slips available. **Jamaica Bay Inn,** Basin E, 4175 Admiralty Way, Marina del Rey 90292, tel. (213) 823-5333; small boat launching ramp. **Marina Beach Hotel,** Basin E. 4100 Admiralty Way, Marina del Rey 90292, tel. (213) 301-3000. **Marina del Rey Hotel,** 13534 Bali Way, Marina del Rey 90292, tel. (213) 301-1000; slips available. **Marina International Hotel,** Basin E, 4200 Admiralty Way, Marina del Rey 90292, tel. (213) 301-2000.

Restaurants
Akbar, 590 Washington St., tel. (213) 822-4116. **Benihana of Tokyo,** 14160 Panay Way, tel. (213) 821-0888. **Casa Escobar,** 14160 Palawan Way, tel. (213) 822-2199. **Casola's Fish House,** 4211 Admiralty Way, Marina del Rey,tel. (213) 823-5339. **Charley Brown's,** 4445 Admiralty Way, Marina del Rey, tel. (213) 823-4534. **Cheesecake Factory,** 4142 Via Marina, tel. (213) 306-3344. **Cyrano's,** 13535 Mindanao Way, tel. (213) 823-5305. **Don the Beachcomber,** 13530 Bali Way, tel. (213) 823-5435. **El Torito** (Fisherman's Village), 13715 Fiji Way, tel. (213) 823-8941. **Fish Market,** (Fisherman's Village), 13723 Fiji Way, tel. (213) 823-8444. **Jamaica Bay Inn,** 4175 Admiralty Way, tel. (213) 823-5333. **Red Onion,** 4215 Admiralty Way, tel. (213) 821-2291. **Shanghai Red's,** 13813 Fiji Way, tel. (213) 823-4522.

Church Services
Second Community Baptist Church, 1041 Washington Blvd., Venice, CA tel. (213) 392-5632. **Saint Mark's Catholic Church,** 940 Coeur D'Alene Ave., Venice, tel. (213)

821-5058. 20th Church of L.A., 132 Brooks Ave., Venice, tel. (213) 396-1390. **Marina del Rey Episcopal Chapel,** 4201 Via Marina, Marina del Rey, tel. (213) 823-8643 or 670-4777. **Beth Shalom Jewish Temple Reformed,** 1827 California Ave., Santa Monica, tel. (213) 453-3361. **First Lutheran Church of Venice,** 815 Venice Blvd., Venice, tel. (213) 821-2740. Non-denominational **Church of the Marina** meets every Sunday morning at 9 in the Burton Chace Park Community Building. For information call (213) 823-9598.

Emergency Services

Sheriff's Harbor Patrol offices are adjacent to the Department of Beaches and Harbors Administration Offices at 13837 Fiji Way. Harbor Patrol offices are staffed 24 hours, every day of the year, and can be reached by calling (213) 823-7762 or 911 (emergency) to report a fire or to request the paramedics.

REDONDO BEACH AND KING HARBOR

Redondo Beach's **King Harbor** continues to grow more popular and more crowded each year. The harbor can handle more than 1,500 pleasure boats. Between boaters and visitors to the Redondo Municipal Pier, the International Boardwalk, and Monstad Pier, King Harbor attracts lots of people, especially in the summer. There are four marinas in King Harbor. None maintain transient docks; however, arrangements can be made if slips are available.

King Harbor Marina

Located in Basin One and Two, mailing address is 819 North Harbor Dr., Redondo Beach, CA 90277, tel. (213) 376-6926. Laundry, restaurant, and cocktails close by.

Port Royal Marina

Located in Basin Two, mailing address is 555 North Harbor Dr., Redondo Beach, CA 90277, tel. (213) 376-0431.

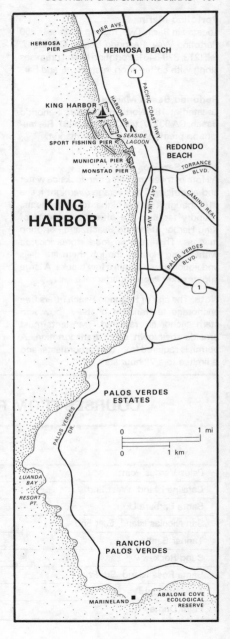

Portofino Marina

Located in Basin Two, mailing address is 260 Portofino Way, Redondo Beach, CA 90277, tel. (213) 379-8481. Portofino Inn on premises along with coffee shop, restaurant, and bar.

Redondo Beach Marina

Located at 189 North Harbor Dr., Redondo Beach, CA 90277, tel. (213) 374-3481. Restaurant on premises, close to fish market.

Marina Services

All four of these marinas offer dockside water and electricity. The average overnight fee is $10, though it can be higher for larger boats. Laundry facilities are offered to guests of King Harbor, Redondo Beach, and Portofino marinas. There are no food stores located within King Harbor, though there are delis and liquor stores within a few blocks. A large supermarket is one-quarter mile away.

Note: The city of Redondo Beach offers free anchorage to transient boats. A bow and stern anchor are required. Transients must provide their own shore transportation. A permit is required from the harbormaster and is limited to a 72-hour stay.

Restaurants

King Harbor is encircled with fine restaurants. The pier at the south end of the harbor offers a plethora of good dining and entertainment.

Marine Services

King Harbor Marine Center is in Basin One, next to King Harbor Marina, at 831 North Harbor Dr., Redondo Beach 90277, tel. (213) 374-8923. The boat yard is open Monday through Friday 7:30 to 5. The marine store is open seven days a week; 24-hour emergency service is available. The fuel dock, Portofino Oasis Petroleum, is located at the entrance to Basin Two, 310 Portofino Way, Redondo Beach 90277, tel. (213) 374-9858; open daily 6 to 6 with marine supplies, ice, cold drinks, and snacks.

LOS ANGELES HARBOR ATTRACTIONS

Catalina Boat Terminal

Boats to Catalina Island leave from Catalina Landing in downtown Long Beach and from San Pedro at the Catalina Air and Sea Terminal under the Vincent Thomas Bridge, dai-

COURSES FROM REDONDO BEACH

To:	Magnetic Course	Reverse Course	Distance Nautical Miles
Palos Verdes Point	191	011	4.5
Catalina Island, West End	191	011	24.0
Santa Barbara Light	221	041	38.0
San Nicolas Island, East End	218	038	62.0
Tanner Bank	193	013	77.5
Begg Rock	231	051	70.5
Santa Rosa Island, So. Pt.	257	077	85.0
Anacapa Light	267	087	49.0
Point Dume	279	099	27.0

ly year-round. For complete information see "Getting There" in the main "Introduction."

Cabrillo Marine Museum
The original Cabrillo Marine Museum at 3720 Stephen M. White Drive was begun in 1920, rather a casual affair instigated by the local lifeguards of the area. Today, the museum has grown up and is headquartered in a new and larger facility that includes an auditorium, classrooms, laboratories, an exhibition hall with interpretive displays, and aquariums containing marine flora and fauna. The museum is open Tuesday through Sunday from 10 to 5. Call (213) 548-7562 for information

regarding guided tidepool tours at the Point Fermin Marine Life Refuge. The museum also sponsors whale-watching tours, trips to the Channel Islands, grunion run programs, and Cabrillo Day celebrations. For whale-watching charter boats call (213) 832-4444.

***Queen Mary* Complex**
Anyone visiting Long Beach for the first time should by all means take an afternoon and visit the *Queen Mary* and *Spruce Goose.* The *Queen* was originally engaged in crossing the Atlantic between Europe and the U.S. She's a grand example of luxury liners of the past. Close by is the *Spruce Goose,* the brainstorm

COURSES FROM POINT VINCENTE

To:	Magnetic Course	Reverse Course	Distance Nautical Miles
14-Mile Bank	120	300	29.0
60-Mile Bank	146	326	68.5
Catalina Island, East End	153	333	26.0
Gallagher Cove, Catalina Island	157	337	22.8
White's Cove, Catalina Island	158	338	21.0
Lone Pt., Catalina Island	158	338	20.0
Isthmus Cove, Catalina Island	178	358	18.6
Emerald Cove, Catalina Island	183	003	17.6
San Nicolas Island, East End	222	042	60.0
Santa Barbara Island, North End	228	048	35.0
Anacapa Island	275	095	50.0
Pt. Hueneme	285	105	46.0
Pt. Dume	292	112	24.5
Avalon, Catalina Island	152	332	24.0
Coronado Island	128	308	99.0
San Diego, Entrance Buoy	123	303	90.0
Del Mar	107	287	60.5
20-Mile Bank	118	298	30.0
Newport Entrance Buoy	093	273	29.5

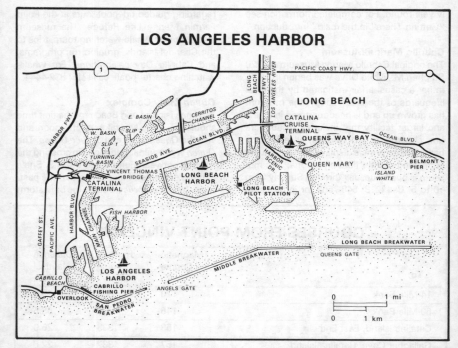

LOS ANGELES HARBOR

of the eccentric though brilliant Howard Hughes. The *Goose* is the largest plane ever to get off the ground, and that's about as much as it did, getting just airborne. In the geodome that houses the giant plane, exhibits and films give the public the history and events that brought about the construction and follow-up of Hughes' brainchild.

Ports O' Call Village And Whalers Wharf
A favorite for out-of-towners is to stroll through the "re-created" atmosphere of Ports O' Call, an old California seaport and then into Whalers Wharf, a 19th century New England seaside community. Both offer shops, restaurants, harbor excursions, and a view of the main channel of the harbor. Open 11 a.m. to 9 p.m. all year.

At **Abalone Cove Ecological Reserve**, investigate the tidepools. **Point Fermin Lighthouse**, closer to the harbor, was built in

1874. Visitors are not allowed into the lighthouse, but the park and grounds surrounding it are a perfect spot from which to watch the whales during their yearly migration. Along with picnic facilities, playground, and small amphitheater, you'll find the **Cetacean and Community Building**. The whale station offers a free 20-minute whale movie; open Saturday and Sunday 9 to 4.

LONG BEACH AREA

Though the Long Beach Marine Stadium was used for the 1932 Olympics, it was built in the 1920s. A mile long and a mile wide, this connection to Alamitos Bay is perfect for a multitude of water sports.

Cerritos Bahia Marina
Located at 6289 E. Pacific Coast Highway, Long Beach, CA 90803, tel. (213) 431-6575.

COURSES FROM SAN PEDRO

To:	Magnetic Course	Reverse Course	Distance Nautical Miles
Newport Bay Bell Buoy	096	276	20.0
San Diego Entrance Lighted Whistle Buoy	126	306	82.0
14-Mile Bank	131	311	22.0
Horseshoe Kelp	145	325	3.2
60-Mile Bank	153	333	65.0
Catalina Island, East End	172	352	24.0
Avalon, Catalina Island	174	354	21.7
Gallagher Cove, Catalina Island	178	358	21.0
White's Landing, Catalina Island	183	003	19.8
Lone Pt., Catalina Island	183	003	18.6
Isthmus Cove, Catalina Island	202	022	19.8
Emerald Cove, Catalina Island	208	028	19.8
Catalina Island, West End	219	039	22.6
San Nicolas Island, West End	229	048	65.0
Santa Barbara Island, North End	236	056	40.5

No transient slips are available. There is a food store on the premises that's open 24 hours. Water is located at every dock. Marine supplies available 7 to 6. Fuel dock available 6 to 6.

Restaurants
Chart House, 221 Marina Dr., tel. (213) 598-9411. **Edgewater Inn,** 6400 E. Pacific Coast Highway, tel. (213) 434-8451. **Golden Sails,** 6285 Pacific Coast Highway, tel. (213) 430-0585. **Hof's Hut,** 6257 E. 2nd St., tel. (213) 498-2110. **Jolly Roger,** 168 Marina Dr., tel. (213) 598-9431. **Rusty Pelican,** 6550 Marine Dr., tel. (213) 594-6551. **Schooner or Later,** 241 Marina Dr., (213) 498-3185. **Todd's,** 190 Marina Dr., tel. (213) 597-7771. **Windrose,** 110 Marina Dr., tel. (213) 597-3607.

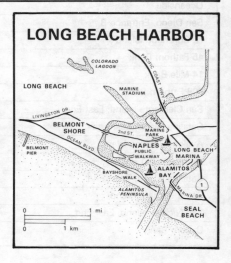
LONG BEACH HARBOR

COURSES FROM
LONG BEACH HARBOR

Long Beach Breakwater to:	Magnetic Course	Reverse Course	Distance Nautical Miles
Avalon, Catalina Island	183	003	23.5
Isthmus, Catalina Island	208	028	22.5
Horseshoe Kelp	194	014	4.5
14-Mile Bank	140	320	21.5
San Clemente Island, East End	174	345	54.5
Newport Bell Buoy	105	285	17.5
San Diego Entrance Buoy	130	310	81.0
Catalina Island West End	220	040	26.0
Santa Barbara Island	236	056	44.5
San Nicolas Island, East End	229	049	68.0
Point Fermin	236	056	5.5

Long Beach Marina East Breakwater Light to:	Magnetic Course	Reverse Course	Distance Nautical Miles
Oceanside	116	296	48.0
San Diego, Entrance B	131	311	80.0
N. Coronado Island	136	316	87.0
45 Fathom Bank	157	337	64.0
14-Mile Bank	145	325	21.0
209 Fathom Bank	145	325	40.0
San Clemente Island, East End	176	356	55.0
Catalina Island, East End	183	003	26.0
Avalon, Catalina Island	187	007	24.5
Isthmus, Ship Rock C.I.	213	033	24.0
Catalina Island, West End	223	043	28.0
Santa Barbara Island	238	058	47.0
San Nicolas Island, East End	229	049	70.0
Osborn Bank	229	049	50.0

West Seventh Street Landing

Located at 1550 West 7th St., Long Beach, CA 90813, tel. (213) 432-5062. No transient slips available; slip fees average $6 per foot. The nearest food store is two miles away, open 9 to 5. Fresh water available. Restaurant located on premises. Close to downtown Long Beach.

Alamitos Bay Marina

Located at the Pacific Ocean and the San Gabriel River. Mailing address is Long Beach Marine Bureau, 205 Marina Dr., Long Beach, CA 90803. tel. (213) 594-0951. There are 60 transient end ties available. Slip fees are 50 cents per foot per night. The nearest food store is Lucky Market, one-half mile away, open 8 to 9. Fresh water at each end tie, bring a hose; dock carts are provided. Marine supplies are available at **West Marine Products Store** from 9 to 6. Marine services are available at **Marina Shipyard** from 8 to 5. Fuel at the **76 Dock**, open 8 to 8. No laundry facilities; restaurant located on premises.

Downtown Shoreline Marina

Located at the Pacific Ocean and Los Angeles River (near the *Queen Mary*). Mailing address is 450 E. Shoreline Dr., Long Beach, CA 90802, tel. (213) 437-0375. There are 66 transient end ties available; 50 cents per foot per night. Water available at end ties; bring a hose. Nearest food store is Safeway, one mile away; open 8 to 8. Marine supplies are available from 9 to 6. Fuel dock is open 8 to 6. Restaurant located on premises. Special attractions: Shoreline Village, *Queen Mary*, and the *Spruce Goose*.

Queensway Bay Marina

Located near the bow of the *Queen Mary* and *Spruce Goose,* behind the Viscount Hotel. Mailing address is 900 Queensway Dr., Long Beach, CA 90801, tel. (213) 436-0411. There are 40 transient Catalina-style moorings available; mooring fees range from $12 to $20 per day. Nearest food store is one mile away, fresh water available. Marine supply store open from 10 to 6. Fuel dock available across

The Viscount Hotel overlooks the Queensway Bay Marina.

the river, open 6 to 5. No laundry facilities. Water taxi service to the *Queen Mary,* Shoreline Village, and town; full use of Viscount Hotel swimming pool and tennis courts.

LONG BEACH ACCOMMODATIONS

Viscount Hotel

On Queensway Bay, stay at the Viscount Hotel (700 Queensway Drive, Long Beach, CA 90801, tel. 213-435-7676, for reservations from U.S. and Canada call 800-255-3050) in a modern, world-class hotel. The Viscount is a short walk from the *Queen Mary* luxury liner and Howard Hughes' *Spruce Goose.* The hotel has a swimming pool, tennis courts, non-smoking rooms, and rooms designed specifically for the woman traveler. On the premises, Adolph's Restaurant serves scrumptious fresh seafood, and tables on the patio offer a delightful view of passing boats. The Viscount is an ideal place to overnight when you're going to and from Catalina Island. Both helicopter and boat service are just a 10-min. drive from the hotel.

ORANGE COUNTY COASTAL AREAS

HISTORY

Indians

California Chumash Indians of the Gabrielino and Jauneno groups lived along the coast of what is now Orange County for hundreds of years before the coming of the Spaniards. San Juan Capistrano, several miles inland from the ocean at San Clemente, was the seventh mission (circa 1776) along the California coast. This mission and its priests along with all the other missions established up and down the coast drastically changed the lifestyle of the Indians. Because of this change and the exposure to new diseases brought by the outsiders, most of the Indian population didn't survive very long after the coming of the Europeans. Surprisingly, an exception to this is a small group of Juaneno Indians still living in Orange County. Not too many years ago, a few archaeological artifacts dating back to the first Juanenos were found at the site of the new Crystal Cove State Park.

Settlers

The first whites settled in Orange County around 1859 in the Anaheim area. Inland farmers, away from the swampy coastal regions, were successful at raising orange trees, peanuts, barley, corn, pigs, and sheep. From there the colonists spread out and it wasn't long before there was a small dusty village called Newport next to the sea. It was tough going for the adventurous settlers during those early years. The landscape provided few natural materials to help them establish a town. (The Indians had solved the housing problem by building their oval huts from branches and tule grasses found along the rolling hills that bordered the Pacific.) The settlers brought everything overland in bumpy wooden wagons.

Shipping

In Newport, McFadden's Wharf—the first along this part of California's southern coast—was built at about the same time as the first orange groves were planted inland.

The wharf helped to initiate the shipping and trade industry early on, a boon to farmers shipping their products. Wool alone was big freight from about 80,000 merino sheep grazing the fields close by. It wasn't long before the American entrepreneurial spirit rose to the occasion: Why bring an empty ship from the north to the southern part of the state when picking up wool and other agricultural products? And so in 1873, a forward thinker gambled on a load of redwood aboard a southbound ship; just what was needed to fence off areas of farmland south of Santa Ana in order to keep wild horses out. Timber was a hot seller and in great demand—the shipping industry in Southern California was growing up. By 1889 steamships were doing a booming business carrying freight and passengers between San Diego and San Francisco with a stop in Newport. But the trains would change all that very shortly. The same farsighted men that developed the shipping business in Orange County also introduced the railroad for both passengers and freight. The premier line was an 11-mile run between Santa Ana and Newport. It cost 50 cents per person, and took 30 minutes going north, 40 minutes going south. The difference was a 10-minute stopover at artesian wells to pick up water. (Until 1905, Newport had to import all of its drinking water.) New railroad lines were built, connecting all the cities of California and the southern state grew by leaps and bounds!

Newport

With the advent of the railroad, the quiet little village of Newport began a transition that would ultimately make it a popular resort destination. A moderate year-round climate attracted people from all over California to its long white beaches, craggy cliffs, and beautiful clear ocean. For years (till the mid-1950s) outlying acreage in Orange County remained untouched until another American with great foresight gambled millions of dollars to build an amusement park in Anaheim, many miles from the established business centers of Southern California. The man was Walt Disney, and he called his unique park Disneyland. Since that time, Orange County has developed into a thriving metropolis. Hundreds of thousands of people and many big corporations left busy inner cities to go to the sunny countryside. The nearby coastal areas were also affected—new ports and marinas are added each year, with Newport the oldest and perhaps the queen of the Orange County coast.

Newport Harbor

ORANGE COUNTY ATTRACTIONS

Marine Events

If visiting an Orange County port for the first time, you may wish to leave the boat docked at the marina for a day and evening or two or three and visit one of the many fine attractions scattered about. Close by is the **Orange County Marine Institute**, where, through classes and talks, visitors get an opportunity to view and understand the natural marine life of this coastal area. Young people spend a day and night aboard the brig *Pilgrim* learning history, basic shipboard tasks, and standing watch.

The ship is a replica of the brig which carried Richard Henry Dana to these waters in 1834. Dana's experiences are recounted in the classic, *Two Years Before The Mast*. Another program is held onboard the tall ship *Californian*, replica of a 19th century revenue cutter. The **Nautical Heritage Society Museum** offers seamanship training for young people aged 16 to 25, focusing on California maritime history. If you happen to be visiting during whale-watching season, February to March, beginning mid-February the **Festival Of The Whales** continues for a month. In addition to daily whale-watching cruises, lectures, movies, displays, and demonstrations are open to the public.

Amphitheaters

Fine year-round entertainment is presented at many open-air amphitheaters. Check the schedules for **Irvine Bowl**, 650 Laguna Canyon Rd., Laguna Beach, CA 92349, tel. (714) 494-1145. Home of the summer presentation, Pageant of the Masters. **Pacific Amphitheatre**, corner of Fair Dr. and Fairview in Costa Mesa (next to the Orange County Fairgrounds), tel. (714) (714) 546-4875. Seating 19,000, it's the largest outdoor amphitheater in California, and presents concerts and name entertainment.

Fine Arts

Laguna presents the prestigious **Festival of Art** yearly, tel. (714) 494-1145. **Idyllwild School of Music and Arts**. P.O. Box 38, Idyllwild, CA 92349, tel. (714) 659-2171. **Segerstrom Hall**, Costa Mesa, CA 92626, tel. (714) 556-2121, is a 3,600-seat multipurpose theater.

Theaters

Spend an evening at one of the many fine theaters, such as **Cabrillo Playhouse/San Clemente Community Theatre**, 202 Avenida Cabrillo, San Clemente, CA 92672, tel. (714) 492-0465. **Costa Mesa Civic Playhouse**, 661 Hamilton St., Costa Mesa, CA 92626, tel. (714) 650-5269. **Irvine Community Theater**, 12 Fuchsia, Irvine, CA 92658, tel. (714) 857-5496. **Laguna Moulton Playhouse**, 606 Laguna Canyon Rd., Laguna Beach, CA 92629, tel. (714) 494-8021. **Newport Theatre Arts Center**, 2501 Cliff Dr., Newport Beach, CA 92660, tel. (714) 631-0288. **South Coast Repertory Theatre**, 655 Town Center Dr., Costa Mesa, CA 92626, tel. (714) 957-2602. *Two Years Before The Mast* and other theatrical productions are presented onboard the *Pilgrim* each year.

Dinner Theaters

For a complete evening of entertainment including a good dinner visit: **Elizabeth Howard's Curtain Call Theatre**, 690 El Camino Real, Tustin, CA 92645, tel. (714) 838-1540. **Harlequin Dinner Playhouse**, 3503 S. Harbor Blvd., Santa Ana, CA 92628, tel. (714) 79-5511. **Southampton's Dinner Theatre**, 140 Avenida Pico, San Clemente, CA 92672, tel. (714) 498-7576.

Special Attractions

Don't forget the old favorites, **Disneyland**, 1313 S. Harbor Blvd., Anaheim, CA 92835, tel. (714) 999-4565; and **Knott's Berry Farm**, 8039 Beach Blvd., Buena Park, CA 90679, tel. (714) 220-5200. **Balboa Island** is a picturesque community on a small island with trendy shops and specialty restaurants reminis-

historic Balboa Pavilion

cent of the New England coast. And the favored way to get there is onboard the **Balboa Island Ferry**. This is a small ferry for a short trip holding only three cars, passengers, and bikers traveling between Balboa and the "fun zone" of the Balboa Peninsula. Step into the past with a visit to **Mission San Juan Capistrano**; if it happens to be March 19, you'll witness the annual return of the swallows; the mission is only a 10-minute drive east of Dana Point.

Nature Treks
Explore the **Corona del Mar Tidepools** at Big Corona State Beach, and Little Corona Beach. It's one of the few places in Orange County where you can observe firsthand the intriguing organisms of the sea. Or visit the **Orange County Marine Institue**, 35502 Del Obispo, Dana Point, CA 92629, at the far end of Dana Point Harbor. This is an educational facility for exploring the ocean environ-

ment. Bird watchers check out the **Bolsa Chica Ecological Preserve** and **Upper Newport Bay Ecological Reserve** (see map). The Bolsa Chica Ecological Preserve consists of 1,200 acres of marshland. From two parking lot viewing areas you may see three birds on the endangered species list: the clapper rail, California least tern, and the savanna sparrow. Take the loop trail across from the beach entrance; interpretive signs along the way. Note: most of the marsh is private land, so stay within the viewing areas; one is at Pacific Coast Highway across from the main Bolsa Chica Beach entrance, and the other is at Pacific Coast Highway and Warner Avenue. The Upper Newport Bay Ecological Reserve is an estuary. Contact **Friends of Upper Newport Bay** offering interpretive bird tours Saturdays during the winter: P.O. Box 2001, Newport Beach, CA 92663. Are you docked at Dana Harbor and getting cabin fever? Take a walk to the northern end of the harbor to the jetty and offshore **Dana Point Marine Life Refuge**.

Events Along The Orange County Coast
Some events are held annually in the communities of Orange County. In March the **Orange Coast Jazz Festival** presents top-name entertainers for three nights at the Robert Moore Theatre on the Orange Coast College Campus. Workshops are held daily, 2701 Fairview Rd., Costa Mesa, CA 92628 tel. (714) 432-5527. Ticket prices range from $8 to $12. In April, sailboats from both local and distant ports arrive to take part in the **Newport Ensenada Race,** an annual sailing race from Newport Harbor to the waters of Ensenada, Mexico, tel. (714) 640-1351. **Around the Bay in May** is an annual event celebrating the coming of summer with 10-mile jogging/running races around the Newport Beach area, tel. (714) 644-8211. An annual event celebrating the musical heritage in Corona del Mar is held in June and called **Baroque Music Festival**. The **Newport Beach Bike Tour** in June is a six-mile ride around the back bay returning to East Bluff Park (and a picnic), tel. (714) 650-1000. It's fun to play in

the sand in October's **Sandcastle Contest** at Big Corona Beach in Corona del Mar. Here you'll see some fabulous sand sculptures done both by individuals and groups. Each December brightly decorated boats follow an eight-mile parade route through Newport Harbor nightly for two weeks in the middle of December, during the **Festival of Lights Parade.** For details about getting your boat into the fun, call (714) 644-8211.

ORANGE COUNTY MARINAS

Sunset Aquatic Marina
Located at the end of Edinger Avenue in Huntington Beach, P.O. Box 538, Sunset Beach, CA 90742. For reservations or information, call (213) 592-2833 or (714) 846-0179. Transient slips are available, four plus a guest dock. Slip fees are 34 cents per foot up to 30 feet. No food store on the premises; the nearest is two and a half miles away. Hours are 9 to 5 daily. Water hookups located at all slips and guest dock. Washers and dryers are located in restrooms.

Harbormaster: (213) 592-2869 or (714) 846-2873 or (714) 834-3800. A rescue boat is

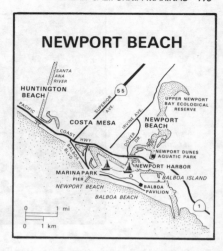

based here and may be contacted on channel 16. If no contact is made, call KDG Newport on 156.8 mHz.

NEWPORT HARBOR MARINAS

Balboa Marina
Located at 201 E. Coast Highway, Newport Beach, CA 92660. One hundred thirty-two slips are available, live-aboards are not allowed. Fees according to size are 20 to 55 feet, $9 to $9.50 per foot monthly. Also available: water, electricity, dock box, phones, showers, restrooms, pump-out, parking. There's a waiting list. Contact Daryl Landrum, tel. (714) 644-9730.

Balboa Yacht Basin
Located at 829 Harbor Island Dr., Newport Beach, CA 92660, tel. (714) 673-1761; 171 slips are available, no live-aboards allowed. Slip fees according to size are 31 to 75 feet, $9.50 per foot. Facilities include water, electricity, dock box, phones, showers, restrooms, pump-out, parking, garage-walk-in and hardware store. Absolutely no dry storage. There's a waiting list; contact Don Jones.

A sunny day brings out small and large vessels in Newport Harbor.

Bay Shores Marina
Located at 2572 Bay Shores Dr., Newport Beach, CA 92660, tel. (714) 944-9730; 134 slips available, live-aboards not allowed. Slip fees according to size are 18 to 82 feet, $8.50 to $9.50 per foot monthly and facilities include water, electricity, dock box, phones, showers, restrooms, pump-out, parking. There's a waiting list according to length. Contact Daryl Landrum.

Bayside Marina
Located at 1137 Bayside Dr., Coronado del Mar, CA 92625, tel. (714) 644-9730; 250 slips available, no live-aboards. Slip fees according to size are 18 to 75 feet, $9.50 per foot monthly; facilities include water, electricity, dock box, phones, showers, restrooms, pump-out, parking. There's a waiting list according to length. Contact Daryl Landrum.

De Anza Bayside Marina
Located at 300 East Coast Highway, Newport Beach, CA 92660 tel. (714) 673-1331; 265 slips available, no live-aboards allowed. Slip fees according to size are 14 to 50 feet, $7.75 per foot monthly; 21 to 30 feet $9.50 per foot monthly; 31 feet and up, $9.75 per foot monthly. Facilities include water, electricity, dock box, phones, laundry, message service,

dry storage, showers, restrooms, paging service, parking, no waiting for some, a year's wait for others. Contact Shirlene Burrill.

Little Inn On The Bay
Located at 617 Lido Park Dr., Newport Beach, CA 92663, tel. (714) 673-8800; 14 slips available, live-aboards not allowed. Slip fees range $10 to $11 per foot per month; facilities include water, electricity, dock box, phones, mail/message service, showers, restrooms, restaurants, security. There's a waiting list of six months. Contact Mike Saber.

Marina Dunes
Located at 101 N. Bayside Dr., Newport Beach, CA 92660, tel. (714) 644-0126; 230 slips available, 10 live-aboard. Slip fees are 24 to 45 feet, $6 per foot by length or boat slip length, whichever is longest. Facilities include water, electricity, phones, mail/message service (for live-aboards only), showers, restrooms, paging service, parking, security. There's a waiting list. Contact Tom Ginger.

Newport Arches Marina
Located at 3333 W. Coast Highway, Newport Beach, CA 92663, tel. (714) 642-4644; 76 slips available, five live-aboard. Slip fees are 25 to 66 feet, $12 to $15 per foot monthly. Facilities

include water, electricity, dock box, phones, mail/message service. Fuel dock available with mini mart, showers, restrooms, restaurant, parking, security, brokerage. Availability varies, some slips currently available. Contact Judy Owens.

Twenty-eighth Street Marina
Located at 2602 Newport Blvd., Newport Beach, CA 92663, tel. (714) 673-6606; 25 slips available. Fees are $11 to $14 per foot monthly. Facilities include water, electricity, dock box, phones, showers, restrooms, parking, security. No waiting list, contact Mike Singer.

NEWPORT YACHT CLUBS

Bahia Corinthian Yacht Club,
1601 Bayside Dr., Corona del Mar, CA 92625,
tel. (714) 644-9530

Balboa Island Yacht Club (and Ferry)
410 S. Bay Front, Newport Beach, CA 92662
tel. (714) 673-1070

Balboa Yacht Club
1801 Bayside Dr., Corona del Mar, CA 92625
tel. (714) 673-3515

Newport Harbor Yacht Club
720 W. Bay Ave., Balboa, CA 92660
tel. (714) 673-7730

Shark Island Yacht Club
1099 Bayside Drive, Newport Beach, CA 92662
tel. (714) 760-0221

South Shore Yacht Club
2527 W. Coast Highway, Newport Beach, CA 92660
tel. (714) 631-9969 (Port)
tel. (714) 646-3102 (In house)

Other Area Marinas
California Recreation Co., 1137 Bayside Dr., Corona Del Mar, CA 92625, tel. (714) 644-9730. **Lido Yacht Anchorage,** 717 Lido Park Dr., Newport Beach, CA 92663, tel. (714) 673-9330.

Area Restaurants
Ruby's Diner, 1 Balboa Pier, Newport Beach, tel. (714) 675-7029. **The Cannery,** 3010 Lafayette Ave., Newport Beach, tel. (714) 675-5777. **Amelia's On Balboa Island,** 311 Marine Ave., Balboa Island, tel. (714) 673-6580.

DANA POINT

Once a major port for square-rigged ships, the new harbor was named for Richard Henry Dana, author of *Two Years Before The Mast.* The classic novel is an account of the true adventures of a young man from the east coast of the U.S. working onboard a merchant ship that plied the waters of the West Coast in the mid-1830s. The flavor of early California is depicted in a very real manner. Richard Henry Dana would be amazed and proud to have this harbor named in his honor. It isn't only a gathering spot for modern pleasure boats, but is a popular dock from which to join whale-watching excursions and research vessels. Here at Dana Point in 1986, significant fact-finding was accomplished on the subject of whales' voices and underwater communication. One of the largest and most popular waterfront festivals in Orange County, the **Tallships Competition,** is held here each year; what a beautiful sight!

MARINAS

Dana West Marina
Located at 24500 Dana Point Harbor Dr., Dana Point, CA 92629; 1,462 slips available. Fees: 23 to 63 feet are $4.56 to $7.05 monthly. Water, electricity, dock box, phones, laun-

dry, pump-out, parking, showers, restrooms, security. If you wish to add your name to the waiting list call (714) 496-6137.

Dana Point Marina Company
Located on the east side of **Dana Point Harbor**, it is 60 miles equidistant between Los Angeles and San Diego. Mailing address is 24705 Dana Dr., Dana Point, CA 92629, tel. (714) 496-6137. Call the harbormaster for guest berth assignment. Anchorage is available for visitors but vessel must be attended at all times. Transient slips available: 24 side ties for boats 28 feet and under. Slip fees: $5.26 to $7.65 per foot per month. A number of restaurants and small shops are located in the harbor.

Marina office hours are Tuesday through Saturday 8 a.m. to 12 p.m. and 1 to 5 p.m. Fresh water available at each slip. Marine supplies available 8 to 5. Marine services open 8 to 5. Fuel dock hours are weekdays 8 to 5; weekends 6 to 5. Laundry facilities available 24 hours daily.

Restaurants
The Brig, 25010 Del Prado (Mariner's Village), tel. (714) 496-9046. **Casa Maria,** 25052 Del Prado, tel. (714) 496-6311. **Harpoon Henry's,** 25200 Del Prado, tel. (714) 493-2933. **Jolly Roger's,** 25100 Del Prado, tel. (714) 496-0855. **Quiet Cannon,** 34344 Street of the Green Lantern, tel. (714) 496-6146. **Skippers Galley,** 25116 Del

COURSES FROM NEWPORT BAY

To:	Magnetic Course	Reverse Course	Distance Nautical Miles
Dana Point	121	301	11.0
San Diego Bell Buoy	136	316	66.2
60-Mile Bank	170	350	56.3
14-Mile Bank	192	012	13.0
San Clemente Island, East End	192	012	52.5
San Clemente Island, West End	213	033	50.0
Tanner Bank	214	034	83.2
Catalina Island, East End	216	036	27.0
Avalon, Catalina Island	222	042	26.4
Gallagher Cove, Catalina Island	225	045	26.9
White's Landing, Catalina Island	229	049	27.0
Lone Pt., Catalina Island	230	051	26.4
Isthmus Cove, Catalina Island	239	059	31.5
Emerald Cove, Catalina Island	242	062	33.5
Catalina Island, West End	244	064	36.6
Santa Barbara Island, North End	249	069	58.2
Pt. Fermin Buoy	272	092	21.5
San Pedro Breakwater	276	096	20.0

Prado, tel. (714) 496-0424. **Wind & Sea,** 25152 Del Prado (Dana Wharf), tel. (714) 496-5959. **Beach Cities Pizza,** 34473 Golden Lantern, Dana Point, 496-2670.

Marine Facilities
Dana Point Fuel Dock, 34461 Puerto Place, Dana Point, CA 92629, tel. (714) 496-6113. Summer hours, weekdays 6 to 6, weekends 6 to 5. Off-season hours 8 to 5. **Balboa Marine,** 34467 Golden Lantern, Dana Point, CA 92629, tel. (714) 496-3640, for marine hardware, charts, electronic sales and service. **Dana Marine Engines and Boats,** 34760 Pacific Coast Highway, Capistrano Beach, CA 92624, tel. (714) 496-4370. **Dana Book and Navigation,** 24402 Del Prado, Suite B, Dana Point, CA 92629, tel. (714) 661-3926. Open daily 10 to 5:30 for nautical magazines, books, charts, instruments. **Dana Point Shipyard** (north of the fuel dock), 34671 Puerto Place, Dana Point, 92629 CA, tel. (714) 661-1313; travelift capacity 50 tons, crane capacity 7 tons. For boat and engine maintenance, repairs, parts, prop and

shaft repairs; open Monday through Saturday 8 to 5. **Black Bart's Aquatics,** 34145 Pacific Coast Highway, Dana Point, CA 92629, tel. (714) 496-5891, for diving supplies, sales rentals, fishing license, air refills, charter dive boat, and marine hardware.

Important Information
Harbormaster: 25005 Dana Dr., Dana Point, CA 92629, tel. (714) 496-2242 or (714) 834-3800. Emergency tel. (714) 496-1121; the harbormaster assigns guest berths. The **speed limit** is five mph in Dana Point Harbor. **Dockmaster's** office is located at 24701 Dana Dr. in the southeast part of east basin. **Dana Point Harbor Patrol** is equipped with rescue and fire-fighting equipment and stationed in the harbor; they maintain a 24-hour radio watch on VHF-FM channels 12 (156.60 mHz) and 16 (156.80 mHz). During late hours contact the Newport Harbor Patrol via VHF channel 16, or use emergency phone at foot of Harbor Patrol stairs (most southeasterly building seen once through the breakwater).

SAN DIEGO COASTAL AREAS

History

San Diego is sometimes referred to as the Cradle of California Civilization. Juan Cabrillo's discovery of San Diego in 1542 was the beginning of the Spanish influence that has remained part of California's lifestyle. Mission San Diego de Alcala, built in 1769, was the first in a chain built by Father Junipero Serra, the beginning of the *Camino Real* ("Royal Highway"). Ultimately 21 missions were built, all a day's walk from each other going from San Diego toward northern California. San Diego was organized as a town in 1834, and by 1850 was incorporated as a city.

San Diego Harbor is considered one of the finest natural harbors in the world. For years the biggest fleet was that of the U.S. Navy. Today, the biggest fleet is the fleet of pleasure boats that fill its many marinas. Vessels vary from simple and small to luxurious and large. The temperate climate is perfect for the sailors that either make San Diego their home base, or just a favorite port of call.

OCEANSIDE

The second mission constructed in California was Mission San Luis Rey, in 1798 in Oceanside—San Diego County's second sister. A large group of Native Americans called this home. The missions were generally built near large Indian villages since the object was to convert them to Christianity. More boaters are discovering the 10-million-dollar marina and small craft harbor. Being equidistant between San Diego and Newport Beach has its advantages for boaters, whether for permanent docking or for a good transient "halfway house." The boat harbor accommodates 900 permanent boats with slips reserved for transient boatmen. Other facilities include good restaurants, shopping, marine supplies, launching ramps, fuel docks, boat repairs, good fishing supplies, and a quarter-mile-long fishing pier. All slips are handled through the Harbor District.

Oceanside Harbor Marina

Located at Oceanside Harbor in the city of Oceanside, mailing address is 1540 Harbor Dr. North, Oceanside, CA 92054, tel. (619) 722-1418. Boaters will find 51 transient slips. Slip fees vary according to season from May 1 to September 30, 45 cents per foot. October 1 to April 30, 40 cents per foot. Water hookups are at each slip. A marine supply store is open 8 to 6. Marine services are available 8 to 5. Fuel dock is open from sunrise to sunset; laundromat open 24 hours. A mini mart on the premises is open from 8 to 6. **Note:** Boaters wishing an overnight slip or docking, please check at the Headquarters Building, 1540 Harbor Dr. North.

Marine Services

Oceanside Marine Centre, Inc., 1550 Harbor Dr. North, Oceanside, CA 92054, tel. (619) 722-1833, is open year-round, weekdays 8 to 5; Saturday 9 to 4:30, Sunday 10 to 3. Fifteen-ton travelift available plus hardware, engine repair, maintenance, sales, and brokerage. **Oceanside Sailboats** is at 1400 Harbor Dr. North, Oceanside, CA 92054, tel. (619)722-3509. Chandlery and brokerage; new and used are available. **Oceanside Fuel Dock,** 1380 North Pacific St., Oceanside, CA 92054, tel. (619) 722-5853. Open all year except Christmas, New Year's Day, and Thanksgiving afternoon. Hours May through October are 7:30 to 5, November through April, 8 to 4:30.

Area Accommodations

Villa Marina Resort is at 2008 Harbor Dr. North, Oceanside, CA 92054, tel. (619) 722-1561.

Nearby Restaurants

The **Chart House,** 314 Harbor Dr. South, tel. (619) 722-1345. **Cape Cod House,** 258 Harbor Dr. South, tel. (619) 722-5556. **Harbor Deli,** 272 Harbor Dr. South, tel. (619) 722-7228. **Harbor Fish & Chips,** 282 Harbor Dr. South, tel. (619) 722-4977. **Harbor Light,** 264 Harbor Dr. South, tel. (619) 722-4855.

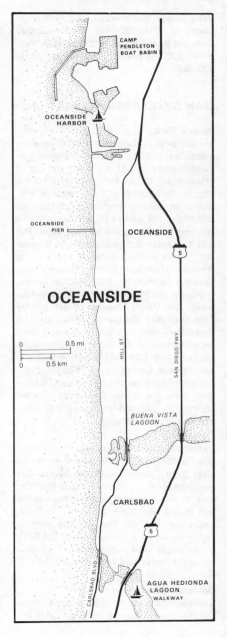

Jolly Roger Restaurant, 1900 Harbor Dr. North, tel. (619) 722-1831. **Monterey Bay Canners Seafood**, tel. (619) 722-3474. **Pappy's**, 270 Harbor Dr. South, tel. (619) 439-9648.

SAN DIEGO AREA ATTRACTIONS

Balboa Park

It would be possible to stay in San Diego for a month and take in a different outstanding attraction every day (if you didn't run out of money first!). Balboa Park, in the heart of the city, is the location of 1,074 acres of museums, art galleries, theaters, sports facilities, and one of the world's largest zoos. What's left over is green grass and tall trees. The park's museum and gallery complex is amazing. Within walking distance you find the **Reuben H. Fleet Space Theatre and Science Center**, the **Hall of Champions, Museum of Man, Natural History Museum, San Diego Museum of Art**, and the **Timken Art Gallery**. Most of the Spanish/Moorish buildings in the park were originally part of the Panama-California Exposition of 1915-16 and the California-Pacific International Exposition of 1935-36. Every day the 100-bell carillon chimes each quarter hour from the lovely **California Tower**, another city landmark and example of Spanish/Moorish architecture.

Cabrillo National Monument

The Cabrillo National Monument overlooks what Juan Cabrillo called San Miguel Bay and what today is called San Diego Bay. The monument was established to remember the first man to visit the entire California coast, beginning in 1542. Stop by the visitor's center for an exhibit which tells of Cabrillo's explorations and discoveries. Programs about the monument are presented daily.

Gaslamp Quarter

Step back in time to the 1890s and one of San Diego's newest historic districts. You'll get the sights, sounds, and feeling of a bustling California waterfront before the turn of the century. One of the best ways to learn about the Quarter is via walking tours offered every Saturday from 10 a.m. to noon and 1 to 3 p.m. Custom tours can be arranged by calling (619) 233-4694.

Sea World

A desolate marshland several miles north of downtown San Diego has been brilliantly transformed into a 4,600-acre aquatic playground called **Mission Bay Park**. In the heart of this complex, Sea World offers visitors one of the finest marine-life facilities in the world. Along with a high-flying killer whale named Shamu, there's the Penguin Encounter in a 5,000-square-foot re-created Antarctic neighborhood behind a 100-foot viewing window, exhibiting a 28-degree temperature home for more than 400 penguins.

Sea World is one of the fun places to visit while in the San Diego Area.

lions and tigers and bears — at the renowned San Diego Zoo

In the California Tidepool exhibit, visitors may pick up and examine starfish and sea urchins, or wander around to see dolphins, sea lions, otters, and even a walrus. Plenty to see and do for the whole family.

Animals

For the animal lover a trip to **San Diego Wild Animal Park** at 15500 San Pasqual Valley Rd., Escondido, CA 92027, tel. (619) 231-1515, is well worth the time. You'll find 1,800 acres of natural habitats for more than 2,200 animals roaming free as they would in their birthplace. The park, 30 miles from downtown San Diego, includes an African village as well as a five-mile (50-minute) monorail trip (with narrator-guide) that glides silently through expansive Asian and African enclosures. Don't miss the Nairobi Center with its lowland gorilla colony. Along with its Animal Care Center, the park has achieved national acclaim with its condor program. Of the 27 condors in the U.S., 13 were hatched at Wild Animal Park. This is one of the few preserves in the world where the animals run free and the people are contained! The park is open every day of the year.

Closely related in operations is the **San Diego Zoo** at Balboa Park in downtown San Diego. One of the highlights is the Children's Zoo. Double-decker buses with narrator-guides takes visitors on a 40-minute trip through three miles of safari land, including sprawling canyons and mesas. Open daily.

More Attractions

Old Town is the site of the first European settlement in California. In 1967, the state provided two and a half million dollars to buy six blocks in the heart of Old Town. It has been restored and the **State Park Old Town Historical Society** offers walking tours led by park rangers at 2 p.m. daily from the Machado y Silvas Adobe across from the plaza. For more information, call Old Town State Park, (619) 237-6770. The **Maritime Museum** is a trio of ships, each telling its story of the past. The most familiar, the *Star of India,* is the oldest merchant sailing vessel afloat. The steam-powered ferryboat *Berkeley* was the first successful propeller-driven ferry on the West Coast and was responsible for carrying thousands to safety during the 1906 earthquake. The 1904 steam yacht *Medea,* built for a wealthy Scot and later owned by members of Parliament, served in both world wars. Moored on the Embarcadero, the "fleet" is open daily from 9 to 8, admission $4, tel. (619) 234-9153. The Mexican border at **Tijuana** is a 25-minute trip ($1.50 RT) on the trolley from downtown. From the border

The sunny shores of San Diego attract boaters, windsurfers, and picnickers.

it's another 20-minute walk to Avenida Revolucion in downtown Tijuana where there are dozens of shops. No passport or visa is required of U.S. citizens for a stay of less than 72 hours, within 75 miles of the border. You may bring $400 in retail value of duty-free goods back into the States. A good destination for visitors to Tijuana is the **Cultural Complex,** where in the Omnimax Theatre you re-live Mexican history. On the grounds also visit the **Anthropological Museum** and the **Performing Arts Center.** For the sportsman there's **horse racing, jai alai,** and **bullfighting** in season. For non-boaters interested in a small ocean cruise, take a three-hour ride on a 72-foot catamaran to Catalina Island. Complimentary breakfast going over and hors d'oevres coming back. For information call Catalina Cruisin', tel. (619) 235-8600; the boat departs from B Street Pier year-round. Fare: adult $39 RT, senior and military $33, child 12 and under $23. Security parking is $4 daily.

Water Sports
San Diego offers a multitude of aquatic activities, from the obvious — sailing and power boating — to water skiing, windsurfing, swimming, wet biking, and deep-sea fishing. Sport-fishermen know they have a good chance (in season) to catch albacore, bar-

racuda, bluefin tuna, marlin, yellowtail, swordfish, mackerel, and white sea bass. Without going too far out to sea (three to 14 miles), bottom fishing is another favorite pastime with fishermen, bringing in kelp bass, rock bass, ling cod, rock cod, grouper, halibut, black sea bass, sheepshead, and sole. And don't overlook fishing from your skiff in Mission Bay, where you'll have access to croaker, smelt, bass, halibut, flounder, perch, and sea trout.

MISSION BAY AREA

Mission Bay Marina
Located on the northwest corner of Quivira Basin, next to the harbor patrol and hospitality point. Mailing address is 1500 Quivira Way, San Diego, CA 92109, tel. (619) 222-6488. The number of transient slips varies. Slip fees range from transient, 50 cents per foot; to permanent slips, $6.25 to $8 per foot per month. Fresh water is located at each or every other slip. Clean restrooms and showers, as well as free hookup to master TV antennae, dock boxes, and telephone service available to guests. Marine supplies are available Monday through Saturday 8 to 5, Sunday 10 to 3. A full-service boat yard, Knight Carver Yacht Center, is open week-

days 7:30 to 5; fuel dock is nearby. No laundry facilities available. Boaters will find a deli, liquor store, several restaurants, and a seafood market nearby. The closest food store is about one and a half miles away, open weekdays 8 to 5, weekends 8:30 to 4:30. (May close on Sundays in the winter.)

Seaforth Marina

Located on Quivira Basin in Mission Bay. Mailing address is 1677 Quivira Rd., San Diego, CA 92109, tel. (619) 224-6807. Slip fees are $6.25 per foot. There's a freshwater hookup at each slip and a marine supply store is open from 9 to 5. Marine services and repairs available are from 9 to 5. A fuel dock is

located one block away. The nearest food store is also one block away; no laundromat. A restaurant is located on the premises.

Sea World Marina

Located at Perez Cove in Mission Bay, next door to Sea World. Mailing address is 1660 S. Shores Rd., San Diego, CA 92109, tel. (619) 226-3915. **Harbormaster:** 2581 Quivira Court, San Diego, CA 92109, tel. (619) 224-1862. The number of transient slips available varies; slips will accommodate boats from 24 to 50 feet. Slip fee is $15 per night. At each slip guests find electricity, phone hookup, dock boxes, and fresh water. A food store on the premises is open from 7

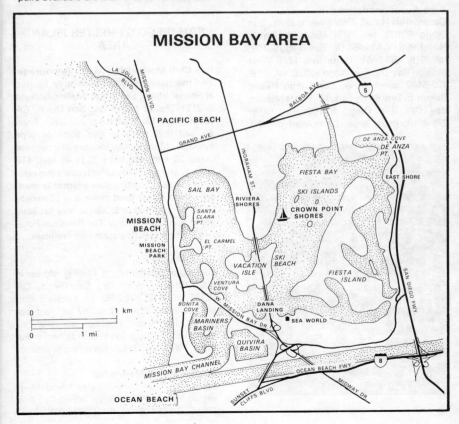

MISSION BAY AREA

to 7 in the summer and 8 to 5 in the winter. Marine services include washdown, wax, and hull-painting service. Fuel dock available, hours: 7 to 7 summer, 8 to 5 winter. No laundry facilities available. Sea World Marina is within easy walking distance of Sea World. There is no fee to tie up for the day and visit Sea World. Special 20 percent Sea World admission discounts are provided to marina tenants. The marina is 10 minutes away by car from San Diego International Airport, downtown San Diego, and most major resort hotels and restaurants. Special events: hydroplane racing, bathtub races, the Christmas Parade of Lights.

Area Accommodations
Catamaran Hotel, 3999 Mission Blvd., San Diego 92109, tel. (619) 488-1081. **Bahia Hotel,** 998 W. Mission Dr., San Diego 92109, tel. (619) 488-0551. **Dana Inn,** 1710 West Mission Bay Dr., San Diego 92109, tel. (619) 222-6440; guest docks. **San Diego Hilton Beach & Tennis Resort,** 1775 East Mission Bay Dr., San Diego 92109, tel. (619) 276-4010; guest slips. **Campland on the**

San Diego skyline

Bay, 2211 Pacific Beach Dr., San Diego 92109, tel. (619) 274-0601.

Nearby Restaurants
Atlantis, 2595 Ingraham St., tel. (619) 224-2434; guest dock at Sea World Marina. **Bahia Hotel,** 998 W. Mission Dr., tel. (619) 488-0551. **Catamaran Hotel,** 3999 Mission Blvd., tel. (619) 488-1081. **Dana Inn,** 1710 W. Mission Bay Dr., tel. (619) 226-6440; guest dock. **Islandia Hyatt House,** 1441 Quivira Rd., tel. (619) 224-3541; guest dock. **Trade Winds (Hilton Hotel),** 1775 E. Mission Bay Dr., Mission Bay, tel. (619) 276-4010; guest dock. **Vacation Village Hotel,** 1404 Vacation Rd., tel. (619) 274-4630.

SAN DIEGO'S SHELTER ISLAND AREA

Bay Club Marina/Half Moon Anchorage
Two marinas next door to each other, located at Shelter Island, San Diego. Mailing address is 2131 Shelter Island Dr., San Diego, CA 92106, tel. (619) 222-0314 or 224-3401. Boaters will find three to five transient slips available. Monthly slip fees are $12 per foot under 30 feet; $15 from 30 to 40 feet; $18 from 40 and up. Freshwater faucets and electricity on docks (sometimes a pigtail is needed). The nearest food store is a 10-minute walk; hours are 8 to 5:30. Laundry facilities are at Bay Club Marina. The Bay Club Hotel and Humphrey's Restaurant on premises.

Kona Marina Inn
Located on Shelter Island. Mailing address is 1901 Shelter Island Dr., San Diego, CA 92106, tel. (619) 224-2489. No transient slips are available. Slip fees are $7 per foot per month. Freshwater hookups are near the boat slips. Nearest food store is two miles away. Restaurant is located on the premises.

Shelter Island Marina Inn
Located at Point Loma, Shelter Island. Mailing address is 2051 Shelter Island Dr., San Diego, CA 92106, tel. (619) 223-0301. Num-

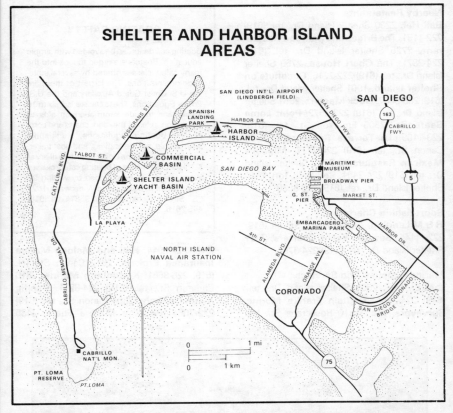

SHELTER AND HARBOR ISLAND AREAS

ber of transient slips varies. Slip fees range from $10-30. Live-aboards are allowed. There's a freshwater hookup at each slip. Nearest food store is one mile away, open from 9 to 5. Laundromat is open 24 hours a day. There's a restaurant on the premises. Special services include meeting and banquet facilities to accommodate groups from 20 to 500 people.

Sun Harbor Marina
Located near Shelter Island, Point Loma, in San Diego. Mailing address is 5104 N. Harbor Dr., San Diego, CA 92106, tel. (619) 222-1167. No transient slips available; slip fees are $6.50 per foot per month. The near-

est food store is three blocks away, open 9 to 4:30. You'll find a freshwater hookup every three slips. There is a restaurant on the premises. Special attractions include sportfishing.

Nearby Accommodations
Humphrey's Half Moon Inn, 2303 Shelter Island Dr., tel. (619) 224-3411. **Kona Inn,** 1901 Shelter Island Dr., tel. (619) 222-0421. **Kona Kai Club,** 1551 Shelter Island Dr., tel. (619) 222-1191. **Posada Inn,** 5005 N. Harbor Dr., tel. (619) 222-0561. **Travel Lodge Point Loma,** 5102 N. Harbor Dr., tel. (619) 223-8171.

Nearby Restaurants

Bali Hai, 2230 Shelter Island Dr., tel. (619) 222-1181. The **Brigantine Seafood Restaurant,** 2725 Shelter Island Dr., tel. (619) 224-2871. The **Chart House,** 2760 Shelter Island Dr., tel. (619) 222-2216. **Coconuts on Shelter Island,** 1901 Shelter Island Dr., tel. (619) 286-6887. **Dock Masters,** 2051 Shelter Island Dr., tel. (619) 223-2572. **Point Loma Seafoods,** 2805 Emerson St., tel. (619) 223-1109. **La Terraza Restaurant,** 2830 Canon St., tel. (619) 224-2777. **Miguel's Mexican Restaurant,** 2912 Shelter Island Dr., tel. (619) 224-2401. **Red Sails Inn,** 2614 Shelter Island Dr., tel. (619) 223-3030.

Sport-fishing Charters

H & M Landing, 2803 Emerson St., tel. (619) 222- 1144. **Set Sail Yacht Charters,** 2051 Shelter Island Dr., tel. (619) 224-3791.

Marine Supplies And Services

C.M.E., Inc., 2565 Shelter Island Dr., tel. (619) 224-2764. **Captain Franke Marine Surveyors, Inc.,** 1310 Rosecrans St., tel.

BOATING SAFETY

Boating accidents can be avoided with simple education. Boaters are urged to look into the many safety classes offered by several statewide organizations. The largest of these are the U.S. Coast Guard Auxiliary and the U.S. Power Squadrons. These classes last six to 16 weeks and include information on aids to navigation, rules of the road, charts and compasses, boating regulations, marlinspike seamanship, marine engines, and boat trailering practices. Call the Coast Guard Auxiliary at (213) 590-2217. A list of boating safety classes in your area will be provided by writing to: Department of Boating and Waterways, 1629 "S" Street, Sacramento, CA 95814, tel. (916) 445-2616.

---

(619) 224-2944. **Hall and Malone Marine Insurance Brokers,** 2812 Canon St., tel. (619) 226-8661. **Kettenburg Marine,** 2810 Carleton St., tel. (619) 224-8211. **Pacific Marine Supply,** 2804 Canon St., tel. (619) 222-7084. **Pearson Marine Fuels,** 2435

San Diego's boating population grows each year.

COURSES FROM SAN DIEGO

Courses from: San Diego Whistle Buoy to	Magnetic Course	Reverse Course	Distance Nautical Miles
Oceanside	332	152	35
Dana Point	320	140	56
Newport	316	136	66
Los Angeles Light	306	126	82
Catalina-Avalon	293	113	70
San Clemente-Pyramid Cove	266	86	58
Cortez Bank	248	068	95
Sixty Mile Bank	222	042	60
North Coronado	181	001	12
South Coronado	167	347	14

Shelter Island Dr., tel. (619) 222-7084. **San Diego Marine Exchange, Inc.,** 2636 Shelter Island Dr., tel. (619) 223-7159. **Tonga Fuels, Inc.,** 2385 Shelter Island Dr., tel. (619) 224-3090. **Driscoll Custom Boats,** 2438 Shelter Island Dr., tel. (619) 224-3575. **Marine Management Company,** 1050 Anchorage Lane, tel. (619) 222-0325. **Mauricio & Sons, Inc.,** 2420 Shelter Island Dr., tel. (619) 223-3191. **Shelter Island Boatyard,** 2330 Shelter Island Dr., Suite 1, tel. (619) 222-0481.

SAN DIEGO'S HARBOR ISLAND AREA

Harbor Island West Marina

Located on San Diego Bay, Harbor Island. Mailing address is 2040 Harbor Island Dr., San Diego, CA 92101, tel. (619) 291-6440. Number of transient slips varies; slip fees ramge from $10.50 to $19.25 per night. Water available at each slip except side ties; dock carts are provided and on docks. Marine supplies for sale from 9 to 6. Fuel dock open 7 a.m. to 10 p.m. Laundromat open 8 a.m. to 10 p.m.

Cabrillo Isle Marina

Mailing address is 1450 Harbor Island Dr., San Diego, CA 92101, tel. (619) 297-6222. Transient slips are available; the number varies. Guest slip fees from $16 to $33 per day, from 30 feet to 56 feet. Special charges for live-aboards. Fresh water is available at each slip along with lockable dock boxes, telephone, concrete docks, clean restrooms. Marine supplies available within one mile from marina. Marine services and repairs available; fuel dock one-quarter mile away. Laundry facilities available. Deli and restaurant located on premises and open from 7 to 7; supermarket is one mile off. Special attractions: Vacationland of the West, Sea Port Village.

Marina Cortez

Located on San Diego Bay; mailing address is 1880 Harbor Island Dr., San Diego, CA 92106, tel. (619) 291-5985. Number of transient slips available varies. Slip fees are $25 per night. Fresh water available at docks. Marine supply store open 9 to 5. Fuel dock open 7:30 to 6. Laundromat, restaurant, and food store located on premises. Open 8 to 7 during the summer.

Area Restaurants

Anthony's Fish Grotto, 1360 N. Harbor Dr., tel. (619) 232-7408. **Bali Ha'i**, 2230 Shelter Island Dr., tel. (619) 222-1181. **Barnacle Bill's**, 1880 Harbor Island Dr., tel. (619) 297-1673. **Boat House** (Harbor Island Marina), 2040 Harbor Island Dr., tel. (619) 291-6440, guest dock. **Boll Weevil**, 2743 Shelter Island Dr., tel. (619) 224-2871. **Brigantine**, 2912 Shelter Island Dr., tel. (619) 224-2871. **Chart House**, East Harbor Dr., tel. (619) 223-7391, guest dock. **Chart House**, 2760 Shelter Island Dr., tel. (619) 222-2216. **Chart House** (Glorietta Bay), 1701 Grand Way, Coronado, tel. (619) 435-0155, dinghy

FUEL DOCKS

Chevron Oil Company
High Seas Fuel Dock
2510 Shelter Island Drive
tel. (619) 224-5522

Chevron Oil Company
Pearson Marine Fuels, Inc.
2435 Shelter Island Drive
tel. (619) 222-7084

Cortez Fuel Dock
1880 Harbor Island Drive
tel. (619) 296-2331

Pelican Marine Sales
2040 Harbor Island Drive
tel. (619) 297-3735

Tonga Marine Fuel Dock
2385 Shelter Island Drive
tel. (619) 224-3090

sightseeing in the harbor

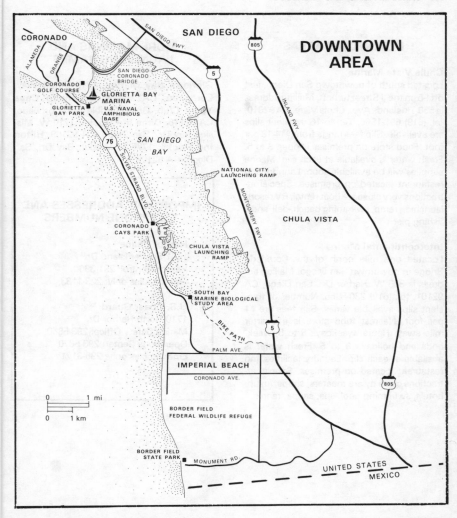

dock. **Doc Masters (Shelter Island Marina Inn)**, 2051 Shelter Island Dr., tel. (619) 223-2572, guest dock. **Tom Ham's Light House**, 2150 Harbor Island Dr., tel. (619) 291-9110, guest dock. **Humphrey's**, 2241 Shelter Island Dr., tel. (619) 224-3411, guest dock. **Intercontinental Hotel**, 385 W. Harbor Dr., tel. (619) 234-1500 or 231-0972.

Lael's, Maison Anne-Marie, Las Cascadas, guest dock. **Red Sails Inn**, 2614 Shelter Island Dr., tel. (619) 223-3030. **Rueben E. Lee River Boat,** 880 Harbor Island Dr., tel. (619) 291-1974. **Sheppard's** (at Sheraton Harbor Island Hotel), 1380 Harbor Island Dr., tel. (619) 291-2900. **Tarantino's**, 5150 Harbor Dr., tel. (619) 224-3555.

DOWNTOWN AREAS

Chula Vista Marina

Located south of downtown San Diego, just off I-5 on the J Street turnoff. Mailing address is 550 Tidelands Ave., Chula Vista, CA 92010, tel. (619) 691-1860. Ten to 15 transient slips are available. Slip fees range from $14-18 per foot. Food store on premises is open 8 to 5. Fresh water is available at each slip. Marine supplies will be available soon. Laundry and restaurant located on premises. Special attractions very close are boat rental, RV resort, launching ramp, swimming beach, deli, and a fishing pier.

Intercontinental Marina

Located one mile north of the Coronado Bridge in downtown San Diego. Mailing address is 385 W. Harbor Dr., San Diego, CA 92101, tel. (619) 230-8955. Number of transient slips available varies. Slip fees are $1 per foot. Nearest food store is a quarter mile away. Hours: weekdays 8 to 5; weekends and holidays 9 to 5. Fresh water is available at each slip. Laundry facilities and restaurant located on premises. Special attractions close by are theaters, shops, luxury hotels, swimming pool, spa, sauna, tennis.

MORE MARINAS AND LAUNCHING RAMPS

Glorietta Bay Marina, 1715 Strant Way, Coronado, CA 95443. **Coronado Cays Yacht Club**, Grand Carible Isle, Coronado, CA 92118. **Dana Inn Docks**, 1710 W. Mission Bay Dr., San Diego, CA 92109. **Hilton Inn Docks**, 1775 E. Mission Bay Dr., San Diego, CA 92109.

IMPORTANT ADDRESSES AND TELEPHONE NUMBERS

Harbor Police
1401 Shelter Island Dr.
Harbor Control: 291-3900.
Emergencies only: 223-1133.

U.S. Coast Guard
1710 North Harbor Dr.
Marine Safety Office: 293-5860.
Operations Center: 293-5870
Emergencies only: 295-3121

THE CHANNEL ISLANDS

THE LAND

There are eight islands in the Channel Islands group, which extend off the California coast in a chain from Santa Barbara south to the Oceanside area. All share similar geologic origins, but each has evolved over the millenia into its own special environment with its own unique history. Geologists now disagree over what once was accepted as fact: that from 70 million years ago to less than 20,000 years, the four northern Channel Islands were one colossal "super-island" connected to the Mainland by a land bridge. The theory was that the Anacapa end of this supposed island was joined to the Mainland at Point Mugu and was part of the Santa Monica Mountains. There is a question as to whether a land bridge existed. One of the reasons earlier scientists believed in the possibility of a land bridge is the presence of

land animals; the bridge gave them a logical explanation for how the fauna traveled to the islands. Many other theories are now being studied that would be plausible explanations for wildlife on the islands without a land bridge.

Other geologists believe that the islands were formed 14 million years ago when volcanic activity along the southern California coast was at its maximum. Islands, peaks, and ridges rose out of the sea, only to settle down again as the volcanic activity subsided. Ultimately, this left what we now call the Channel Islands. With the coming of the Ice Age over a million years ago, freezing water and then subsequent melting eroded the offshore peaks. Geologic stresses of all the changes caused buckling, folding, fractures, and tears in the earth. Cliffs were formed, ridges slid into the sea, and islands appeared and disappeared into the ocean.

Geology buffs, while traveling around the Channel Islands, study the cliffs, bluffs, terrain, and underwater floor. In most cases it's rugged and craggy with horizontal and vertical strata, and flat terraces above and below the sea. To a scientist this tells the story of many changes in levels of the ocean over the

centuries. A relatively shallow submarine shelf at an average depth of 300 feet extends three to six miles around each of the islands. Here, the mingling of the cold current of the north with the warmer counter-current of the south, along with the unique topography of the ocean bottom, contribute to making this one of the richest marine environments in the United States.

FLORA

Coreopsis

All eight Channel Islands have many natural similarities. On each of the islands many of the same plant communities thrive. One of the most common, coreopsis, also called sea dahlia and sunflower tree, has been described as a dwarf or miniature tree. The grotesque, odd plants average two feet in height but can grow as tall as 10 feet. In the fall, the clustered plants, bare of blossom or leaf, look like a dwarfed, misshapen, mysterious forest, all black and brown with knobby branches. But with winter rains, a change spreads over the hills; delicate fern-like fronds begin to appear. By spring, the plant blooms profusely (depending on the amount of winter rainfall) though just for a short time, bearing brilliant

yellow/orange flowers; this splash of color is seen clear to the Mainland. The coreopsis is found on most of the islands (not on San Clemente), spreading a bright carpet along the gentle hills of Santa Barbara Island, poking up even from craggy pockets and crevices of Anacapa and San Miguel. Rabbits destroyed many of the coreopsis on Santa Barbara, eating all the greenery they could reach, and then even girdling the trunks of the trees, ultimately destroying the plant and its bright flowers.

Wildflowers

The purple **blue-eyed grass** flowers have six graceful petals with yellow star-like centers. The **western thistle** blooms a bright pink on

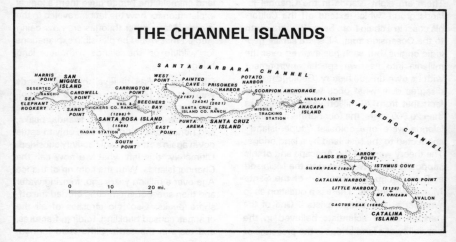

THE CHANNEL ISLANDS

coreopsis

spring bursts forth on the islands, and even the sand dunes come alive with blue **lupine** and golden **California poppies**. Dudleya, grayish green and similar to common ice plant, grows side by side with the orange-blossomed **mimulus** or monkey flower, on the steep walls of rocky cliffs with a southern exposure. White **morning glories** steadfastly climb over and around **sea cucumbers** and **island sage**. Ferns and mosses grow at the bottom of steep canyons.

Cactus

This common Channel Island cactus, an *opuntia* species, is seen over much of the southern part of California and on into Mexico. The oval, disk-like pads are edible, as is the fruit—the pear. The plant bears a beautiful satiny yellow blossom that withers and drops as the fruit begins to develop. The fruit becomes sweet and juicy if allowed to ripen on the plant, and is commonly eaten not only on the Channel Islands, but in Mexico, Central America, and parts of Africa as well. An account given in "The Diary of A Ship Captain's Wife," by Margaret Holden Eaton who lived on Santa Cruz Island with her husband

and baby girl from 1909, tells of making syrup for pancakes from the prickly pear. The trick is to peel the spines very carefully, then it's ready to enjoy. Oddly enough, sheep were known to eat the pear, prickly spines and all. As noted before, the land was severely overgrazed—that's real hunger! A relative of the prickly pear growing on the islands is the **cholla cactus**, with a different shape but just as deadly with its curled barb-like spines. It too produces a flower, a delicate pink blossom sprouting at the joints of the cactus. Long trails of **snake cactus** hang from rocky walls and canyons on the islands.

Trees

Island cherry, island oak, and **ironwood trees** grow on California's offshore islands. One of the most unusual of nature's quirks is a stand of Torrey pines on Santa Rosa Island. This is the only example of these pines outside of those at Torrey Pines State Park, north of San Diego. These, along with the Santa Cruz Island pine, are remnants of an archaic Pleistocene forest that have survived a multitude of climatic changes over thousands of years.

FAUNA

Island Fox

The unique island fox, a relative of the Mainland gray fox, is an inhabitant of the six larger Channel Islands (not Anacapa or Santa Barbara). The animal differs from his Mainland relative in several ways. It's small—about the size of a house cat; in fact it has many feline characteristics, a scampering movement, and a yowl resembling a domestic cat's. It lives on a diet of mice, fish, birds and their eggs, crabs, fruit, insects, berries, and yes, even prickly pears. The fox has little fear of humans and a great curiosity (another catlike characteristic); it will stop and give you a good look if you meet on a mountain path. There's no certainty about how he arrived on the islands. One possibility is rafting on a tree trunk washed out to sea from the

Island fox

Mainland during a heavy rainstorm; another is he could have been brought to the islands by Indians traveling from the Mainland. The fox also suffers from the introduction of "exotic" grasses. Wild oat seeds (the kind that stick on your shoelaces when you hike the hills) get into the foxes' eyes and blind them. The island fox is just a little different on each of the Channel Islands; a little bigger or smaller with slight color variations.

Rodents

The **white-footed mouse**, also known as the deer mouse, is endemic to the particular island it inhabits and is an important part of the food chain. The fox is the chief predator of the mouse. The rodent has white undersides, oversized feet, a hairy tail, and wide ears. It eats a varied diet—seeds, bark, twigs, fruit—and if it can get into a camper's tucker, it recognizes gourmet heaven. The mice reproduce readily and survive nicely in nooks and crannies of the rocky coastline, meadows, or sandy shore. They can be found on all eight of the Channel Islands. As with the fox, each island has developed a subspecies with subtle differences. Those on Santa Rosa and Santa Barbara have even developed their own variety of ticks and fleas. Other small rodent relatives found on the islands are the **meadow mouse** and the **harvest mouse**. It is said that there is an **island shrew**, but it must be extremely shy, since it has only been spotted a couple of times over a hundred years. The **ground squirrel** is also part of the island family and lives in underground burrows in the meadow areas.

Wild Goats

This feral animal was introduced to the islands sometime during the Spanish arrival. It's believed that goats were dropped off so the ship's crew would have fresh meat the next time they passed through. It doesn't take many generations for the goat to revert to its wild stage, and they reproduce quickly; the female generally delivers two kids a year. On Catalina and San Clemente the goats increased freely for many years, building up large free-running flocks. They are destructive animals with voracious appetites. Since ecologists have begun to see the need to preserve these islands in their natural state, many of the goats have been hunted or removed. On Catalina the occasional hunt keeps the herds down to a reasonable number. On San Clemente, the Navy Wildlife Biology staff has been trying to rid the island of the animal through hunts and live removal to Mainland sites. The staff has had not only the spritely goats to contend with (they can scamper up the tiniest trail and walk sideways where few humans dare to tread), but also animal lovers that feel goats have a right to life on San Clemente. So while the environmentalists and the animal lovers argue, the goats keep right on reproducing and devastating the landscape with their natural eating habits.

BIRDS

An enormous variety of birds nest on the rocky cliffs and shores of the Channel Islands. Here it is easy to see that the **brown pelican**, only a few years ago in danger of being destroyed, is now flourishing. These large birds fly in a wedge formation gracefully flapping their wings close to the wave tops. Spotting a fishy morsel they dive into the sea, and

forgetting all grace, scoop up as many fish as their large beaks will hold, ending up a crumpled heap on the water's surface. Not too long ago, pelican reproduction slowed down to a point of concern. Egg shells were so thin they could not support the weight of the brooding mother, cutting down dramatically on the number of chicks hatching each year. It was discovered that the problem was caused by DDT found in small fish ingested by the pelican. The pesticide accumulated in the tissues of the bird and eventually reached such high levels that it affected, among other things, the shells of the eggs. Since DDT has able comeback and can be seen in large healthy numbers on Channel Island rookeries.

Pelicans have a few bad habits that get them into other troubles. One is trying to steal fish from fishermen—often right off the hook. If a pelican should get caught on your hook *do not* just cut the line at your end. If you do, you're condemning the bird to death; the line almost always ends up wrapped around the bird's body, including his wings, leaving him helpless, unable to fly, and doomed to starvation. Rather, don't be afraid to reel the pelican in. See following page.

Other Birds

Along with a flourishing brown pelican rookery on Anacapa Island, thousands of other birds have found that the Channel Islands are nirvana. With little outside influence to disturb them, the relatively shallow nearshore waters around the islands supply 11 species of breeding seabirds with a rich food source of fish and invertebrates. On Santa Barbara, bird enthusiasts will find the largest colony of **Xantus' murrelet** and **black storm petrels** in the U.S. These timid seabirds are usually noticed only on or above the open ocean; they return to shore but once a year to breed and nest. Migratory fowl and other birds such as **loons, grebes, herons, plovers, ducks,** and **geese** are also seen on the islands. Some stop just to rest on their long journey, while others take time out for

UNTANGLING A PELICAN FROM YOUR LINE

1. Keep reeling! Although he'll struggle and flap his wings, remember you know what's best. As large as the bird appears, it only weighs about six pounds and is quite harmless if handled correctly.

2. When you've got the bird close enough, grab the closed bill and hold it securely with one hand. The inside edges of the bill are sharp, but unless you rub your hand up and down the edge, a pelican bite will not hurt you.

3. Fold up the wings into their normal closed position and hold them there. This quiets down the bird and it should stop struggling.

4. Turn the bird's head around so it lies along the middle of its back (that's how pelicans sleep) and the bird is easier to handle. Tuck the pelican under your armpit or between your legs while removing the fishing line and hook. But remember, keep a firm grip on the bird's bill. Certainly, it would be easier for two people instead of one, but one person can do it.

5. The most important thing you can do for the bird is to cut off every bit of the fishing line. Do not throw scrap pieces into the water to ensnare another bird or wrap around a boat's prop shaft.

6. If the hook is embedded in the pelican's flesh, try to cut off the barb and back the hook out. Or cut off the loop end of the hook and push the rest of the hook through. If you lack wire cutters, remove the line from the hook and push it forward. Do not rip the hook out; if impossible to remove the hook, leave it in. Pelicans do not seem to get infections and the bird's skin will heal around the hook.

7. Set the bird down, step back a few feet and release it. You just did a very good deed for one of Mother Nature's favorites.

nesting and breeding before continuing on. Other feathered inhabitants of the islands are the **Brandt's cormorant,** a powerful web-footed diver that swims underwater after its pelagic prey. The **western gull** is a noisy old friend seen all over the West Coast, which vigorously nests on the Channel Islands high above the sea. **Sandpipers** are seen not only on the sandy shore, but also on the rocks and cliffs above, where nature has provided ample food and few predators.

MARINE CREATURES

Upwelling

An action of the sea called upwelling occurs along the California coast. Actually it happens all over the world, near the equator as well as in the Antarctic. In simple terms, coastal upwelling occurs when water from deeper levels of the ocean is brought to the surface to replace the surface waters when they are moved offshore by heavy winds. Upwelling fertilizes coastal waters by replacing surface water. The upwelled water is colder and contains richer nutrients such as nitrates, phosphates, and silicates. These nutrients act as fertilizer for marine plants, and ultimately help the fishing industry. Sometimes large areas of the sea become red, green, or brown from the rapid reproduction of microscopic plant and animal organisms called plankton. During this "plankton bloom," these tiny organisms are grazed upon by small animals. The smaller animals are fed upon by larger animals, including fish, who are in turn food for the larger fish. And when whales graze in these colorful "pastures," they consume up to a ton of plankton per mouthful.

Tidepools

It's hard to describe the myriad marine creatures of the Channel Islands without first mentioning the tidepools that thrive along their rocky shores. A tidepool is a pocket of the sea trapped regularly after the tide has gone out. The mini-worlds that exist in each of these tiny pools are a replica of sealife in the larger picture. The fight for existence against such mighty forces as the pounding surf in high tide, drying sun and smothering heat during low tide, ultraviolet radiation from the sun, rain that dilutes the salinity, and ever-present predators presents ongoing adversity for the sturdy survivors that inhabit the pools. One major predator is man and his inventions. The creatures of the sea have not yet evolved a defense system to fight such calamities as oil spills or chemical pollution. It's up to us to do everything in our power to protect these fascinating creatures. When exploring or studying tidepools, each person has a responsiblitiy to leave it as found. Apparently, it does no harm to the tiny creatures to pick them up (carefully), or turn them over, or scoop them up in a jar to watch them swim freely, as long as everything is returned *exactly* the same.

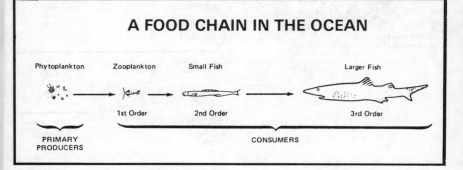

A FOOD CHAIN IN THE OCEAN

Phytoplankton	Zooplankton	Small Fish		Larger Fish
	1st Order	2nd Order		3rd Order
PRIMARY PRODUCERS		CONSUMERS		

Note: Wear sturdy rubber-soled shoes that you don't mind getting wet, as most of the rocks around the intertidal zone are slick. Be sure to check the tide table in the local paper or marine store, and keep track when you're meandering at low tide; it could be difficult to return when the tide is barreling back in, especially in a rocky area.

Intertidal Zone

The intertidal zone is the area between the highest high tide and the lowest low tide. It's created by the coming and going of the ocean current each day. The currents also change with the time of the month, the year, and the quarter of the moon. This creates a continuum of habitats from high rocks that regularly get the splashing surf at the highest tides to the deepest level of pools that are only exposed during the lowest tides at certain times of the year. All of the species in the zone have learned to live with the ocean and its capricious nature. Those with the least tolerance to atmospheric pressure are found at the lowest part of the zone or closest to the sea. Tolerant ones live toward the tops of rocks or reefs. The poor little creatures that get washed into the sea (and probably eaten) every time a large wave crashes into their rocky home occupy the protected pockets and crevices on the lee side of the rocks. Nature thinks of everything.

The following intertidal organisms are found along the entire Pacific Coast from the top of Alaska to the southern edge of Mexico. For an excellent pocket guide of identification and explanation while exploring Pacific tidepools, get a copy of *Pacific Intertidal Life,* by Ron Russo and Pam Olhausen, Nature Study Guild, Box 972, Berkeley, CA 94701.

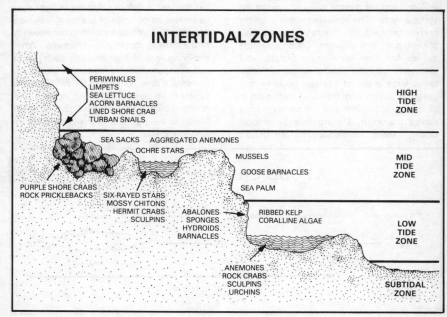

INTERTIDAL ZONES

PERIWINKLES
LIMPETS
SEA LETTUCE
ACORN BARNACLES
LINED SHORE CRAB
TURBAN SNAILS

HIGH TIDE ZONE

SEA SACKS   AGGREGATED ANEMONES
OCHRE STARS

MUSSELS

GOOSE BARNACLES

SEA PALM

MID TIDE ZONE

PURPLE SHORE CRABS
ROCK PRICKLEBACKS   SIX-RAYED STARS
MOSSY CHITONS
HERMIT CRABS   ABALONES
SCULPINS   SPONGES
HYDROIDS
BARNACLES

RIBBED KELP
CORALLINE ALGAE

LOW TIDE ZONE

ANEMONES
ROCK CRABS
SCULPINS
URCHINS

SUBTIDAL ZONE

TIDEPOOL ORGANISMS

shield limpet	dogwinkle	crab
ribbed limpet	octopus	shrimp
owl limpet	sea slug	eel
plate limpet	anemone	bristleworm
horned slipper shell	sea star	ribbonworm
black abalone	sun star	flatworm
chiton	brittle star	green alga
mussel	green urchin	brown alga
black turban snail	giant red urchin	red alga
leafy hornmouth	isopod	sponge
checkered periwinkle	barnacle	hydroid

Sand Creatures

The smooth sand constantly brushed by the incoming/outgoing sea hides a multitude of organisms. Everyone has seen the tiny **sand crab** burrowing his way into the wet sand of the backwash of each wave, straining for tidbits of food. Other small creatures (all different) come in many sizes and shapes: some have antennae, some hop sideways, some are gray, white, or the color of the sand. At night swarms of tiny **sandhoppers** leap onto kelp fronds in search of food. These, too, are part of the food chain with their own set of predators.

Marine Flora

Some brown algae (seaweed) called kelps form large tangled forests consisting of **giant kelp, feather boa kelp, bull whip kelp,** and **elk kelp.** All of these brown algae depend on the gas-filled bulbs, called pneumatocysts, to buoy their long, swaying stems, and blades that transfer energy material from the sun into the dim depths of the bottom regions of the "holdfasts," which anchor the kelp to the sea floor. These kelp forests are habitats for a great variety of marinelife that depend on

them for food and shelter. The fish that live within the forest are colorful and varied.

Among the most flamboyant algae is **giant kelp**, growing as much as 100 feet from the sea floor to the surface. They grow amazingly fast, as much as three feet a day, fed by the rich nutrients of the colder water brought in by "upwelling," and plenty of sunshine. A new plant usually doubles its size every three weeks. The long stems are buoyed up by brown, tear-shaped bulbs filled with gas. From the surface, the kelp resembles a jumbled mass of brown rubber-like stems and vines and tobacco-like leaves, a place you want to stay away from. In reality this is just the canopy; the remainder of what continues to grow just gets longer and lays on the surface of the water. From the diver's point of view, the stems grow a good distance apart from each other or the sea floor, and indeed resemble a forest of tall trees. The holdfast is not a root in the sense of a land plant, gathering nutrients from the surrounding soil. Rather, it is simply an anchorage. The alga takes nourishment directly from the seawater through all exposed surfaces. Reproduction is through microscopic cells known as spores, produced by a female plant and fertilized by a male; free-floating spores then germinate and begin to form separate new plants. Some seaweeds produce mini-plants which eventually separate and become new plants. Eventually giant kelp becomes so top heavy that the holdfast lets go and the entire plant ends up floating on the surface of the sea until caught by a current and thrown in a heap on a beach or rocky shoreline. However, it continues to nurture, harboring a variety of crabs, worms, clams, starfish, and other invertebrates.

Just as tidepool life exists because it can sustain itself despite drying, temperature change, salt level, and tide level, so it is with kelp. One of the more hardy, able to resist and persist, is a green alga called **sea lettuce**, which can lose up to 75 percent of its tissue water and recoup to fine fettle once in the water again. A brown alga, common **branched rockweed**, can withstand up to 48 hours of exposure without drying out. On the other hand, most red algae are extremely sensitive to heat and light and exist in the low intertidal zone because they cannot survive more than two or three hours of exposure.

Algae Aquaculture

Aquaculture is the farming of aquatic plants and animals, and is practiced by many countries in the world. In Japan and other Oriental countries it has been a flourishing business for years; in the United States it's still in developing stages. A multimillion-dollar business in algae harvesting is one area of aquaculture that has been very successful in the U.S. Algin, a derivative of kelp, is found in many products that you see in the supermarket every time you shop. Next time you buy ice cream, chocolate milk, pudding, salad dressing, cheese, or fruit juice, take a close look at the ingredients. Algae deriva-

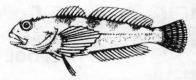

tives furnish a gel used to emulsify and stabilize foods. It's used in diverse ways, in dental molds, brewing beer, fertilizer, animal feed, paint, cosmetics, and approximately 15 percent of the world's iodine comes from Japan where it is manufactured from kelp. The kelp beds off California are leased out by the state. They in turn accept bids from companies that do the actual harvesting in specially designed ships that often harvest 400 tons of kelp a day. San Diego is a very popular area for kelp harvesting because of good year-round weather conditions. Under the auspices of the Department of Fish and Game, kelp can be cut up to a maximum of four feet below the surface of the water. Opening up the surface directs more sunshine beneath the sea and onto the plants, encouraging new growth. Harvesting is a healthy process.

Seaweed Dishes

Some countries (Japan, Hawaii, China, and the Philippines) have recognized the value of eating seaweed for centuries. These algae are nutritious and rich in vitamins A and E. Add to that the red, green, and brown algae, also very high in niacin and vitamin C, B-12, and B-1. They contain digestible proteins—the red and green are the highest. Three ounces of red algae supplies one-half the daily adult protein requirements. Common sea lettuce is high in iron, protein, iodine, magnesium, vitamins A, B-1, and C, and sodium. Pluck or cut the blades from rocks at low tide, wash well, dry at room temperature, and then use as a soup base.

Be aware that *except* in state parks and reserves, gathering algae for non-commercial use does *not* require a California fishing license or permit. In a state park or reserve, you must obtain a permit from the state Department of Parks and Recreation. In the

SEAWEED RECIPES

Some seaweed is good raw, others cooked. Some make good additions to salads combined with cucumber and radish. All, including the seaweed, should be finely chopped.

KELP *NEREOCYSTIS* CAKE

3 eggs
2 C. sugar
1½ tsp cooking oil
1 tsp baking soda
1 tsp baking powder
1 tsp cinnamon
½ tsp powdered ginger
1½ C. grated kelp
1 C. crushed pineapple, drained

Use portion of "head" or float of nereocystis, the brown alga (kelp) frequently found on beaches in California. A float about four inches in diameter will not be too old or tough. Cut into pieces, peel with vegetable peeler, and grate or chop finely. Wash (to remove excess salt that is released in grating) and drain well in colander.

Beat eggs until thick and lemon colored, gradually adding sugar. When combined, add cooking oil and stir briefly. Stir together flour, baking soda, baking powder, cinnamon, and powdered ginger. Add to egg mixture, then fold in the finely grated kelp and crushed pineapple. Bake at 350 degrees F for 45 minutes in a greased and flour-dusted 10 X 10 or 9 X 12 inch pan.

This recipe makes a moist spice cake which may be frosted with butter-lemon frosting or left unfrosted with powdered sugar sifted over the top, according to taste. (From I.A. Abbott)

KIM CHEE

Based on the Korean method of preparing their famous pickled cabbages, using a red alga, *gracilaria*.

2 lb. *gracilaria* chopped into 2- to 3-inch pieces
handful of coarse salt
2 cloves garlic chopped per quart of wilted seaweed or to taste
1-2 chopped bulb onion or ½ C. chopped green onions
chili pepper, chopped, or ½ tsp cayenne (to taste—should be hot)
½ tsp paprika

Wash and clean the seaweed. Salt and wilt by letting it stand overnight. Drain off liquid; add garlic, onions, chili pepper, and paprika. Pack tightly in jars, seal, and refrigerate. Let stand a few days before using. (From Abbott and Williamson)

course of collecting algae in intertidal areas, you will find many invertebrates including clams, crabs, worms, and snails living among the seaweeds. These animals can be taken only in legal seasons, and with a fishing license. Outside of bureaucratic permission, all you need is a sharp knife, a bucket, some plastic bags, and don't forget your rubber-soled shoes. A good guidebook is handy to have along. The best time to collect is at low tide—in California tides reach high and low levels twice a day. Tidal charts are found in many beach community newspapers, or check at your local sporting goods store or bait and tackle shop. Rocky shorelines are your best bet for collecting algae; the sides of the rocks are richer in plant life than the top. To get the freshest seaweed, take it direct from the place of attachment. Don't get lazy and grab a bunch that's been washed ashore—it's seldom fresh and will be full of debris. Take only what you need.

MARINE MAMMALS

Marine Mammal Protection Act

More than 25 species of marine mammals inhabit the Channel Islands Sanctuary. After being nearly demolished by the extensive

northern Alaska fur seal

hunting in the 18th and early 19th centuries, seals, sea lions, and a variety of fur seals have made a remarkable comeback. The Marine Mammal Protection Act of 1972 was passed with the intention of protecting the mammals, and management was transferred from the coastal states to the federal government. Many feel this law was enacted primarily to protect whales, but it was written to include all marine mammals—to the dismay of many. There's much controversy among fishermen who feel that the sea lion and sea otter are interfering with their business. According to divers, the sea otter eats a tremendous amount of abalone each year. Commercial fishermen complain that the growing sea lion population is taking a larger share of fish, often right from their nets, not only creating a decrease in income, but fouling up expensive gear, creating "down time," and worst of all (according to the fishermen), they cannot destroy an animal that persists without first obtaining a special permit from National Marine Fisheries Service. Ecologists argue that nature provides its own means of thinning the herds: many newborn pups are trampled to death each season in the rookeries as the herd multiplies. But fishermen are still demanding the right to destroy a seal that is making a nuisance of itself in the nets. Right now, there are no clear-cut answers. The law says it is illegal to harass a marine mammal. Harassment is interpreted as human activity which changes the behavior of the animals. You cannot harm, capture, kill, interfere with or enter a rookery, or closely pursue (a whale) with a boat.

Pinnipeds

Pinniped means "featherfeet," and refers to the modification of the front and hind feet to form flippers. Many of the seals, such as the **harbor seal**, spend six to eight months at sea. Others, such as the **northern fur seal**, spend considerable time on land. These creatures have thick hides with heavy layers of fat underneath and in some cases fur to protect them from the cold.

northern elephant seal

The pinniped family includes two basic groups, the **eared seals**, which include fur seals and sea lions, and the **hair seals**, so-called true seals — harbor seals, ribbon seals, and elephant seals. Eared seals have small external flaps for ears. They move rapidly on land since they can turn their hind flippers forward, almost like feet. They use their large forward flippers to swim quickly in the water. These mammals return year after year to special breeding areas called rookeries, commonly on offshore islands. Breeding season is a noisy, hectic time at the rookery. Males fight for territories and to the victors go groups of 25 or more females, accurately called "harems." Males go more than two months without feeding during breeding time.

Hair seals have no external ears. They have small front flippers, and use their hind flippers for swimming. They cannot turn their hind flippers forward, making them very clumsy on land. Five species of pinnipeds gather to breed, pup, and nurse their young in the Channel Islands: the harbor seal, stellar sea lion, California sea lion, northern fur seal, and elephant seal.

Sea Otters

After being around for at least three million years, the sea otter was almost totally annihilated (see p. 250) in the middle 1800s. It was quite a thrill when, in 1938, a large herd (100) of sea otters was discovered about 15 miles south of Monterey. The marine mammal, part of the weasel family, can grow to about four and a half feet long, and reach a weight of 60-87 pounds. Their hind feet are large and webbed, with the fifth digit (comparable to man's little toe) the longest. The tail is used to help guide the animal while swimming, which it can do very efficiently. Its most impressive feature, however, is its beautiful soft fur, which in the past made many coats and nearly caused its extinction.

The otters' front paws are stubby with retractable claws. However, the animals are quite adept with them, using them much like a human uses fingers. Anyone that has ever tried to remove an abalone attached to a rock knows that it is impossible to do without a metal bar. The otter, however, is quite an accomplished underwater hunter, easily capturing abalone and other shellfish. It is commonly seen floating on its back with a rock in one paw, holding a shellfish in the other, pounding away at the shell till it frees the flesh and it's ready to be nibbled. Though the otter floats on its back at leisure, when swimming it turns on its belly and in time of danger has been clocked at speeds up to five miles an hour. It's capable of staying underwater for periods of up to four minutes. The otter has no blubber as do seals and sea lions; its fur is not efficient enough to maintain its

body temperature at 100 degrees, so it has a high metabolic rate and must consume large quantities of food each day. It forages (very efficiently) day and night. As the herds grow, the prognosis is that certain fishing industries will be greatly affected: Pismo clam, abalone, sea urchin, shallow water red and rock crab, Dungeness crab, lobster, razor clam, and all open mariculture (marine farming) projects. The otter lives about 20 years, and produces one pup approximately every two years. Its only enemy (besides man) is the white shark.

The first record of sea otters was made in 1741, after Vitus Bering (the explorer from whom the Bering Sea took its name) spotted them in the Commander Islands and eastward in the Aleutians. The famous explorer was accompanied by a German naturalist, George Wilhelm Steller. The group obtained about 800 pelts from the Indians that hunted them for the pelt and food in reasonable numbers. These were taken home to Europe—the first time Europeans were exposed to otter pelts. In 1778, English explorer James Cook returned from extensive travels along the north Pacific coast and revealed to the world the potential profit awaiting the hunter. Thus, the sea otter fur trade began, which would attract people in ships from many parts of the world, weakening and ultimately loosening the hold of the Spanish flag on California.

Whales

When whales are mentioned, most West Coast dwellers think of the **gray whale**, which is enthusiastically observed as it migrates along the Pacific Coast from the Bering Sea to Baja and back each year. Others remember fondly the fun and games created by "Humphrey the Humpback" that led the Coast Guard and many boaters on a romp up the Sacramento Delta in 1986. But many more species of this usually gentle, giant mammal (part of the cetacean family) live in and around the coast near the Channel Islands. Although one thinks all whales are gigantic, the **pygmy sperm** grows to only 13 feet maximum, and some of the **beaked whales** only grow to 15-17 feet. The **false killer** isn't a true whale, but belongs to the dolphin (Delphinidae) family and gets huge, 18 feet. The **killer** grows to 31 feet, and the **pilot**, 22 feet.

Various sources say there are 78-91 species of cetaceans in the world. The cetaceans store thick layers of blubber under their skins. This provides insulation against cold, and some scientists believe it enables them to go for long periods without food. It's becoming more evident that the gray whale feeds heavily during the four months spent in the Bering Sea, and feeds lightly during the eight months of migration to and from Baja. Rather amazing, considering the energy it must take

AVOIDING SHARKS

Boaters, swimmers, surfers, and divers by the millions safely enjoy California's beaches and coastal waters. However, once in a great while a shark attack is reported. Be aware of the facts without stressing out while you're in the water of the Pacific. One of the easiest precautions is to avoid areas where sharks are known to roam, particularly places where seals and sea lions congregate. Another place *not* to go is the location of a previous shark attack. Since 1926, there have been 65 shark attacks recorded off the California coast, 44 attributed to great whites. Two of the attacks were at San Miguel Island, and three off

Point Conception. Most of the other confrontations occurred north of Point Conception, which should help put Southern Californians at ease. Sharks seem to avoid kelp beds, which should make skin divers exploring the beds around the Channel Islands feel a little more relaxed. A few statistics: most attacks took place near a deepwater area; attacks on humans occur at the surface (not because the person looks like a seal as some believe, but for territorial reasons); and in Northern California, most attacks took place in clear water under 60 degrees rather than in warm or murky waters.

finback whale

California gray whale

to swim thousands of miles, and on the return, nurse a baby as well (if it's a blue whale, the baby could be 25 feet long and weigh up to two tons at birth!). Most whales feed on plankton, minute organisms floating in the sea, straining it through baleen plates, the fine net-like apparatus in their mouths. Although they have been known to snack on a passing school of anchovies or other small fish, plankton supplies the bulk of their diet. So the largest animal on earth feeds on the smallest organisms—lowest on the food chain where the supply is more abundant. When in captivity, the animals are fed a variety of soft-boned fish that includes mackerel and squid.

The killer whale is the only known enemy of the great whales—along with man. But attacks are not as common as some would think. Pods of killer whales have been known in isolated instances to attack a lone whale; but its reputation as a killer whale rises mostly from tales related by ships that have had their slaughtered whales (under tow) attacked by killer whales. The killer is ordinarily a fish eater. Great whales appear to be unusually healthy animals; the slow movers attract acorn barnacles, which are really just "hitchhikers" and do no physical harm. Parasites

on the other hand can be a disabling menace, maybe even causing the strange act of "beaching." Though considered an aberrant behavior, scientists have found large quantities of parasites on these beached mammals.

Whaling

For centuries the whale has been a source of food and oil (and for a while, whalebone), especially for the polar region natives. Seven thousand years ago, Eskimos on the east coast of Canada were using toggle harpoon heads. In the mid-19th C. they were "invented" again by the American Yankee whaling fleet. Whaling began off the coast of California by Yankee whalers in the early 1800s. By the late 1800s, the gray whale was thought to be extinct. Shore whaling (referred to as whaling by hand) is part of California's history, and the first whaling station was built in Monterey in 1854. Others were built up and down the California coast and down to Baja—but were short lived. In 1874, Charles Melville Scammon (the whaler who discovered and exploited Scammon's Lagoon in Baja) wrote: "This particular branch of whaling is rapidly dying out, owing to the scarcity of the animals which now visit the coast."

CALIFORNIA WHALES

northern right	finback	beaked or bottlenose
fin or rorqual	humpback	Baird's beaked
minke	gray	Hubb's beaked
sei	sperm	Cuvier's beaked
blue or sulphurbottom	pygmy sperm	orca or killer
	dwarf sperm	

During this time, the Americans dominated the whaling industry. Their chief target was the **right whale**, so called because he was the "right" whale to catch: it was slow moving, didn't sink when killed, contained valuable baleen used for women's corset stays (big business in those days), and of course was a great source of valuable oil used for lamps and smokeless candles. (Thank heaven petroleum was discovered in 1859, and Edison came through with the incandescent bulb in 1879; we may never have had the privilege of seeing a whale.) When overhunting pretty well wiped out the right whale, the new target was the **sperm whale**; these were taken for oil and ambergris (used to make perfume).

The industry was really making inroads into the population of whales with the development of the explosive harpoon gun in 1868, fast steam-powered catcher boats, and later with the use of floating factory-ships. The whaling industry methodically went about its business, destroying one species of whale after the other. After 1880, whaling was just about finished. However, interest was revived again in the States between 1940 and 1965. Whales were slaughtered and used mostly for pet food until it was no longer economically feasible to hunt them. Only two nations — Japan and Russia — continue to hunt, and they aim primarily at the sperm whale for its oil. Whale meat is eaten in Japan, but it accounts for only two percent of the fishing industry, and is steadily declining. Russia takes a small number each year for the subsistence of Siberian natives. Except for Eskimos, it is illegal for Americans to hunt whales under both the Marine Mammal Protection Act and the Rare and Endangered Species Act. Whaling is also prohibited in a 200-mile zone of U.S. waters by the Fisheries Conservation Act of 1976. The last "killer" ship registered in the U.S. was the *Sioux City,* now used for marine research.

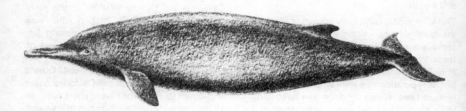

Baird's beaked whale

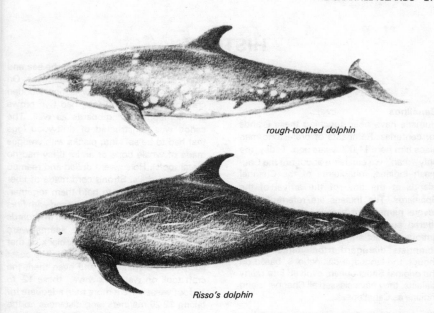

rough-toothed dolphin

Risso's dolphin

Dolphins And Porpoises

If there were a popularity contest for sea animals, hands-down winners would be porpoises and dolphins. They always appear to have a smile on their faces, their squeaky "talk" is a happy sound, they impart a playful attitude, and certainly their friendly rapport with human beings in marine parks around

the U.S. has endeared them to millions of people. Also of the cetecean family, many of their habits are similar to their big brother whale. The terms *dolphin* and *porpoise* are continually confused. Strictly speaking, the dolphin is the long-beaked variety. The porpoise is the snubby-nosed form. Porpoises and dolphins have intrigued man for centuries. They have been written about, sung about, drawn, and fought over. Aristotle compared them to man: "...dolphins are born of a womb, take milk from nipples, breathe with lungs, make a variety of sounds, copulate rather than spawn, and care for their young, often with the help of an 'auntie.' "

When you see "dolphin" on menus, it is not a cetacean, but is actually a fish called *mahi-mahi* or dolphinfish. Around the Channel Islands, it isn't unusual to see hundreds of **white-sided dolphins** cavorting in the wake of a fast-moving boat. The largest herds are seen from August to January — or individual performers can be seen at San Diego's Marineland.

PACIFIC DOLPHINS AND PORPOISES

common or white-belly
Pacific pilot
Risso's
Pacific white-sided
harbor
Dall
false killer
striped
rough toothed
Pacific bottlenose

HISTORY

INDIANS

Canalinos

Humans have been touching these islands for centuries. Remnants of prehistoric man place him here 11,000 years ago. Today, the only "man" we can learn about are the Chumash Indians, inhabitants of the Channel Islands at the time of the arrival of the Spaniards. The Indians are referred to by several names. But because these islanders shared such similar culture (due to continuous contact and trading), most modern scientists disregard tribal names. Even though the language distinctions, based on the original Shoshonean, evolved into many dialects, they have classed all Channel Island Indians as Canalinos.

These particular Indians are considered to have possessed higher than average technical abilities. They are credited with many contributions to the culture of the time, but the most outstanding was their wood-plank canoe called a *tomol*. Before this boat was developed, there is evidence that a primitive craft made from large bundles of tule grass was used. It had obvious disadvantages: it

Canalino Indians built huts from branches and tule grass.

only lasted one or two times in the sea and long distances could not be undertaken. On the other hand, the *tomol,* a fine wooden craft, was sturdy and fast, had two prows and sometimes wing-boards as well. The canoe was constructed of driftwood logs that had to be split into planks with wedges made of whale bone or antler (they had no metal tools). Holes were drilled and reamed with stone drills. Strong cord made of fiber was strung through to hold them together. They were then buried in wet sand with fires built over them to steam and bend the boards to the desired shape. The seams were caulked with asphaltum (thick black oil that oozes at certain rocky areas along the coast such as in Carpinteria), and even then, the craft took on water. However, these 12- to 16-foot vessels were more than adequate for taking 12-20 mariners long distances, to the Mainland and from island to island — even though they had to include a youth or two to bail water.

The Canalinos were hunters and fishermen. They hunted sea lions, otters, and seabirds. They fished from their wood-plank boats and used shiny hooks carved from abalone shells that fooled the big fish into thinking the hook was a little fish — the first man-made lure? It apparently worked well, as indicated in the many kitchen middens found all over the Channel Islands — obviously seafood was an important part of the Canalino diet.

The Indians were talented in other areas also. They wove sturdy, handsome baskets from plant fibers, varnishing those they wished to make waterproof. They painstakingly made tiny beads from the marine snail (purple olivella) among other shells. These were strung and valued for trade with Mainland Indians. Besides beads, islanders traded otter skins, seal pelts, shellfish, and carved stone figures (often depictions of whales or seals) used as charmstones. The island Indians had quantities of stone to work with, as on Catalina where there's an abundant supply of soapstone and obsidian. These island objects were traded for Mainland goods not easily available on the islands such as acorns, rabbits, deer, a hard rock called chert, and other strictly Mainland goods.

Indian Cult

All the villages of the Channel Islands were independent of each other, each with a *wot* (chief) and a shaman (medicine man). The life of the Indian villager was controlled by these two men. There were rules and ceremonies and the chief depended on the mysterious prowess possessed by the shaman to help him through difficult times, such as drought or eclipse. A few important ceremonies consistently held in the village dealt with birth, death, and puberty for both boys and girls. Puberty ceremonies were so universally celebrated among the hunting and gathering Indians that historians believe them to have been brought from Asia itself.

The boys went through a rigorous ceremony involving the ingestion of a narcotic, called the *toalache* cult (see p. 7). The girls' rite was more in the nature of a debut, a presentation to society of a marriageable young woman. It was a time of moral lectures and a test of virtue. First, virtue was tested with the girl swallowing a ball of tobacco. If she could retain it without regurgitating, she was indeed a virtuous Indian maiden; if she regurgitated, she was considered a fallen woman and held in contempt. Sad for the girl with a queasy stomach! During the three-day rite, some of the old taboos remained, such as not eating meat, and using a stick to scratch her head instead of her fingers. But mostly it was a preparation for life as a wife, mother, and efficient member of the community—and for her future health. These qualities were enhanced by practically baking her in a pit for three days and nights, protected from hot stones only by a mattress of branches of such plants as the California mugwort and the western ragweed. During this time she was the center of attention, and although she did fast from all food, she could drink, was bathed with warm water, and was the central figure in hours of dancing and singing and the distribution of gifts.

After three days, her face was painted by the wife of the visiting official (guests from a neighboring village) in charge of the ceremony. Anklets and bracelets of highly valued human hair and shell necklaces were placed on her. A sand painting was made on the ground and she was given moral lectures, instructed on how to act in order to be socially acceptable. She should be industrious and not a gadabout, bathe each day, be hospitable, have a straightforward manner with no malice in her heart. At the end of the ceremony, she was givien a ball of sage meal and salt that she then spit into a hole in the center of the ground painting and she watched as the entire "painting" was brushed into the hole and the earth packed in on top of it—her future life was sealed.

The Indians of the Channel Islands were all part of the cult called Chingichnich that originated on Catalina Island. The medicine men exercised (what would be called today) incredible exploitation of the people. The shaman was considered a wizard, a powerful man deserving of the respect of the people. He induced spells, producing items from his mouth that he said were sent to him from the heavens. He would take credit for magically causing the death of an enemy in another village. The medicine man also explained the signs of nature to the people; a rainbow was a sign of good fortune, while an eclipse was a certain omen of calamity. During an eclipse the people were reduced to shouting and weeping, pounding with sticks on the ground, all to scare away the monster trying to steal the moon or sun. The shaman must have been right, since in each instance they eventually managed to scare away this evil monster that was eating their celestial body. Falling stars were children of the moon; the morning and evening stars were the Big Stars, and Polaris was the "star that does not move."

The Advent Of Modern Man

It appears that life went on among these Indians for centuries with very little outside intrusion. This was destined to change shortly after the Spaniards claimed the west coast of the continent for the king of Spain in the mid-1700s. It was shortly after this time that the Russians and Americans discovered that the west coast was home to a precious little sea creature, the otter, that was desirable for its velvet-like fur with a ready market in Asia and Europe. The otter hunts that would change the destiny of a country (Spain) and a culture (the Indians') began. For awhile the Russians and Americans were competitors, each trying to outhunt the other. After realizing what was happening, the Spaniards, too, began hunting the otter, at the same time placing strict embargos on all foreign ships, ordering them to leave the territory. These orders didn't stop either the Russians or the Americans, nor for that matter ships from other countries that were beginning to enviously eye the beautiful California coast.

The Spanish didn't have the manpower to police the entire Pacific coast, and outsiders had their way. The beginning of the end for the Spanish regime was on the horizon; the hunts continued. The otter was slaughtered on a grand scale and soon it was all but wiped out. But neither the Americans nor the Russians considered that, and in fact they ultimately joined forces, employing experienced hunters, the ruthless Aleut Indians with their sleek *bidarkas* — kayaks made from seal skins stretched over whalebones. The Aleuts made temporary camps on the islands while they massacred the sea otter for its fur. The hunters found there was also a market for certain species of pinnipeds and then virtually destroyed the Guadalupe fur seal, northern fur seal, and northern elephant seal, which was prized for its superior grade of lubricating oil. One large bull might produce more than 200 gallons of this oil, while his whiskers fetched a handsome return in China as opium-pipe cleaners. In the midst of all this turmoil, the Channel Island Indians were caught up in the outsiders' frantic search for money. The peaceful Canalino Indians were no match for the aggressive Aleuts. Their women were raped, the men murdered, and entire families commandeered by the savages from the north while they stayed on the islands. White man's diseases were rampant; syphilis and measles were responsible for the deaths of most of the Indians that weren't murdered. The few that remained agreed to go to Mainland missions. By 1857, there were no Indians left on the Channel Islands. It was the end of an era. Modern man's entrance to the California coast was totally destructive.

Pioneers

In a different spirit, even the pioneers wrought havoc on nature's balance. In the latter half of the 19th century settlers began to arrive with their sheep. What better place? There were no fences needed, no other farmers to disturb, just massive grazing areas. These voracious animals were allowed to roam and reproduce freely — overgrazing destroyed native plants. The introduction of oats and other ''exotic'' crops further damaged the natural vegetation of the islands. People have tried to tame these bits of land, but in most cases the greatest equalizer of all, nature's elements, have maintained the upper hand. Today, bowing to this natural power, man has wisely chosen to preserve most of these islands as they are and were in prehistoric times.

Chinese

The Chinese were heavily discriminated against during and after the gold rush. They were often smuggled into the country by dishonest sea captains to sell (yes, like slaves) for cheap labor. It was sometimes necessary for these ships from the Orient to lay over or hide the Chinese on the Channel Islands in order for the captain to complete his nefarious dealings and sneak by wary customs agents. While spending time on the islands, the Chinese discovered the profusion of abalone along the islands' shores. After the sea otter slaughter (sea otters eat thousands of abalone each year) and the destruction of the Indians (who also harvested their share of the shellfish) the abalone was ignored and allowed to replenish for many years. At the first opportunity, the Chinese returned and harvested cove after cove of the delicately flavored abalone meat that had been prized by Orientals for centuries. This quietly administered industry (California's first organized fishing industry, if you don't count the Indians) flourished in all of the Channel Islands and by 1879 more than four million pounds a year of dried abalone meat were being exported. The hardworking Orientals were driven away by other immigrants: Italian, Portuguese, Yugoslavs, and Japanese. By 1890 Chinese fishing villages were nonexistent. Commercial divers over the past 30-40 years have made their dent in the population as well. Abalone has become more scarce each year; now the meat is sold at local fish markets for around $48 a pound!

The First Oil Boom

Southern California's first oil boom took place in the late 1800s. Much like the gold rush, it brought economic rewards to the state, and everyone wanted to get into the oil business. The industry was a baby. It wasn't until the 1890s, with technical improvements

in drilling, storing, and refining, that it became a viable business. As the years passed, Southern California continued to upgrade the industry until it was producing 25 percent of the world's oil. Offshore leases of the Outer Continental Shelf were first obtained in the 1950s. Today, San Pedro and Long Beach Harbor still bustle with the comings and goings of large oil tankers from all over the world; the pro-ecology groups keep their fingers crossed that each year will be "spill-free."

Channel Islands National Park

San Miguel, Santa Rosa, Santa Cruz, Anacapa, and Santa Barbara, the five northernmost of the eight Channel Islands, make up Channel Islands National Park, established on March 5, 1980, when President Carter signed a bill into law creating the National Park and Marine Sanctuary to preserve the delicate ecology of the area. The entire Channel Islands National Park is a reserve included in the Man and the Biosphere Program, an international effort to define and solve worldwide environmental problems and issues. National marine sanctuaries are under the administration of the National Marine Sanctuary Office, the National Oceanic and Atmospheric Administration (NOAA), and the U.S. Department of Commerce, and are managed by the National Park Service and the California Department of Fish and Game under an agreement with NOAA. The Sanctuary includes the land areas of Anacapa, Santa Barbara, San Miguel, and most recently acquired (1987) Santa Rosa, plus a band of sea extending six miles around each of the five northernmost Channel Islands.

PRACTICALITIES

Camping

Camping is permitted on Anacapa, San Miguel, and Santa Barbara with a free permit from Park Headquarters at 1901 Spinnaker Dr., Ventura, CA 93001, tel. (805) 644-8262. Visitors planning to take their boats should study U.S. Coast and Geodetic Survey Charts 18720, 18729, and 18756. Anchoring at either Anacapa or Santa Barbara islands can be hazardous due to sea conditions. A maximum of 30 people per day may camp at each island, and only in designated areas. Everything for your stay must be hauled in, including water and fuel. When you leave you must take all trash with you. The facilities at the campgrounds include pit toilets and tables. No open fires are allowed. If you plan to cook you must bring a small stove. There are restrictions on using the stoves, all meant to control the possibility of a wildfire on the arid islands. There is no fire department, and a blaze would destroy the years of effort by the National Park Service to restore the land to its original condition. Also, discharge of firearms and fireworks is not allowed in the park or within the one-nautical-mile seaward boundary of ocean within the state ecological reserves.

Activities

When you get right down to it, there's not a whole lot to do on the Channel Islands. In fact there are probably many people that would not be interested in this kind of a trip at all. Let's find out how you rate. Do you need electronic entertainment, a regular bed, and a close-by fast-foodery to make your getaway worthwhile? If you answered yes to any or all of these questions, cancel your trip to the Channel Islands—*right now.* On the other hand, does the shock of a black velvet sky sparkling with brilliant stars always bring a lump to your throat? Can you gaze fascinated, for hours at a time, into a small rocky pool filled with the colorful minutiae of marinelife? Do you somehow mistake the sound of the sea crashing onto a rocky shore for a lullaby? If you answered yes to any or all of *these* questions, you will have the time of your life on the Channel Islands.

All visitors to the islands should know that most of what you get from a visit is a glimpse of life before the advent of modern man. Because of the importation of domestic animals and the intrusion of "exotic" plants, including fast-growing grain types such as oats, barley, and sea grasses, the native vegetation was choked out almost entirely. Introduced seeds were broadcast in open

---

SPECIAL TRIPS TO THE CHANNEL ISLANDS

For a slightly different approach to the Channel Islands, a cruise aboard the schooner *Shearwater* can be arranged. Multiple-day cruises can be arranged on a charter basis, or a one-day trip where you have the option of going ashore to the closer Channel Islands National Park. For more information contact Ocean Passages, Inc., 380 Shamrock Dr., Ventura, CA 93003, tel. (805) 643-7299. Another option is a trip aboard the Baltimore clipper, *Swift Of Ipswich,* built around 1778. The *Swift* plans several one-day barbecue trips each year to Scorpion Ranch on Santa Cruz Island. The romantic ship also makes half-day coastal sails as well as a harbor cruise. These are not daily trips; call for schedules and prices from Island Packers. Another special trip is a two-day trip to San Miguel Island. You sleep aboard your vessel while crossing the channel, arriving at San Miguel's Cuyler Harbor early in the morning. For those in good condition, a 14-mile hike is led by a ranger. This trip offered by Island Packers also makes a stop on Santa Rosa Island. For prices and schedules write or call 1867 Spinnaker Dr., Ventura, CA 93001, tel. (805) 642-1393.

plowed fields by well-intentioned farmers, further crowding out the native grasses This combination of events all but destroyed the original landscape. Today, with a lot of TLC, the native plants are returning. With this in mind, hiking on the islands (where permitted) is restricted to formal paths.

Getting There

The ocean around the northern Channel Islands can change from placid to rough and choppy very quickly, especially in the afternoon. It's wise to study local conditions and be prepared. **Island Packers Boat Company** provides regular transportation to both Anacapa and Santa Barbara islands; reservations should be made at least a week in advance. There are seasonal schedules. Contact them at Box 993, Ventura, CA 93002, tel. (805) 642-1393, for details. Several commercial boat companies operate open party and charter trips the rest of the year, especially during the whale-watch season, January through March. For more detailed information call Park Headquarters, (805) 644-8262.

San Miguel And Santa Rosa

A permit to visit San Miguel is free through Park Headquarters in Ventura. Access by excursion boat only. For permission to land on Santa Rosa Island contact Park Headquarters. To visit Santa Cruz, contact Santa Cruz Island Co., 515 S. Flower St., Los Angeles, CA 90071, tel. (213) 483-8022. To land on Santa Cruz Island east of the property line between Chinese Harbor and Sandstone Point, contact Mr. Pier Gherini, 1114 State St. #230, Santa Barbara, CA 93101, tel. (805) 966-4155.

Day trips are available to several of the islands. For further information write to: Channel Islands National Park Visitor Center, 1901 Spinnaker Dr., Ventura, CA 93001, tel. (805) 644-8262. Boat transportation and package tours are provided by Island Packers, 1867 Spinnaker Dr., Ventura, CA 93001, tel. (805) 642-1393. Sailing charter trips are available from Navigators Channel Island Cruise, 1621 Fernald Point Lane, Santa Barbara, CA 93108. Twilight and sunset cocktail harbor cruises are offered at Captain Jack's Landing, 4151 S. Victoria Ave., Oxnard, CA 93030, tel. (805) 985-8511 and (213) 457-9221.

ANACAPA ISLAND

Anacapa lies off the California coast 11 miles southwest of Oxnard, 14 miles south of Ventura, and 26 miles southeast of Santa Barbara. Isolated and remote, it stretches five miles across the sea, but has a total acreage of only one square mile. Anacapa is actually three separate islands separated by narrow channels, inaccessible to each other except by boat. West Anacapa, largest of the islands, is punctuated with sea-etched caves and craggy peaks. On Middle Anacapa, surrounded by high cliffs, meadows of green grass display giant coreopsis with their distinctive yellow flowers that, when in bloom (on a clear day), can be seen on the Mainland and far out to sea.

Geology

This volcanic rock called Anacapa is riddled with labyrinthine caverns in the submarine lava flow easily observed at the island's base. The island is made up almost entirely dense deposits of Miocene volcanic rock, lava ash, and breccia (rock consisting of

sharp fragments embedded in compacted sand, clay, or lava ash). As time, wind, and sea continue to erode the cliffs, gravel and pebbles of different minerals are exposed. Near Frenchy's Cove, look for a large vein of almost-white chalcedony (a translucent quartz, commonly pale gray or blue with a wax-like luster), and on the south shore of West Anacapa near Cat Rock the geology buff can spot San Onofre blue-green breccia. While browsing Cat Rock, notice the surge channel, and the adjacent blow hole that makes beautiful photos with a little patience.

The famous Arch Rock, a natural "bridge" formed by constant sea erosion, is at the easternmost extension of the island. This is Anacapa's trademark and the sight most people remember after visiting all the Channel Islands. It was first brought to the attention of the public when sketched by Whistler during his time in the Coast Guard. Arch Rock is 80 feet high and the archway is 50 feet high—product and victim of the pounding sea. Along the island's coast, the erosion from the perpetually crashing waves has created blow holes, surge channels, caves, and benches; the black sand seen on a few beaches during low tide is actually tiny flakes of the black lava of which the island is made. Earthquake faulting, folding, lifting, and the ancient volcanic eruptions (from a still unknown source) created steep-sided cliffs that fall precipitously into a deep sea. The rugged splendor of Anacapa is one of those lifetime events not soon to be forgotten.

FLORA AND FAUNA

There are practically no trees on Anacapa. The landscape is reminiscent of California's high desert, with only low-growing scrubby shrubs that include cholla, dudleya, and coreopsis. The most readily noticed animals are the birds. You'll see cormorants, scoter ducks, black oystercatchers, western gulls,

Seagulls trail an excursion boat as passengers feed them on their return from Anacapa Island.

and brown pelicans gliding low over the sea and high along the rugged cliffs. The once nearly extinct brown pelican uses the slopes and cliffs of West Anacapa as its only large nesting site on the west coast of the United States. Because West Anacapa has been designated a research nature area for the pelican rookery, no landings are permitted without written permission from the superintendent.

Brown kelp hugs the shoreline, providing a haven for a myriad collection of fish, invertebrates, and other curious sea creatures. This is a favorite place for divers to photograph, explore, and see abalone, lobster, and scallops. Fishermen (with a valid fishing license) will find sheepshead, rockfish, perch, and sand dabs. Sea lions and seals frolic in the surrounding waters, and the top of the cliff on Middle Anacapa is an ideal viewing location during the January-March migration of the gray whales that pass close to the island.

HISTORY

Indians
Because there is no water source, most historians believe that the Canalino Indians didn't live on the island permanently. Instead they used Anacapa as a hunting ground for shellfish, sea lions, and seals. They also used the ready supply of sturdy minerals to make arrowheads. Many kitchen middens have been found, and other remnants of the past can still be seen on Anacapa. Remember, everything on the islands is protected by federal law, so don't take any souvenirs— whether Indian, animal, plant, or mineral.

Europeans
The first outsiders to see Anacapa were the crew of Cabrillo's ship that anchored near the small island in October 1542. It wasn't mentioned again until 1769 when Portola made notes in his log, calling it *Las Mesitas* ("Little Tables"). But it was Juan Perez, supply ship captain of the Portola expedition, who named

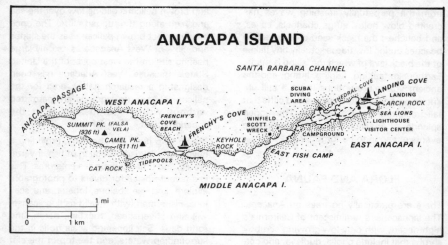

ANACAPA ISLAND

SANTA BARBARA CHANNEL

ANACAPA PASSAGE
WEST ANACAPA I.
SUMMIT PK. (FALSA VELA) (936 ft)
CAMEL PK. (811 ft)
CAT ROCK
TIDEPOOLS
FRENCHY'S COVE BEACH
FRENCHY'S COVE
KEYHOLE ROCK
WINFIELD SCOTT WRECK
EAST FISH CAMP
SCUBA DIVING AREA
CAMPGROUND
CATHEDRAL COVE
LANDING COVE
LANDING
ARCH ROCK
SEA LIONS
LIGHTHOUSE
VISITOR CENTER
EAST ANACAPA I.
MIDDLE ANACAPA I.

0   1 mi
0   1 km

it *Falsa Vela* ("False Sail"). This name is still in use today for the tallest point on Anacapa. On a clear day seamen have a remarkable view of the 930-foot peak. The island was renamed Anacapa by Captain George Vancouver, sailing under the British flag on his journey down the California coast in 1793.

The closest islands to the Mainland, the Anacapa group was probably the easiest for smugglers to reach in the mid-1800s, as well as ruthless sea captains who deposited their deported Chinese slaves here till buyers could be found. As a result, the industrious Chinese gathered abalone, a money-making bonanza that abounded in West Anacapa's tidepools. These flat-shelled marine mollusks thrived on the coves and rocky shores, since their chief predators—the sea otter and the Indian—had all but disappeared.

Navigation

It is believed that the Indians traveled between islands in their *tomols* (wooden canoes) at night after the westerly winds calmed down. Open fires on island promontories were tended by the Indians as navigational aids. By the early 1800s, the Indians were gone from the Channel Islands, and Europeans began settling the California coast. As traffic increased, maritime disas-

ters became commonplace. Now, as then, fog appears when least expected and a calm sea becomes a churning chaos—often too quickly for a ship to escape its torment. Though the Channel Islands were on the course traveled between New Spain (Mexico) and the Philippines, Spanish galleons soon learned to give these formidable rocky bits of land a wide berth. For years ships went aground near the islands and it was evident that a lighthouse was needed.

The East End Lighthouse

Only after a disastrous accident (December 2, 1853) brought attention to the channel's need for a lighthouse was it seriously considered. A 225-foot sidewheel steamer, the *Winfield Scott,* went aground in a thick fog on Middle Anacapa's rocky coast. Two hundred and fifty passengers (and $800,000 in gold bullion) waited eight days on the barren island with virtually no food, water, or shelter before they were rescued. In 1854, a United States Coast Survey team agreed that Anacapa was the ideal spot for a lighthouse, but after careful exploration concluded that it was impossible to build on the steep-cliffed island. Many years passed before something more than talk took place. In 1912, an unattended automatic acetylene beacon was built; in 1932, the present lighthouse was erected by the United States Lighthouse Service (later to become the U.S. Coast Guard).

When first built, the lighthouse was attended by a group of Coast Guardsmen accompanied by their families. In 1969, the light was automated, and at an elevation of 277 feet is one of the most powerful on the California coast. The catadioptric light has 1,200,000 candlepower and can be seen 23 miles in all directions. Housed in a traditional white cylindrical structure, a foghorn sounds every 15 seconds in foggy weather. A radio beacon close by transmits with a full range of 10 miles. The Anacapa light on East Anacapa continues to serve as a beacon for the many ships that pass, endangered by the fog that often shrouds these rocky islands. Today the lighthouse is attended by personnel stationed in Port Hueneme on the Mainland coast. A park ranger lives year-round in one of the former Coast Guard houses on East Anacapa, still white with a red-tiled roof. Another house has been transformed into a museum for visitors to the island.

ISLANDERS

The Websters

Anacapa's history includes very few permanent residents. And like all the other Channel Islands, it was sheep that brought the first settlers to Anacapa. In 1907, Heaman Bayfield (Bay) Webster (son of the Ventura postmaster of the era), his wife Martha, and their two young sons Morris and Harvey bought the lease to Anacapa from the Department of the Interior for $75. They set up housekeeping and lived on the island for the following 10 summers. They raised sheep and opened a tourist resort, calling it the Webster Sheep Ranch and Fishing Camp. It was primitive—with sand-flushed toilets. (A trap door on the windward side of the outhouse received gusts of wind-blown sand—flush courtesy of Mother Nature.) Water was brought from the Mainland in five-gallon jugs. With no fresh water on Anacapa, it's curious how the sheep survived—one bit of lore claims that each morning after heavy night-fog had soaked their wool, the animals licked the moisture from one another's coats. A good part of their diet was the dudleya plant, a low-growing succulent that provided some liquid.

Webster instigated one of the first package tourist trips on the California coast. For a budget sum, he brought families to the island in one of his boats, offered them fishing, swimming, hunting, hiking, and Indian artifact hunts; a smokehouse was available for fishermen. Who wouldn't jump at the chance for that vacation on the Channel Islands today! Entrepreneur Bay Webster was way ahead of his time.

Frenchy The Hermit

Born Raymond Ledreaux in Brittany, his colorful past is said to include a bitter experience of aborted studies for the Catholic priesthood, followed by a seaman's life that took him around the world and from China to America. Contentment was cut short by the death of his young wife during the 1918 influenza epidemic. Perhaps it was these tragedies that first turned Frenchy to his reclusive life on tiny Anacapa Island in 1928. The Frenchman survived alone over the years through fishing and by using his ever-ready supply of seafood to trade for other necessities with local fishermen and occasional campers. All who knew Frenchy enjoyed a visit to the rocky island, and never arrived without a jug of wine to loosen his tongue. Their evening might include a dinner of cioppino and lobster (he was a good cook) and tall tales of the sea, or perhaps discussions of classic literature and fine music. Frenchy was a diamond in the rough, and though he lived a life far from the madding crowds (with a crowd of cats), he didn't fit the stereotype of a hermit; he was always happy to have the company of visitors to the island. In 1954, Frenchy turned 68 and the Park Service employees decided he should be moved ashore after 26 years on Anacapa Island. A lovely cove on West Anacapa north shore bears his name.

GETTING THERE

Being the closest to the Mainland, East Anacapa is the island most frequently seen by visitors. Camping, hiking, and picnicking in small groups are encouraged by Channel Islands National Park Service.

Island Packers, a commercial carrier, provides transportation between Ventura and East Anacapa ($40 pp), with seasonal schedules available. The boating company offers a variety of trips to other parts of Anacapa as well as the rest of the Channel Islands. Some are day trips; some are multi-day island adventures. A favorite trip takes passengers to Frenchy's Cove Landing on special low-tide days to explore the tidepools for several hours. Island Packers also delivers campers to East Anacapa and makes arrangements to pick them up on a designated day ($60 pp). You can't change your mind—remember, there's no phone on the island! However, the Park Service has a radio for emergencies—only. For further information, prices, and schedules, contact Island Packers, 1867 Spinnaker Dr., Ventura, CA 93001, tel. (805) 642-1393. For information about other commercial carriers, contact Channel Islands National Marine Sanctuary, 1901 Spinnaker Dr., Ventura, CA 93001, tel. (805) 644-8464. Sport-fishing and scuba-diving boats frequent the island and all boaters are invited to anchor offshore.

ACTIVITIES

Hiking On East Anacapa
The first thing you must do when arriving on East Anacapa Island is to climb a steep stairway of 154 steps up the side of the mountain—after that you've really arrived. The park ranger is very helpful, and with advance planning through the Park Service, you may arrange for tours, walks, and other programs. A self-guiding trail acquaints you with the magic of nature on Anacapa. The walk is short (one and a half miles), and the park requests that you stay on the trails in the interest of protecting fragile island resources—and for your own safety. If you happen to visit on a foggy day and the foghorn is on, *do not* visit the lighthouse. Severe hearing damage may result. Picnicking is allowed, but you must carry all trash off the island. Latrines are available, but there is no fresh water, so bring along whatever water you think you'll need.

hiking the dry hills of San Miguel Island

CAMPING

Anyone wishing to camp on the Anacapa group is restricted to the campground on East Anacapa. Facilities are free on a first-come first-served basis and limited to 30 persons or six groups. Therefore reservations and permits are a must. The permit gives you 14 days on the island; reservations may not be made more than 60 days in advance. Bring everything you need; there is nothing on Anacapa Island except the artistry of Mother Nature. But travel light; remember, you haul everything up the side of the cliff (shelter, food, fuel, water, etc.) and then walk another quarter mile to the campground. You'll find picnic tables and fireplaces; however, from May through October, and under adverse weather conditions, all open fires are prohibited, so bring a portable stove if you plan to cook. Bring your own wood for the fireplace. Be prepared in the event a strong wind comes up (it frequently does), and bring a tent that can be well anchored. Note: there's no room to run free, or throw a football or even a Frisbee. Expect time on Anacapa to be spent tuning in to nature and enjoying the solitude, a subtle interaction with what life must have been like hundreds of years ago. This is unique, life on a desert island with its many changing moods and faces. Pets are not allowed.

Weather

The weather is something to be considered when planning a camping trip on the Channel Islands, because in most cases you can't just pack up and go home. The wind often blows for several days at a time—even in summer—at speeds up to 20-30 miles per hour. Your only protection will be the shelter you bring along; tube tents are not recommended; a small mountain tent is best. Wet, thick fog can also set in for several days. Spring and winter rains turn the trails into thick quagmires of mud, and when the sun shines there are no shade trees to provide relief. If all of these possibilities don't discourage you, you'll have the time of your life.

What To Bring

Bring an extra day's supply of food in case the weather turns bad and you cannot leave when planned. Plan a gallon of water per person for each day. Take an extra change of clothes in case you take an unplanned swim. Bring at least one heavy jacket, a rain poncho (the boat ride can be wet), and a wool cap. Bring also a ground cloth, windbreak, and medium-weight sleeping bag. A backpacker's stove is recommended since wood or charcoal is heavy to pack, and gathering live or dead plant life on the island is prohibited. Use biodegradable soap *only*. Do not pour waste in the ocean or on plants; dispose of it in gravel areas. You'll be glad you brought a brimmed hat, sunscreen, first aid-kit, binoculars, and camera. Bring all the usuals: matches, flashlights, etc.

Swimming, Fishing, And Diving

Beaches on East Anacapa are inaccessible, but on hot, still summer days, swimming is great in the Landing Cove. This means you'll enter the water from the landing dock several feet above the water. Snorkelers will find kelp beds not too far from the dock. A favorite scuba spot, the water is crystal clear, though many areas are thick with seaweed. Here marinelife flourishes with the usual and unusual darting in and out of the brown leaves and bulbs of the tall kelp forest. Note: The waters for one nautical mile around each of the park's islands are a California State Reserve. State fish and game laws apply. Some areas in these reserves are available for sport-fishing only. Check with your local Fish and Game officer or the park ranger and remember to come with a valid California fishing license. Spear guns are not allowed.

FOR BOATERS

As your boat approaches East Anacapa and you begin to look for the park entry, watch for a cluster of white buildings on the bluff. A white painted wall marks a small dent in a cliff used as a landing for traffic in and out of East Anacapa. Though there's room for a good-sized vessel, there's usually a surge. Put on your muscles; a dinghy can and should be hoisted the 11 feet to the platform because the surge and movement from the blow hole will surely bounce the dinghy against the dock. This is the loading area for supplies for the National Park Service personnel. Everything is hauled up the cliff with the help of a crane. Boaters will see two buoys off the dock, but overnight mooring is definitely discouraged.

Cathedral Cove

This cove is considered a marginal fair-weather anchorage, but is one of the loveliest coves on the island. Some boatmen leave their boats anchored here when going ashore to the ranger station, a half mile east. Be prepared for thick kelp along the coast. Underwater nature trails are in the planning stages for Cathedral Cove. For adventurers, Cathedral Cave is a multi-chambered sea cave and can be explored by skiff in calm weather; beware of surge.

Frenchy's Cove

Frenchy's Cove has a great beach, good picnic spot, and outstanding snorkeling area. And for nature lovers, this is the place to explore the extensive tidepools at low tide. Most sailors agree that Frenchy's is the most sheltered anchorage on Anacapa—in calm conditions. When the sea rises, there isn't a good anchorage on the island. Frenchy's is popular, not only for its tidepools, but also for the caves in the cliffs northwest of the cove. In calm water you can land a dinghy on the beach; there are no facilities. If the sea is surging, landing can be touchy. The vaulted interior of the nearby caves (Frenchy's and Indian Water Cave) can be explored by skiff.

The *Winfield Scott*

Close by, divers will find the *Windfield Scott,* a steamer that grounded and sank here in 1853. Clear water in the area makes ideal conditions for good underwater photos. Just take pictures, no souvenirs please!

Cat Rock Anchorages

On the south side of West Anacapa, three quarters of a mile west of the West Passage, head at least 200 yards west of Cat Rock for a safe anchorage. Expect some kelp. East anchorage is under the lee of the land east of Cat Rock. Pick your way through the kelp and you'll find deep water close to the shoreline.

East Fish Camp

East Fish Camp is a popular anchorage with fishing boats. Here you'll find protection from west to north winds—but expect an occasional surge in the anchorage. In a calm sea this is an adequate overnight refuge. East Fish Camp shore is usually thick with kelp.

SANTA BARBARA ISLAND

Of the eight Channel Islands, Santa Barbara is the smallest, roughly one by one-half mile, covering a total of 640 acres. The island is 38 miles west of San Pedro, and 25 miles west of Catalina Island.

THE LAND

The tiny triangle-shaped rock is a remnant of an ancient Miocene volcano and geologically associated with the Guadalupe Islands of Mexico. It's a marine terrace on top of steep, jagged cliffs, some as high as 500 feet. From the cliffs, two peaks gently swell from the center of the island: the highest, Signal Peak, rises to 635 feet. The second highest, at 562 feet, is North Peak. The island shares the rough-hewn look of the other Channel Islands with caves, coves, blow holes, rocky ledges, and dramatic drops to the sea.

CLIMATE

Santa Barbara Island is mild, with daytime temperatures varying from 50-80 degrees Fahrenheit. Frost is almost unheard of, but fog is another matter. The island is often shrouded in fog early in the morning and in the evening. As on the Mainland close by, rainfall averages 10-12 inches yearly, falling mostly in the winter months. The winds can be devastating, rising quickly and blowing hard across the desolate landscape.

FLORA AND FAUNA

Because of the lack of water and the frequent mighty winds, the island has no trees and only low-growing scrub vegetation. The closest thing to a tree is the **coreopsis** plant that often grows to 10 feet on the island, showing bright yellow, daisy-like flowers across the landscape in the spring. Even the coreopsis growth has been reduced over the years to just a few stands scattered around the island. Other native plants are the **prickly pear cactus** and **sea blite**.

Non-native plants imported over the years include the devastating **crystalline iceplant** (native to South Africa). No one is certain how it arrived, but since before the turn of the century it's been steadily taking over the terrain. Perhaps a lone seed carried by a migrating bird was the first culprit. Because of its ability to thrive while absorbing salt-laden sea air, it gradually encroached upon the native plants. And when it withers and dies it

Anacapa Lighthouse on Arch Point

deposits its salt-loaded tissues into the soil, further destroying the possibility of survival for the native plants. On the eastern terraces are fields of grasses including **rye, barley,** and **oats** introduced in the days when farmers tried to tame the wild elements of the island by raising farm animals. Due to the lack of rain and frequent high winds it was not a successful venture. With the protection and care of today's National Park Service, native plants are making a slow recovery.

Only two vertebrates make their home on Santa Barbara, the **night lizard** and the **white-footed mouse.** In the early 1900s a large number of feral rabbits and cats roamed the island. The rabbits furthered the destruction of plants and the cats decimated the bird population. The rabbits proved almost worse than the voracious sheep on other Channel Islands. When the rabbits could no longer reach the leaves, they began nibbling the trunk of the coreopsis, girdling it, which caused the plant to die, leaving toppled trunks in their wake. However, the rabbits are

SANTA BARBARA ISLAND

ARCH PT.

SHAG ROCK

LIGHTHOUSE

WEBSTER PT.

ELEPHANT SEAL COVE

NORTH PK.
(562 ft) ▲

LANDING COVE

LANDING

VISITOR CENTER & CAMPING

CANYON VIEW NATURE TR.

CAVE CANYON

ARCH PT. TR

COVE TR.

ELEPHANT SEAL

SIGNAL PK.
(635 ft) ▲

SEA LION ROOKERY

SIGNAL PK. TRAIL

CAT CANYON

SUTIL I.

0   0.5 mi

0   500 m

gone, and the cats were rounded up and the last of them shipped off the island in 1978; the result is now a bird-watcher's paradise. The Audubon Society frequently brings groups to the island for a week of observing **barn owls, meadowlarks, burrowing owls, American kestrels, hummingbirds, orange-crowned warblers, island horned larks,** and **finches.** The skies are thick with coastal birds including a variety of **gulls, cormorants, pelicans,** and the **black oystercatcher.**

Sea Creatures

Webster Point Cove is a haul-out area for sea lions and sea elephants. Watching them frolic in the coastal waters is a good pastime; bring binoculars and a long lens for your camera. If you spend much time here you'll get used to the raspy bark of these sea mammals and even begin to distinguish when it's just a call from mom for the pups to come for dinner, or the harsh, commanding call of the courting male. In early summer you might see pups being taught to swim and fish. They depend on their mothers for food for the first couple of months, but at six or seven months they join groups of the same age and are ready to try their flippers and venture out to sea. Remember, it's against the law to interfere in any way with marine mammals. The rugged shoreline is surrounded with rich kelp beds that make an ideal habitat for a wide variety of sea creatures, including abalone, lobster, sea urchins, crabs, and myriad varieties of fish.

HISTORY

The Indians living on nearby islands were known to have visited Santa Barbara Island and used it as a campsite while hunting seals and other sealife. Evidence of this is found in several middens scattered around the island. But because of the lack of water there was never a permanent settlement. Explorer Sebastian Vizcaino arrived on the island December 4, 1602, which is the special day of

sea elephant

remembering Saint Barbara—and so this little bit of rock was named Santa Barbara Island. As with all of the islands, it was peaceful and undisturbed by the white man until the mid-1800s, when shipping and otter hunting became common along the Pacific coast. In the early 1920s, a group of farming families led by Alvin Hyder tried their hand at farming. They were responsible for clearing large stands of coreopsis to plant barley and hay used to feed about 200 sheep. They also began raising Belgian hares (all of which were gone by 1940). By the mid-1920s the farming venture had failed and the settlers left the inhospitable island. A story has circulated for years about a barefoot wanderer who found shelter on Santa Barbara during the Depression. He cared for the wild cats that had been left behind by settlers long gone. It is said that he eked out an existence by trading fish to passing boats. After his departure the island was left to nature's capricious whims until World War II. The U.S. Navy used the island as an early warning outpost; in the 1950s it was used as a missile tracking station. Santa Barbara Island became part of the National Park system in 1938, and was designated part of the Channel Islands National Marine Sanctuary in 1980.

GETTING THERE

Public transportation is available next to Park Headquarters in Ventura aboard one of several Island Packers sail or power boats. Boats leave for Santa Barbara daily during the summer months. Day trips are available for $40. Round-trip transportation for campers is $60. Winter weather gets rather nasty around this outer island, and few trips are scheduled. Write for yearly schedule: Island Packers, 1867 Spinnaker Dr., Ventura, CA 93001, tel. (805) 642-1393. Private boats travel to the island, but occupants must have a camping permit and reservations before arrival if planning to spend the night.

ACTIVITIES

Camping
Camping is permitted on Santa Barbara Island, but it is a trek for the hardy. The camping area is located next to the ranger's headquarters; the ranger is on the island most of the year. You are off-loaded onto a landing dock and then you must carry all equipment one-quarter mile up a steep trail to the campground. A maximum of 30 people are permitted at five campsites. And be forewarned,

your camp will probably be only a few feet from your neighbor; in other words there's no privacy. Once at the campsite things get a little easier. Remember to bring everything you need: drinking water, camp stove, charcoal, food, garbage bags (yes, you must haul out all your trash), and bring clothes for wide variations in weather. There are toilet facilities, picnic tables, and one fire ring and four grills where charcoal cooking is permitted, but only when open fires are allowed. In times of heavy winds, open fires are prohibited. (See "Anacapa Camping," p. 225). No open fires are permitted from May to October. Yes, this is camping on the proverbial desert island. Permits (free) are required and obtained from Park Headquarters in Ventura, tel. (805) 644-8262. (See "Camping," p. 218). No pets, slingshots, firearms, or fireworks are allowed.

Hiking
Hiking is permitted only on six miles of established trails. Ask the ranger about the **Canyon View Self-Guided Trail** and the booklet that interprets much of what you see. Two trails begin at the campsite. One (to the left) wanders the gentle terrain to a gorge where one of the few stands of coreopsis can be seen. This is good bird-watching country; don't forget the binoculars and bird iden-

Park rangers give visitors an orientation onboard excursion boats headed for Anacapa Island.

tification book. The second trail eventually leads to Signal Peak, the highest on the island. Expect a steady ascent over several hills until finally you reach the summit, with a dramatic view of the sheer drop into the rocks and swirling sea below. From here you can see across the narrow channel to Sutil Island, a huge barren rock. Hikers: please do not wear Vibram-soled hiking boots, as they tear up the fragile landscape.

Water Sports

Access to the sea is at the Landing Cove only. Climbing down the trail from the campsite, you have a choice of a variety of water activities on Santa Barbara Island, such as swimming and snorkeling off the rocky shore, or from the landing dock. The water is crystal clear and makes for fantastic underwater photography. Fishing is permitted off the landing platform; don't forget to bring your fishing gear and license, and note seasonal regulations.

Nature Watching

The best thing to do on Santa Barbara Island is to observe nature. Even if you've never been intrigued with winged creatures before, get out your binoculars and perch on a craggy cliff to view the coastal birds, or hike into the canyon near the coreopsis. You'll be entertained and educated by the antics of these sky creatures. The best time to watch the birds is early in the morning or at dusk when they're looking for food. You can spend hours watching the agile sea lions jumping the waves, diving, and playing much like small children at the shore. At certain times of the year the sea elephant joins in. When a seal moves on land it is called "hauling." The two main hauling areas are on the southeast and northwest shores of Santa Barbara Island.

Tidepools

At low tide you can explore the tidepools on Santa Barbara Island. This is a mesmerizing activity. No doubt you'll see purple sea urchins, limpets, starfish, and many minute organisms. Please take care not to interfere with their life cycle; these delicate life forms are a California treasure that must be guarded for future generations to enjoy. Wear sturdy rubber-soled shoes (no sandals); the rocks you'll be climbing on are very slick. Be aware of when the tide comes back or be prepared to swim to shore.

For Boaters

Boaters planning the trip to Santa Barbara Island should first study U.S. Coast and Geodetic Survey Charts 18720, 18729, and 18756. The trip from Santa Barbara Channel will take you across the Pacific Missile Range, which is often in use. For information about firing times call (805) 982-8841. A Coast Guard lighthouse is located on Arch Point. Anchorage is usually limited to the Landing Cove area, and the dock is not acceptable for boats. Those wishing to go ashore must do so in a skiff or small boat. Be prepared for sudden rising sea and wind, especially in the afternoon and during the fall and winter months. If a strong northeast wind develops, get out immediately. A safe daytime anchorage in calm weather is off the north coast in about 35 feet of water with a sandy bottom. From here you can explore the coastline by skiff and no doubt you'll meet the friendly sea lions that live along the shore. They like to watch you almost as much as you enjoy watching them. A calm day anchored off Santa Barbara Island can be a soothing interlude between you and Mother Nature's creatures.

SAN MIGUEL ISLAND

THE LAND

This most remote island is harassed by north-westerly gales that blast it continuously. Eight miles long and four miles wide, San Miguel Island encompasses an area of 14 square miles and is 26 miles from the closest point on the Mainland. The island's highest points are two peaks in its center just over 800 feet tall. San Miguel is surrounded with treacherous reefs and shoals, and exhibits a shoreline of gentle sandy beaches, as well as rugged rocky cliffs.

Prince Island, a tiny islet close offshore Cuyler Harbor as you approach San Miguel, has steep-walled canyons that drop straight to the sea, adding to the stark landscape as you approach.

In many places the 10,000-acre island is smothered by sand that all but strangles the struggling plant life. To complete this moonscape is a caliche "ghost forest," where macabre remnants of broken trees line up like white tombstones on the desolate, sand-covered surface. The scientific explanation is quite fundamental: caliche is a calcium carbonate sand composed mainly of the shattered lime skeletons of innumerable sea creatures that blows inland from the beaches, engulfing the existing vegetation. Organic acids in the plants react chemically with the sand, cementing the fine grains together. After the inner plant decays, perfect castings remain. Some of these strange forms have been standing for thousands of years while others are new—the process continues. These startling caliche forms can also be seen on Santa Rosa and San Nicolas but are quite rare in other areas of the world.

Climate

This isolated, windswept bit of land lies vulnerable to the capricious whims of nature's violent northwesterly storms, unguarded by the land mass of the Mainland. San Miguel is the westernmost island of the Channel group. Small amounts of yearly rainfall (about 11 inches) add to the island's arid

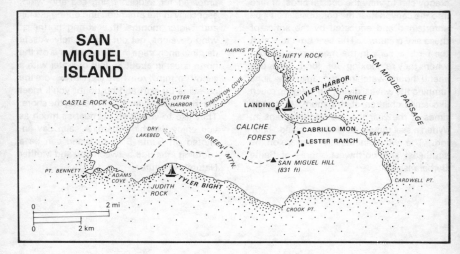

condition, and like the other islands in this unfriendly channel, fog can descend quickly and unexpectedly. Dress for the wind, whether it be hot or cool.

FAUNA AND FLORA

San Miguel is the California coast's largest breeding ground for six species of pinnipeds (fin-footed mammals), the seals and sea lions. The California sea lion, Steller sea lion, northern elephant seal, harbor seal, and northern fur seal return to San Miguel's Point Bennett to haul out, sometimes traveling great distances from throughout the northeastern Pacific. In late spring and early summer the cows come ashore at this sandy peninsula to bear their young and then breed again almost immediately. After a gentle summer of mother's nursing and care, the pups learn to fish amidst a rich supply of food. By autumn most are ready to begin their nomadic life in the sea. Because of the rugged isolated cliffs, three of the major sea bird colonies live here undisturbed. **Auklets, gulls, guillemots, cormorants, snowy plovers,** and many others breed on San Miguel and Prince Island. The few vertebrates on the island include the **island fox** and the **white-footed mouse. Barn owls, peregrine falcons,** and **red-tailed hawks** are among the birds of prey often seen.

A few rare plant species are found on San Miguel: the **live-forever, wild buckwheat,** and **rose mallow.** The bright orange bloom of the **coreopsis** can be seen each spring climbing the hill from Cuyler Harbor. In a wet year San Miguel produces a blazing crop of California poppies.

HISTORY

San Miguel is said to have supported a large community of Canalino Indians. Many middens are known to be on the island, and with relatively little activity over the years, it is hoped that some have been left undisturbed

by pot diggers. Though the wind has been known to unbury Indian graves, hopefully some day these pristine sites will reveal more about the long-gone Canalino Indians.

Most historians agree that "Isla de Posesion" was the name that Cabrillo gave to San Miguel on his voyage of discovery in 1542. It's believed that Cabrillo died in Cuyler Harbor in January 1543. His fellow voyagers changed the name of the island to La Isla de Juan Rodriguez in his honor. Though Cabrillo is reportedly buried on San Miguel, his grave has never been found.

Charts from the later Vizcaino expedition identified San Miguel as La Isla de San Lucas. The final change came in 1770 when cartographer Miguel Costanso changed the

one of San Miguel Island's eerie caliche forms

name to honor himself. In 1793, British Captain George Vancouver traveled south along the California coast and fixed the names of the islands on nautical charts.

The Fascinating People

George Nidever of San Nicolas fame (see p. 251) was the first to try ranching on San Miguel Island in the mid-1800s, grazing cattle, horses, and hogs as well as sheep. After Nidever, a parade of hermits, boatmen, and would-be ranchers came and went, unobtrusively struggling with the land and the tempests. Time was spent building and patching from what they could scavenge from nature's collection of flotsam and jetsam violently thrown on San Miguel's shores. Captain Waters, a salty character who ranched the island during the late 1800s, declared it a separate sovereignty. Obviously that didn't take hold. San Miguel has been owned by the federal government since the signing of the Hidalgo Treaty in 1848 and leased to various ranchers over the years. In 1906, rancher John Russel built a V-shaped fenced compound, outbuildings, and a ranch house from planks, timber, and scraps, much of which was combed from the beach. The building was designed to allow the winds to rush by the house and out to sea without damage, similar to the windshields seen today on large trucks. The man was ahead of his time! By 1930 he was gone.

Probably the name that lingers with the desolate little island more than any of the others is the "King" of San Miguel, Herbert Lester, and his family. Lester and his wife Elise, both New Yorkers, arrived on the island as honeymooners. From the stories that filter down from the past, Herbie and his wife Elise learned to love the island and led a blissful life for a long time. Herbie was thrilled when asked to manage the sheep ranch. Elise and Herbie happily filled their days with the not-so-easy chores of day-to-day living on the lit-

tle island: gathering firewood, dealing with the water situation, trying to keep the constant wind-blown sand out of the house (would you believe a revolving door?), the struggle to make ends meet when there was little money, and very little to make do with. But the Lesters were happy and ingenious and loved the freedom to explore and enjoy their "island paradise." Two daughters were born while the Lesters called San Miguel home. Elise taught the girls, Marriane Miguel and Betsy, in their own small schoolhouse with the help of the 500-volume library she brought with her to the island. It was a life that today many folks would envy. Mostly through the efforts of the Lester family, a small monument was placed on the island to honor the memory of the first visitor to San Miguel — Juan Rodriguez Cabrillo.

The Lesters welcomed many visitors from the Mainland — by sail boat, airplane, fishing boat, and official Coast Guard vessel; Elise kept a guest book and in 12 years recorded several thousand entries. Unfortunately, the story does not have a happy ending. When World War II hit the country, the government began to make plans to take over the "Lesters' island." Eventually two sailors were put on the island as "guards." Apparently the intruders and the thought of leaving his island was more than Herbert Lester could handle; he ended his life with a gun. All three of his girls moved to the Mainland and have never returned to San Miguel.

The sheep were removed and the Navy took over the island for use as an aerial bombing range during WW II and the Korean War and after that a missile target area. The bombing of San Miguel was finally stopped in May of 1960 after protests by ecologists. The National Park Service signed an agreement with the Navy to preserve and manage the island. The breeding colony of pinnipeds at Point Bennett has increased and multiplied since that time. A National Park ranger is stationed on the island most of the year.

Special excursions take visitors on occasional overnight cruises stopping at several of the Channel Islands.

PRACTICALITIES

San Miguel Island is managed by the National Park Service and has a resident ranger for most of the year. The island is open to the public on a limited basis; camping is allowed with a permit. This protects the large seal and sea lion rookeries that are thriving at Point Bennett. Occasionally, an old bomb shows up from the time when the island was used as an aerial bombing target. A free permit is required to visit the island and you *cannot* obtain permits at the island. Get your permit from the Channel Islands National Park office in Ventura, 1901 Spinnaker Dr., tel. (805) 644-8262. San Miguel is well worth a visit, especially to see the rookeries and the unusual caliche. A knowledgeable park ranger will guide you around the island; hiking is restricted to the designated trails. No fishing is allowed from shore.

For Boaters

Anchoring overnight is permitted only at Tyler Bight and Cuyler Harbor. Inexperienced boaters are warned of the dangers of the unpredictable wind and sea conditions. Cuyler Harbor was named after its original government surveyor and was a favorite anchorage for the explorers of the past. The shore is covered by sand dunes on the south side of the anchorage. Cuyler Harbor can be a comfortable and uncrowded anchorage, but it's not unusual for a cranky surge to suddenly appear and for sweeping winds to rage over the cliffs. San Miguel is an island of great extremes; you can anchor in calm conditions at Cuyler one moment and be taken on a roller coaster ride the next. Take all precautions and be alert to the changeable weather. There's a government-designated "Danger Area" over the eastern half of San Miguel Island. Look into the regulations in chapter two of the U.S. Coast Pilot. The coastline at Tyler Bight is covered with large areas of sand dunes. Adams Cove is at the east end of the sandy beach extending east from the point with an indented cove of sloping rocks and sand. San Miguel is a dangerous destination and should be attempted only by the most experienced boaters.

SANTA ROSA ISLAND

THE LAND

Santa Rosa is the second largest of the Channel Islands, about 15 miles long from east to west and nine miles across at its widest point. Its 55,000 acres offer the same rugged landscape of its brother islands, but with the soothing touch of gentle slopes covered with grass sprawling to the edge of the sea, some ending in sand, some ending abruptly in rocky ledges and rugged cliffs. Some say that Santa Rosa resembles the Azores in the mid-Atlantic. Fortunately, Santa Rosa has fresh water year-round which gives it a rosier future. Two high mountains, Soledad Peak (1,574 feet) and Black Mountain (1,298 feet), rise above the deep canyons and high coastal cliffs that dominate portions of the island.

Climate

Santa Rosa doesn't have as much protection from the Point Conception headland as the islands to the east and south, therefore winds can be ruthless; 20-knot winds are common, and winter gales have been clocked at 90 knots. By some meteorological quirk, Santa Rosa receives only half the rainfall of the adjacent coastline. But the consistent fog shrouds the island with moisture, which helps to keep the grasses green, in some areas year-round. In a really wet year, the island spring is alive with the color of California poppies and blue lupine. When planning a visit to the island, be prepared to dress in layers. It can be cold or it can be hot, and it really depends on the wind.

FLORA

As with all the other islands, the advent of animals and plants has been hard on Santa Rosa's own natural environment. Spanish and Russian sailors left pigs on Santa Rosa for future food sources. With their rooting instinct, the pigs destroyed all seedlings and made it impossible for native plants to survive. Santa Rosa has one of only two stands of **Torrey pines** in existence. (The other stand of Torreys is located in the pine groves around La Jolla, a community called Torrey Pines.) Fortunately, the pines have survived the animals' rooting habits. Why and how

Santa Rosa Island's Carrington

thistle

they made it are questions that so far have not been answered. The trees survived monumental climatic changes over the years in *only* these two isolated spots. Even the Torrey pines have mutated somewhat to adjust to island living. Growing in deep-cut canyons and ravines, the wind whips constantly across the tops of the trees; maybe that's why they grow to only about 35 feet. **Coastal, scrub,** and **island oak, willow,** and **Catalina cherry** also survive on Santa Rosa Island.

FAUNA

Except for the introduced animals, the only natives left are the **island fox, white-footed mouse** and the **island spotted skunk.** Other natives include a **salamander,** a **frog,** two types of **lizards,** and the **California myotis,** the smallest bat found on the Channel Islands. The **harbor seal** and the **California sea lion** make yearly stops on Santa Rosa.

HISTORY

Prehistoric Remains
The remains of a dwarf mammoth (only six feet tall) were found on Santa Rosa in a de-

pression which has been called a "fire pit"; in other words the little beast was barbecued. Radiocarbon tests indicate this feast was held 29,700 years ago! This electrifying discovery has opened a door on the past. Some scientists conjecture that this prehistoric cousin to the elephant may have arrived from the Mainland after having been washed out to sea by a torrential storm and by swimming or just keeping afloat (after all, an elephant does come equipped with a built-in snorkel), or perhaps by rafting. But it survived until it reached a friendly shore. Another theory is the familiar old "land-bridge" idea. At some point, sections of this bridge to the Mainland along the coastline sank, creating Santa Rosa Island and stranding the elephant-like behemoth (known to have roamed the west coast of the Mainland during the prehistoric era). Being stranded on a small island with limited food sources and interbreeding may have caused stunting. All of this is conjecture; will we ever *really* figure out what happened so many years ago?

The Spanish Explorers
It is believed that the Vizcaino expedition named the island San Ambrosio and more than likely Juan Perez, who explored the area in the early 1770s, named the island Santa Rosa.

The Earthquake Of 1812
The missionaries had little luck luring the island Indians to the Mainland missions because of the Indians' isolated location. It was not easy for the priests to get to the islands, and the Indians were happy with their lifestyle, at least until the invasion of outsiders hunting the otters. Then in 1812 a destructive earthquake hit the adjacent Mainland and the Channel Islands. Its epicenter was along Santa Rosa's canyon called Canada Lobo. A tear in the earth 1,000 feet long, 100 feet wide, and 50 feet deep still remains as proof of nature's devastating force on that day. To the Indians, the rumbling earth, crumbling boulders, and mammoth waves crashing on-

to the coast are said by historians to be the factors that finally led the Indians to the Mainland missions and Christianity.

Settlers

After the Indian era, the island was part of a land grant from the Spanish Crown presented to Don Carlos and Don Jose Carrillo. Don Carlos gave half the island as a dowry to each of his two daughters when they were married. For many years the families raised sheep on the island and Santa Rosa was known far and wide for the great fiestas at shearing time. Before the turn of the century, most of the sheep were removed by the island's new owners, A.P. and W.H. More, and replaced with cattle and race horse stock. In 1902 Vail and Vickers bought the island and strengthened the cattle herds, still grazing some of the finest cattle in California.

Santa Rosa Island does not show the severe abuse that some of the other islands suffered, proving that with balanced grazing, the ecology can be preserved. In December of 1986 the island was sold (for $29.58 million) and it is now part of the Channel Islands Marine Sanctuary. Over time most of the cattle will be removed, but the Park's representative advises that they are planning to keep a small herd in operation so that visitors will understand the importance of the cattle ranch and its effect on the island for so many years. There are high hopes that the island will soon be open to the public for camping, backpacking, and specialized nature treks. The former owners of Santa Rosa, the heirs of Walter Vail and J.V. Vickers, have retained the ranch house near Becher's Bay for their private use for the next 25 years.

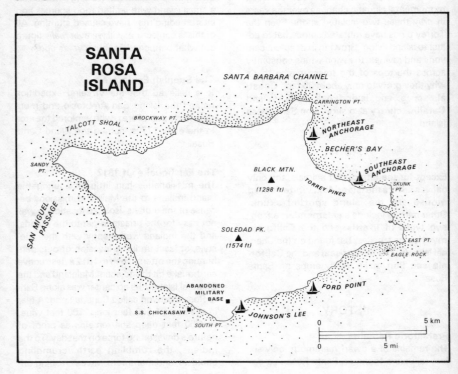

SANTA ROSA ISLAND

ACTIVITIES

Hiking

A landing permit (free) is required to go ashore on Santa Rosa Island. You cannot get a permit on the island; it must be obtained at the Channel Islands National Park Headquarters in Ventura. Visitors are met by the National Park ranger and guided on a three- to five-mile trek with a good historical and geographical lesson given by the knowledgeable ranger. He also points out the interesting facts of the island's flora and fauna. You are not given free run of the island; hikers are restricted to designated paths (which at this time are existing dirt roads left over from the former owners) and taken on a sample hike around the lovely, lonely island.

Fishing And Diving

The thick kelp beds and offshore reefs provide a rich haven for scallops, game fish, abalone, and lobster. The comparatively small number of divers that do brave the poor anchorage find a fish paradise. (Don't forget your license and note the seasons.) On a calm day the water is clear and underwater photography in the kelp forest can be spectacular. These same reefs have proven deadly for a number of vessels that failed to recognize the danger in these waters, where gale-force winds can rise unexpectedly.

BOATING ANCHORAGES

Santa Rosa is without a good natural harbor. Its westernmost extremity is **Sandy Point**, aptly named for the 400-foot white sand dunes that extend from that point inland. **Becher's Bay** is a long open bay four and a half miles across backed by low sandstone cliffs. Though it can be a comfortable daytime anchorage, it's described by some sailors as a wild and interesting spot for an overnight stay. A pier at Becher's is used by the cattle ranch; landing there is by permit only. **Eagle Rock Anchorage** is considered a temporary anchorage under the cliffs with good shelter. **Ford Point Anchorage** is another temporary anchorage in the lee of a small point. It offers little shelter for anything but a short stay. Note the inviting sandy beach nearby. Johnson's Lee is immediately northeast of the southernmost point of the island (there's a light at this end). Experienced sailors call **Johnson's Lee** the best anchorage on Santa Rosa; however, spring and winter can be uncomfortable. On the cliffs above the anchorage notice the old abandoned military barracks. Beware of the dilapidated Navy pier. The shore is lined with thick kelp beds here. The anchorage is fairly comfortable as long as the weather is good. As most boaters already know, there isn't a good safe anchorage at Santa Rosa in bad weather.

PRACTICALITIES

Day trips are now offered and visitors have begun going to the island on Island Packers boats. Right now, part of the adventure is just getting on the island. A dock has yet to be built, so visitors are landed six at a time from a small motorized skiff launched from the larger boat. Becher's Bay can show a strong, turbulent surf, so it's a given that passengers are going to get a little wet (more than likely *very* soaked). In the proper spirit, it's all part of the fun, and visitors are advised to bring an extra set of clothing and to keep cameras in plastic bags until safely ashore. Be sure to bring food, water, film, towels, or anything else with you. The only facility so far is the portable latrine. Landing permits (free) must be obtained from the Channel Islands National Park headquarters, 1901 Spinnaker Dr., Ventura. Commercial transportation to Santa Rosa is with Island Packers Co. (next to the park office). For schedules and reservations call (805) 642-1393; adult $60 RT, child $50.

SANTA CRUZ ISLAND

THE LAND

Santa Cruz Island is a verdant surprise compared with the drier islands of the channel. The usually abundant supply of water has given the island the look of a magnificent green paradise. The beauty of this, the largest of the Channel islands, has attracted boaters for generations. Within its boundaries are rolling meadowlands, rugged slopes, rivers, waterfalls, sandy beaches, thick stands of pine trees, babbling brooks, picturesque old wooden bridges, craggy bluffs, deep wooded canyons and giant caves—a natural wonderland and all surrounded by the beautiful Pacific.

Santa Cruz is in the main volcanic rock. It boasts gigantic sea caves and its tallest peak is 2,400 feet. A few geologists contend that the northern and southern parts of the island were originally on two different small plates of the earth's crust, the southern part having originated near the San Diego area. The island is 25 miles long and two to seven miles wide. It lies 23 miles southwest of Santa Barbara.

FLORA

Ferns add rich beauty to the closed-cone pine forests in the northern and western parts of the island. Eucalyptus trees were brought to the island years ago. With controlled grazing, Santa Cruz seems to have suffered less than some of the other islands. Endemic plants are still found, even though wild boar and at one time over 40,000 feral sheep ran free on certain parts of the island. A native succulent, the dudleya, adds a touch of gray-green against the stark cliffs. A rainbow of colorful wildflowers covers the rolling meadows in spring, including the California poppy, blue lupine, thistles, and many more. Over 600 species of plants are found on the island in 10 different plant communities; 40 species are restricted to the Channel Islands, while eight occur only on Santa Cruz. Some of the more notable examples are Santa Cruz Island ironwood and the island oak.

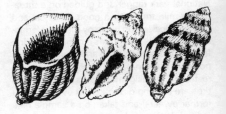

FAUNA

Santa Cruz Island's fauna is more varied than on many of the other Channel islands except Catalina. Along with 10 species of terrestrial mammals, including the white-footed mouse and the big-eared harvest mouse, four kinds of bats inhabit the island. Besides hundreds of Channel Island foxes and the island spotted skunk, you'll find two species of salamanders, one type of frog, three kinds of lizards, and a small group of snakes. More then 140 species of land birds have been identified, including quail, pheasant, ravens, meadowlarks, doves, and an occasional eagle. An example of island endemism is the island blue jay, larger and bluer than its Mainland cousin. The 77 miles of shoreline, cliffs, beaches, offshore rocks, and tidepools provide an important breeding habitat for colonies of nesting sea birds. Hundreds of California sea lions and harbor seals make the isolated coves of the island home. In fact, at Painted Cave you will often find a bull sea lion and his harem on the rocks in the last chamber. Scorpion Rock, near the east end of the island, has become a popular rookery for the pelicans that are coming back strong after a few years' setback during the DDT

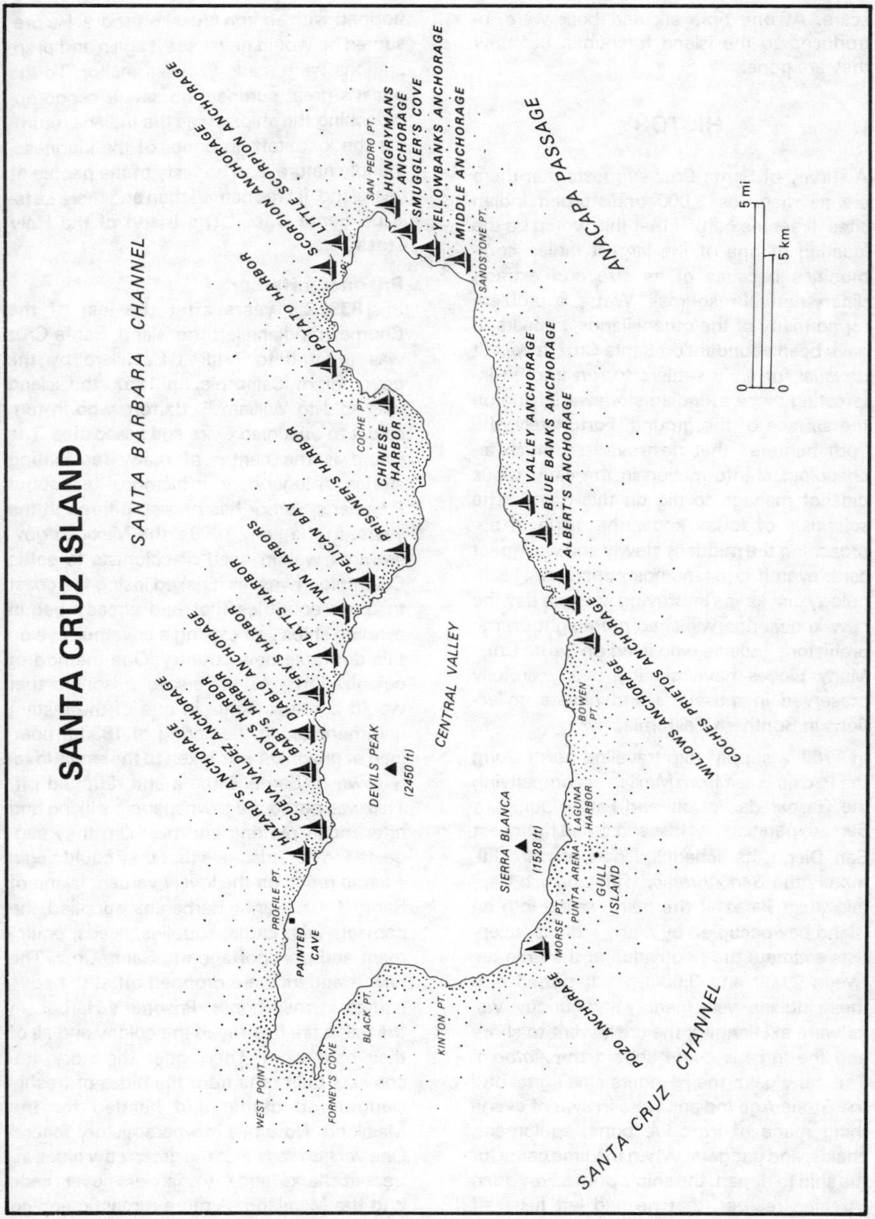

SANTA CRUZ ISLAND

SANTA BARBARA CHANNEL

ANACAPA PASSAGE

SCORPION ANCHORAGE
LITTLE SCORPION ANCHORAGE
SAN PEDRO PT.
HUNGRYMANS ANCHORAGE
SMUGGLER'S COVE
YELLOWBANKS ANCHORAGE
MIDDLE ANCHORAGE
SANDSTONE PT.
POTATO HARBOR
COCHE PT.
CHINESE HARBOR
PRISONER'S HARBOR
PELICAN BAY
TWIN HARBORS
PLATTS HARBOR
FRY'S HARBOR
DIABLO ANCHORAGE
BABYS HARBOR
LADYS ANCHORAGE
CUEVA VALDEZ ANCHORAGE
HAZARD ANCHORAGE
VALLEY ANCHORAGE
BLUE BANKS ANCHORAGE
ALBERT'S ANCHORAGE
COCHES PRIETOS ANCHORAGE
WILLOWS ANCHORAGE
BOWEN PT.

CENTRAL VALLEY

DEVILS PEAK
(2450 ft)

SIERRA BLANCA
(1528 ft)

PROFILE PT.
PAINTED CAVE
BLACK PT.
WEST POINT
FORNEY'S COVE
KINTON PT.
MORSE PT.
PUNTA ARENA
LAGUNA HARBOR
GULL ISLAND

POZO ANCHORAGE

SANTA CRUZ CHANNEL

5 mi
5 km
0
0

scare. At one time elk and boar were introduced to the island for hunts, but now
they are gone.

HISTORY

A survey of Santa Cruz suggests that there
are as many as 3,000 undisturbed Indian
sites. It seems natural that this would be the
location of one of the largest Indian communities because of its size and extraordinary natural resources. Water, a problem
for so many of the other islands, appears to
have been abundant on Santa Cruz. It wasn't
unusual for early settlers to run into an interesting piece of Indian stoneware lying on
the surface of the ground. Fortunately, the
"pot hunters" that destroyed so much archaeological information in the early 1900s
did not manage to dig on this island. The
scientists of today know the value of approaching the middens slowly and with great
care, even if it means postponement. Technology just keeps improving and one day the
new knowledge will shed more light on the
prehistoric Indians who lived on Santa Cruz.
Many pieces have already been carefully
preserved in museums and private collec-
tions in Southern California.

In 1769, a supply ship traveling north along
the Pacific coast from Mexico accompanying
the Gaspar de Portola and Father Junipero
Serra expedition got lost and sailed right past
San Diego, its scheduled port of call. Ultimately the *San Antonio,* with Spanish Captain Juan Perez at the helm, sailed into an
island bay occupied by many Indians (scientists estimate the population at the time between 2,000 and 3,000). As it turned out,
these Indians were friendly and curious. Visits were exchanged; the crew went to shore
and the Indians came aboard the *Antonio.*
The crew gave the islanders small gifts and
the Stone Age Indians were in awe of everything made of iron: weapons, equipment,
chains, and gadgets. When the time came for
the ship to depart, the ship's priest, Fray Juan
Vizcaino realized that he had left his staff

(topped with an iron cross) on shore. He presumed he would never see it again and preparations were made to hoist anchor. To the
priest's great surprise, he saw a canoe approaching the ship: it was the Indians returning the lost staff. In honor of the kindness,
friendly nature, and honesty of the people of
this island, it was named then and there La Isla de Santa Cruz, "The Island of the Holy
Cross."

Prisoner's Harbor

In 1839, 25 years after the last of the
Chumash Indians left the island, Santa Cruz
was granted to Andres Castillero by the
governor of California. In 1857, the island
was sold to William E. Barron, who in turn
sold it to Justinian Caire and associates. The
island is the center of many fascinating
stories. A legendary or historical tale about
Prisoner's Harbor has persisted through the
years. In the early 1800s, the Mexican government was in need of colonists to settle
California towns, as it risked losing the coast
to other countries that had already begun
sending ships and casting a covetous eye on
this desirable new country. One method of
colonization was to release prisoners that
would agree to settle in one of the distant
communities. In the spring of 1830 a boat-
load of prisoners was taken to the small, lovely town of Santa Barbara and dropped off.
This was not to the townspeople's liking and
after much plotting and planning they suggested to the prisoners that they could begin
a cattle ranch on the lovely verdant island of
Santa Cruz. Santa Barbarans supplied the
convicts with cattle, supplies, seeds, equipment and transportation to Santa Cruz. The
new islanders were dropped off at the cove
named in their honor, Prisoner's Harbor. In
the fall, a fire destroyed the colony and all of
their hard work. Then, goes the story, the
convicts built rafts from the hides of freshly
slaughtered cattle, and headed for the
Mainland. Now this is where history falters.
One version says that the green cow hides attracted sharks, and the prisoners never made
it to the Mainland. A more romantic ending

BROWN AND RED ALGAE
OF THE CHANNEL ISLANDS

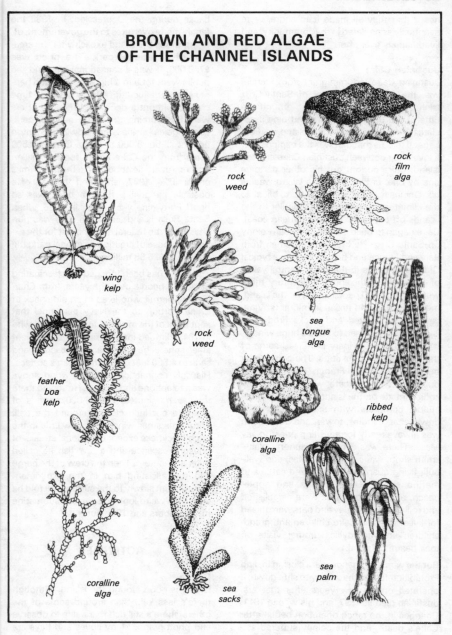

wing kelp

rock weed

rock film alga

feather boa kelp

rock weed

sea tongue alga

ribbed kelp

coralline alga

coralline alga

sea sacks

sea palm

has it that they all made it to shore, were eventually assimilated in the community, and lived happily ever after.

Justinian Caire

Justinian Caire, an immigrant from France, was the original developer of Santa Cruz Island. Living in San Francisco around the time of the gold rush, Caire and nine associates purchased Santa Cruz Island in 1869. Legend tells us that that was the beginning of a love affair between Justinian Caire and the island. Caire bought out his other partners one by one, until in 1887 the island was all his. Originally attracted to the island because the climate and territory were similar to the islands off the French Mediterranean coast, Caire began to build a small European colony on Santa Cruz. He brought craftsmen from Italy and France and began creating a typical Old World estate in the lovely central valley of the island. By the end of the century, there were close to 100 people living on the island, mostly French and Italian immigrants. Vineyards were planted and bricks fired from island clay were used to build a huge winery. It's said that the winery produced some of the finest wine in the state. The community boasted two-story French colonial brick buildings with delicate wrought-iron balconies (made on the island), and a tiny brick chapel complete with stained-glass windows, altar, candles, tower, and bell, which was always ready for a visiting priest to say Mass. There was a bakery, laundry, blacksmith shop, wagon shop, stables, and well-built living quarters. Caire grazed cattle and merino sheep. Olive groves and apple, peach, and pear orchards were established and rolling hills of barley and oats were raised for livestock. The Caire children and grandchildren enjoyed idyllic summer visits on their beautiful island.

But the winds of change were closing in, and Prohibition forced the winery to shut down; it operated only a few years after that era. Justinian died in 1897, and his wife in 1911. Changes in the ranch operation began after Caire's death, and the colony suffered setbacks during the Depression. In 1936 the family made overtures to the government, offering to sell the island explicitly for the creation of a national park. The price was $750,000. It was a sensational idea and the public went for it in a big way. As often happens in bureaucratic affairs, a lot of time passed without a decision. When no offers were forthcoming to form a national park, Los Angeles businessman Edwin L. Stanton bought all but 8,000 of Santa Cruz's 62,500 acres from the Caire estate for one million dollars. An article appeared in the *L.A. Times* on April 24, 1937, lamenting the loss of a possible national park. The price was so right! Forty-nine years later, in 1986, when Santa Rosa Island (similar in size) was purchased by the federal government for the express purpose of creating a national park, the price was $26.58 million.

The island has been touched by a fascinating parade of people over the years, from Charley, the hermit who lived in an old shack at China Harbor, to the Navy personnel that kept track of the missiles, to Otis Barton, who in 1949 climbed into a strange-looking giant steel sphere he called a benthoscope and sank to 4,500 feet below the ocean's surface. His only connection with the world above was a telephone and a cable. He stayed there for seven minutes, with 2,000 pounds of pressure per inch closing around the ball. Through a small window he saw little in the pitch blackness except occasional streaks of phosphorescence and a few fish he called miter and lantern. Then the crew of the barge and tug assisting him in the experiment brought him slowly to the surface. All told he was in his weird-looking spherical submarine for two hours and 19 minutes.

ACTIVITIES

Diving

Diving is good around the island. Although there's less kelp than around some of the others, there's still rich marinelife to observe and photograph. Many coves and bays are

within easy access to the beach, but remember that you are restricted by your permit in where you may go ashore. Lobster and abalone are very popular game on the island; remember your fishing license.

BOATING

Painted Cave
The immense sea caves in various places around the island are fascinating to visit. Painted Cave just west of Profile Point is best entered in a small dinghy or skiff. (You might want to bring a flashlight or two.) The water is usually placid unless there's a swell. It's an easy boat ride for those anchoring in Cueva Valdez to visit the caves. Painted Cave's walls are approximately 80 feet high at the entrance, and the ceiling rises to over 130 feet inside and then slopes to about 20 feet at the back end. It's easy to see why it's been named Painted: beautiful reds, yellows, and greens glow in the low light as you enter. The first section is more than 600 feet into the base of the island; row all the way in and when you reach the back make a hard turn to starboard, which brings you into a side chamber, 150 feet into darkness. But here you'll find a beach and rock ledges with seals and sea lions. If you choose to use a flashlight the pinniped tenants will quickly slide into the water and disappear. Three more caves one and one-tenth miles west of Painted Cave are also great to explore. They all have large entrances.

Hazard's Anchorage
Three-quarters of a mile west of Cueva Valdez anchorage you'll find a sandy beach with limited anchorage at Hazard's Anchorage.

Cueva Valdez
Cueva Valdez is a popular anchorage for beach-loving families. There's a great sandy beach for the kids, and swimming is good, with a few patches of kelp here and there.

Lady's Harbor
This is really two harbors; one is a small cove, and the larger one is great anchorage for just a few boats. This harbor tends to be crowded on a fine summer day. Little Lady's is considered only a fair-weather anchorage and is much smaller. Boats over 35 feet may have trouble turning around once inside the harbor. Landing (with permits) is allowed in both coves. This is lovely terrain with a stream and pools running into the sea.

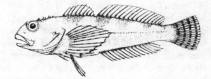

Diablo Anchorage
Immediately west of Diablo Point is Diablo Anchorage and a half mile east is Fry's Harbor. Diablo is rarely crowded and is a good stopover when the weather is quiet.

Fry's Harbor
This is probably one of the most popular anchorages at Santa Cruz Island, and can be crowded. But if you're lucky—maybe in the middle of the week—and it's deserted, you'll find it a beautiful place to be lazy for a few

*about to explore the
underwater world*

days. The rocky cliff immediately southeast of the beach provided the rock for the Santa Barbara breakwater in 1929. You'll notice remnants of the operation. If you have a choice, the best spots to anchor are tucked in under the west cliff. Take a picnic and make a dinghy trip to the small cove immediately east of Fry's or explore the cave 600 feet west of Fry's.

Prisoner's Harbor

Traveling the four miles between Fry's and Prisoner's Harbor is spectacular. More than likely you'll pass a few commercial diving and fishing boats. Along the way you'll see ragged cliffs and sloping hills that become low-lying cliffs, dotted with small coves all the way. Kelp is common for a quarter mile offshore. One of the coves, Orizaba Cove, is a lovely spot in good weather and usually entertains a few harbor seals in the bay. Another pretty place is Twin Harbors; either makes a good lunch stop. For the naturalist, notice the ironwood trees in the wooded canyon of the west anchorage. Along with the rugged cliffs, Prisoner's Harbor has a pier, tall eucalyptus trees, and a few small buildings. This is the main landing for the Santa Cruz Island Company; freight boats arrive on a regular basis. Please note the signs that say *landing closed to permit holders*. Your landing will be on the beach and you must wade ashore.

Pelican Bay

Pelican Bay is a large anchorage and will accommodate a good number of boats on a calm, sunny day. In spring the scenery is beautiful with myriad wildflowers in bloom. This is where Ira and Margaret Eaton lived with their little girl and later operated a hotel. This was also a favorite spot for filming movies in the early days of Hollywood. Some boaters prefer Pelican to any other harbor on the island. (Others say it can be bumpy and prefer Fry's.) In calm weather take a dinghy to Tinker's Harbor or Little Pelican (pull your dinghy out of the grasp of the waves and rising tides). This is a great place to explore the nearby woods and canyons or take a dinghy and investigate the many coves and dents along the coast.

Chinese Harbor

This open bay provides little protection for more than a brief stop. If you see smoke rising from the northeast cliff of the anchorage several hundred feet above the beach, don't be concerned; it's a fumarole, the only one on the offshore islands.

Potato Bay

Formerly known as Tylers, this is a beguiling bay, narrow and between steep cliffs. Not recommended for an overnight anchorage unless in very flat weather.

Scorpion And Little Scorpion Anchorage

Scorpion is the main landing area for the Gherini Ranch. Little Scorpion is the more favored of the two for anchoring with a little better protection. A good trip is exploring the coast in a dinghy in the early hours of the morning, where you'll see spectacular scenery including caves, alluring little coves, and ragged cliffs.

SANTA CRUZ SOUTH

In Brian Fagan's excellent boating guide, *Cruising Guide to California's Channel Islands,* he warns: All south coast anchorages of Santa Cruz are subject to heavy surge from tropical storms off the Mexican coast which can come in without warning, especially in summer.

Smuggler's Cove

Smuggler's Cove is a large open roadstead where a large number of small craft anchor in calm weather. This is a small bight with Caire's old olive groves and tall eucalyptus trees overlooking the cove. Landing is not allowed there's a hazardous beach break.

Yellowbanks

This is one alternative to Smuggler's Cove either in calm or heavy weather. Yellowbanks is not (usually) as crowded as Smuggler's.

Albert's Anchorage

This anchorage is a fairly comfortable one in calm weather, with good shelter from west through north. Some boaters complain that the steep cliff to the west puts the cove in shadow in the late afternoon and it can be dark and coolish. The view of the southeast coast of the island is lovely and you can even see (in the distance) Anacapa Island from Albert's Cove. There's a small beach at the head of the anchorage. Albert's can be bumpy when there's a surge. Landing is on the beach and there's limited access inshore.

Coches Prietos

Another picturesque cove, Coches Prietos ("Black Pigs"), is considered by some the best anchorage on the south side of Santa Cruz Island. There's a great sandy beach and good shelter, and it can be crowded with visitors, especially in the summer. This beautiful semi-circular beach extends into an inland valley. Landing is on the beach.

Willow's Anchorage

This is another popular anchorage and very pretty, but only recommended in good weather. Landing is on the beach.

Temporary Anchorages

Pozo Anchorage has lovely scenery but cannot be recommended for more than a brief stay.

Forney's Cove

Forney's is one of the most popular anchorages on Santa Cruz Island. It's isolated, with breathtaking scenery, great skin diving, and excellent fishing nearby. Landing can be tricky on the beach because of the shallow and irregular surf. Take off your shoes because you'll probably get soaked. Forney's is a boater's paradise and in the spring the riotous color of wildflowers is intoxicating. They have to be seen to be appreciated; bring your camera!

Sandstone Point Anchorage
This is not recommended for an overnight stop.

Potato Patch
An extra warning should be given about the rough area called Potato Patch, which extends two miles west of West Point. This rough water is caused by the meeting of opposing currents in the Santa Cruz Channel and the main channel. Even in the calmest weather you'll have ripples and mild turbulence.

PRACTICALITIES

Santa Cruz is privately owned by two companies and visiting is allowed on a limited basis only. Depending on which end of the island are strictly limited, and must be obtained in advance from the Nature Conservancy. In Santa Barbara call (805) 962-9111 for more information. There are certain prerequisites that must be adhered to. Boaters must have complete sleeping and cooking facilities on board. Landing permits are for day-use only. Permit fees are $15 for 30 consecutive days or $50 for a year. The Nature Conservancy sponsors a limited number of day trips to the island each year

---

20,000-YEAR-OLD-TUSK

A six-foot, nine-inch-long tusk from an imperial mammoth that roamed the continent 20,000 years ago was found in 1984 on Santa Cruz Island. The tusk, found by a young boy, was imbedded in rock. The immense mammoth stood some 14 feet tall at the shoulder and thrived during the late Pleistocene Epoch. It died out as a species at the end of the most recent ice age, about 10,000 years ago. The tusk can be seen at the Santa Barbara Museum.

---

for a fee. For more information contact The Nature Conservancy, Santa Cruz Island Project, 735 State St., Suite 201, Santa Barbara, CA 93101, tel. (805) 962-9111. For those interested in visiting the privately owned eastern tip of the island, contact Island Packers, the only access to Scorpion.

Note: Anyone interested in contributing to the Nature Conservancy's Santa Cruz Island Project can forward checks to The Nature Conservancy/Santa Cruz Island Project. Your contribution is tax-deductible and entitles you to all regular benefits of The Nature Conservancy, including a periodic newsletter on the Santa Cruz Island Project.

SAN NICOLAS ISLAND

If nothing else, San Nicolas Island's claim to fame is a fascinating story about 1,000 Indians that lived here at one time—and about one Indian woman especially, Juana Maria. Today much of the island appears lonely and desolate, with only a few hardy government people enjoying life on this high-tech, windy bit of land.

THE LAND

San Nicolas Island covers 22 square miles, and is 53 miles from the California coast. The island topography, made up of plateaus, terraces, and a few peaks (its highest is 907 feet above sea level), is not very spectacular. San Nicolas forms the outer corner of a quadrangle with the southern Channel Islands, Santa Barbara, Catalina, and San Clemente. Its easternmost point is an everchanging sandspit. Over the last century the continuous attack of the wind and the sea has considerably altered this part of the island.

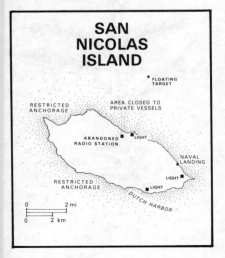

SAN NICOLAS ISLAND

FLOATING TARGET

RESTRICTED ANCHORAGE

AREA CLOSED TO PRIVATE VESSELS

ABANDONED RADIO STATION

LIGHT

NAVAL LANDING

LIGHT

RESTRICTED ANCHORAGE

LIGHT

DUTCH HARBOR

0   2 mi

0   2 km

Climate

The climate is temperate with a mean temperature of 60.4 degrees Fahrenheit, lows and highs averaging within four degrees. Fog keeps the humidity up to about 76 percent. The winds can rage, with the prevailing northwesterlies averaging between 35 and 50 miles per hour almost every day of the year. Sandstorms can happen anytime; the island is often described as a mountain of shifting sand.

FLORA AND FAUNA

Sea Creatures

The rugged coastline of San Nicolas provides stone ledges and platforms where the **harbor seal**, the **California sea lion**, and the **northern elephant seal** bathe in sun and sea. Elephant seals, almost completely depleted during the 1800s, are now found in a large rookery on San Nicolas. In 1950, 168 were counted and they continue to increase their numbers.

Sea Otters

In 1938, when the southern sea otters were presumed to be extinct, a herd of 100 were discovered along the central California coast. Ports at Moss Landing in the north and Port San Luis in the south bracket the otters' 180-mile range. In 1977, the U.S. Federal Wildlife Service estimated that the count had grown to 1,800, and the herd continues to grow. The federal government, under the authority of the Marine Mammal Protection Act, has moved a small population of sea otters from the central California coast to San Nicolas. This move was to protect present numbers of otter slowly coming back from near extinction. The motivation is the fear that an oil spill would wipe out the growing herd, since oil-tanker traffic is heavy along

the California coast. Unlike many marine mammals, the otter does not have a layer of blubber beneath its skin to keep warm in the chilly waters of the Pacific. Instead, it relies on a blanket of air pockets within its fur. When covered with oil, the fur mats down, destroying the air bubbles, and the otter loses its insulation. Within 24 hours, the "oiled" otter will die. At present, the otter is included in the *threatened* species list, and certain environmentalist groups (like Friends of the Otter) would like its status to be upgraded to *endangered.*

Commercial fishermen are lobbying for the otters to be relocated north of Point Conception, since they believe that the otters will spread to other islands nearby, destroying sealife. The otter has a voracious appetite, eating one-quarter of its weight each day. The teddy-bear look-alike dines mostly on the lobster, scallops, and abalone which thrive in the Channel Islands' offshore kelp beds—delicacies of man and a big part of the commercial fishermen's income.

Other Sea Organisms

The west perimeter of the island, called Land's End, is a mass of tidepools alive with barnacles, snails, sea urchins, limpets, and multicolored sea anemones. Rocky pockets and crevices are a gathering spot for purple sea grass, sea lettuce, brown sea moss, and black sea snails.

Land Creatures

Despite the construction of a Navy complex on the island, the sturdy animals seen on all of the Channel Islands persist on San Nicolas. The few endemic animals include the small island fox, the white-footed mouse, the rock hen, a small lizard, and a beetle. For some reason the fox grows slightly longer than related foxes on the other islands, and its coloring is somewhat different. The San Nicolas fox has a black back. The skies and cliffs are rampant with ravens, seagulls, cormorants, and horned larks.

Over the years, the last of the sheep were removed from the island and the land is beginning to recover. With the help of high humidity from the intense fog that prevails much of the time, spring flowers once again cover the landscape. The blue coastal sage blossoms and yellow coreopsis brighten the otherwise dismal panorama. Native plants are regaining the land with the absence of the constantly foraging sheep. Firmly established plants also lessen the erosion and blowing sand.

sticky monkey flower

HISTORY

Indians

It's not certain whether San Nicolas Island was sighted by the Cabrillo party in 1542 or not. In 1602, Spaniard Sebastian Vizcaino followed Cabrillo's path and reclaimed San Nicolas on December 6 (this is a presumption by historians but seems plausible since the sixth is the feast day of St. Nicolas). The Indians on the island were named Nicolenos by the arriving padres. Because so few arrowheads have been found, some scientists claim that the Nicolenos were more peaceful than the other Channel Island Indians. Early sea logs reported that the island supported a large Indian population, and many middens and burial sites have been found. Another fascinating remnant left behind on the south coast of San Nicolas was a sample of the Nicolenos' artistic talent; petroglyphs — large inscriptions of the sea and whales (some as long as six feet) — were discovered in a cave nicknamed by early ranchers the "Cave of the Whales." There are so many questions — and so few answers. Was there some religious significance to these large whale drawings? Why weren't others found? Was this the effort of an early artist? We'll probably never know. Part of the wall fell in 1961 and was given to the Southwest Museum in Los Angeles by the United States Navy.

The Nicolenos seldom saw visitors. It's questionable whether the Spanish actually got off their ships and *explored* the island, since there's very little good anchorage for vessels. The Indians led peaceful lives, and had extensive kelp beds rich with sealife, overrun with otters. Then the otter hunts began, and almost the entire population of Nicoleno Indians was ravaged and murdered — the plight of all the Channel Island Indians — by hunters for the Russian and American traders. In 1835 the few remaining Indians were taken to Mainland missions.

The Abandoned Woman Of San Nicolas

In 1835, the priests discovered that the population was down from more than 1,000 to 17-20 people. A vessel, *Peor Es Nada,* was commissioned by Franciscan padres to relocate the remaining Nicolenos. When Captain Charles Hubbard arrived at San Nicolas to make the rescue, without warning a gale riled the sea. The small schooner bobbed on its anchor as the crew, in haste and confusion, rounded up the remnant group of Indians (mostly women and children) and their modest belongings. The rising sea forced the captain to leave as soon as possible. As the ship was about to set sail with all Indians aboard, a young woman noticed that her child was not among them. In a state of hysteria she leaped into the agitated sea and swam to shore to search for the child. The captain, fearful for the safety of his crew, passengers, and ship, scurried for the Mainland — without the Indian woman or her baby. Captain Hubbard told his story to the padres at San Gabriel Mission and expressed his intention to return for the woman after he completed a voyage to San Francisco. As it turned out, the trip to San Francisco was the last for the *Peor Es Nada.* Less than a month after the trip to San Nicolas the schooner sank, and Captain Hubbard with it. More than a few Mainland people had heard the story of the woman left on San Nicolas, but no one ever tried to do anything about it. Years passed, and the occasional San Nicolas hunter or fisherman mentioned signs of someone living on the island. No one was ever seen so no one investigated, convinced the woman couldn't possibly have survived alone all that time.

In 1850, George Nidever and Thomas Jeffries sailed with a crew of Mainland Indians to San Nicolas to hunt otter, and if possible find the remains of the Indian woman and her child and return them to the Mainland mission. They remained on the island for six weeks, hunting and preparing the otter and seal hides. One night, an Indian working with

Nidever hiked around the island and was convinced he saw a running figure some distance away. He tried to catch up with this surprise visitor, but was unsuccessful. His report put Nidever on the alert, and each time he visited the island he searched for the phantom. Three years later, he and his hunting companions, including Carl Detman, stumbled on a basket filled with a feather dress. Nidever was determined to find the woman this time, and he and his companions conducted a thorough search, cave by cave, beach by beach, every inch of the island. Finally, several days later, Detman followed fresh footprints to one of the high peaks and a grass shelter. Found at last, it was almost unbelievable. The woman appeared to be about 50, healthy and active. She was in a beautiful dress of shiny green cormorant feathers matching the one the men had stumbled upon earlier. Through sign language it was learned that her child had not survived, and in fact had been found dead the day she swam ashore. She had managed quite well over the years, surviving on birds, fish, abalone, seal blubber, and roots. After her early experiences with the vicious hunters that wiped out most of her people, it was no surprise that she was fearful of the otter hunters she had observed on the island occasionally, and she did her best to remain hidden.

After gathering her few possessions (including bone needles and feather dresses that so impressed her rescuers) into a basket, she joined the men and journeyed to the Mainland. The Indian was welcomed into the home of Captain Nidever. The shy woman appeared quite pleased with her new world and enjoyed the many wondrous things that she was introduced to. The rest of her people had been taken 18 years earlier to either the Los Angeles or San Gabriel missions, yet it was almost impossible to find anyone left that could speak her language. Finally, after much searching, an old Indian at Santa Ynez was brought to meet Juana Maria (a name not given to her till she was baptised on her deathbed). After 18 years of desolation, loneliness, and struggling for survival, Juana Maria was being cared for. The story goes that she liked the variety of foods that were new to her, including hardtack bread, fresh fruit, and (especially) sugar. Some blame the foods for her death; but who will ever know? She was treated very kindly, but despite everything, was dead within seven weeks of her rescue, marking the end of five civilizations on San Nicolas Island. She was buried in the graveyard at Santa Barbara Mission; a plaque erected in her memory in 1928 reads:

> Juana Maria
> Indian Woman Abandoned on
> San Nicolas Island eighteen years
> Found and brought to
> Santa Barbara
> by
> Captain George Nidever
> in 1853
> Santa Barbara Chapter
> Daughters of the American Revolution 1928

It was said that her feather dress and possessions were sent to Rome by the local priest, but no one knows where any of these things is today. In 1957, archaeologist Arthur R. Sanger of Los Angeles, who searched the Channel Islands for 30 years collecting Indian artifacts for the Museum of the American Indian in New York and the Los Angeles County Museum, was certain he had the skeleton of Juana Maria's child. He related at the time that this particular infant skeleton was found buried much deeper than the others, and that beads buried with the child had been imported in the 19th century. Anything is possible. An exceptionally fine children's book called *Island Of The Blue Dolphins,* by Scott O'Dell, gives a fictionalized account of Juana Maria's years alone on the island.

Ranching

In 1857, only four years after Juana Maria's removal from San Nicolas, the first rancher, Captain Martin Kimberly, brought in sheep, whose descendants defoliated the island for the next 84 years. San Nicolas didn't go through the line of private ownership as did most of the other Channel islands. However, it was leased to a variety of ranchers, Howland and Vail, L.P. Elliot, Roy Agee, and Martin Kimberly, running thousands of sheep and continuously planting grasses that would survive in the salty, windy environment. Over the years overgrazing was a way of life. In 1840 the island had boasted trees, brush, and moss, but by 1900 San Nicolas was devastated. At one time, the smallest fully accredited school in the county with a full-time teacher (Miss Alma R. McLain) was conducted on San Nicolas Island. The entire student body of San Nicolas Elementary School consisted of two students, Frances Agee and John Scrimiger.

In the mid-1950s, an old sheepherder's shack was torn down and two Navy men found a fascinating piece of parchment with the following message:

At Christmas time when gifts are sent
They're from the saint, a kind old gent.
On an isle which bears his name
Is treasure, hid for you to claim
In an iron chest so strong
Buried where the land is long.
If you walk where the tides do meet
You will find it at your feet.
Coins so rare, coins so old
Coins of silver and of gold.
If he who finds it is my friend,
All my fortune he may spend.
If he who finds it is my foe,
Curses, misery and woe.

This fascinating ditty should whet the appetites of treasure hunters; or is this just another practical joke perpetrated by a bored sheepherder spending a lonely windblown night on San Nicolas?

Navy

In 1933 President Hoover gave jurisdiction of San Nicolas to the Navy. After temporary administration by the Army from 1942 to 1947, Point Mugu regained administrative control of the island for use by the Navy. Since then it has been closed to the public and used for various training programs. Now part of the Pacific Missile Test Center's Sea Test Range, San Nicolas maintains a far different landscape from that of the other Channel islands. The multimillion-dollar government complex includes a 10,000-foot runway with ground-controlled approach facilities that accommodates supersonic target aircraft and planes from the Mainland during operations. The entire program, including sophisticated missile-tracking instrumentation, is closely coordinated with those on the Mainland at Point Mugu. White telescope domes dot the plateau, and approximately 180 military and civilian technicians live on the windswept island.

The marine environment is essential to the testing of airborne weapons from the Pacific Missile Test Center. San Nicolas offers an unobstructed area over which the Navy can test its new weapon systems. This activity is conducted over a rectangular plot of ocean 200 miles long and 80 miles wide, between San Nicolas Island and Point Mugu. All of the information is then fed into complex computer systems and studied by scientists and engineers.

Management

A joint agreement between the Department of the Navy, Department of the Interior, and California Department of Fish and Game provides for the care, management, and protection of the flora and fauna and recovery of the land on San Nicolas. Indian artifacts are protected by the Antiquities Act, which governs historic and prehistoric remains. Excavation and collection is controlled and must be approved by the Department of the Interior. Proposed scientific research is reviewed by a Project Review Board to determine scientific merit, justification, and impact on the environment. The uncontrolled "pot hunters" of the last century inflicted much damage and destroyed large archaeological treasures that could have helped in determining more historic data about the original inhabitants of

San Nicolas. These government bodies are making certain that history does not repeat itself.

PRACTICALITIES

San Nicolas and San Clemente islands are off limits to the general public, as they are military reservations. If you want to visit either, you must adhere strictly to government regulations regarding each island, which can be obtained by writing Naval Air Station, Point Mugu, CA 93042, or call (805) 982-7567.

Boating
Boaters interested in San Nicolas should

check out chart 18755. The restricted naval area extends three miles around the island. An aerolight is 981 feet above the east end. Marine lights are shown from white pyramid-like structures on the south, east, and north sides of the island. A lighted buoy is 1.3 miles southeast of the east sandspit. Another landmark to beware of is **Begg Rock**, 15 feet high and eight miles northwest of the west point of San Nicolas Island. A reef extends north and south of the rock more than 100 yards in each direction. The rock rises abruptly from depths of 50 fathoms and can disappear on a foggy day. A lighted whistle buoy is 500 yards north of the rock. Anchorage around San Nicolas is usually uncomfortable, and in many cases restricted.

SAN CLEMENTE ISLAND

THE LAND

The grass-covered promontories and ragged volcanic cliffs give San Clemente an arid look most of the year. Only in early spring is there a fresh green coverlet on the island, but that lasts only a short time. Twenty miles long and two to four miles wide, San Clemente is the fourth largest of the Channel Islands, covering an area of 56 square miles. Its highest peak is 1,965 feet. The island is a labyrinth of caves; at least one of them reaches up two stories. The shoreline shows masses of bubbled rock formed from ancient volcanic eruptions of sizzling lava that hardened into strange forms when it encountered the cooling sea. Not far from the shore, dozens of steep sand dunes (300 to 1,000 feet high) are located at West Cove.

FLORA AND FAUNA

There are 10 endemic plants on San Clemente, more than on any of the other islands. It is believed that stipa, an endemic bunch grass, was probably the island's main ground cover in the past. Bits of it can still be seen on the weather side of the island in deeply cut canyons. In spring, the island boasts myriad wildflowers, including mountains of succulents called dudleya, the orange flowers of mimulus, prickly pear cactus, wild cucumber, coastal sage, poppies, San Clemente larkspur, San Clemente Indian paintbrush, San Clemente island bush-mallow, San Clemente broom, thistles, lupine, white morning glories, and cholla cactus; ferns and moss are found at the bottoms of sheer-walled canyons hung with long trails of snake cactus. But the colorful flowers last but a brief time. The Navy's Natural Resources Program Office has started a program to restore the previous natural balance with a native plant nursery that includes about 50 species.

Fauna

The most abundant animals are the feral goats that have all but taken over the island. They run free into deep canyons and along ribbon-sized paths and easily outwit the intermittent hunters that the government allows. A program of trapping the goats and releas-

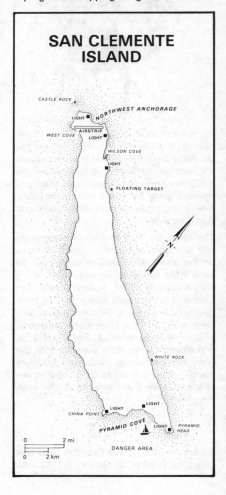

SAN CLEMENTE ISLAND

CASTLE ROCK

LIGHT NORTHWEST ANCHORAGE
AIRSTRIP
WEST COVE LIGHT

WILSON COVE
LIGHT

FLOATING TARGET

N

WHITE ROCK

CHINA POINT LIGHT   LIGHT
PYRAMID COVE LIGHT PYRAMID HEAD

0   2 mi
0   2 km

DANGER AREA

ing them in Mainland areas has been implemented, but the goats multiply and replace the departing animals faster than the trappers can keep up with them. Certain groups of animal lovers have complained loudly about any massive hunts that would thin out the goats, even though they are destroying the flora on San Clemente.

The island fox, two species of island mice, and four types of bats still make their home on the island. An occasional osprey can be seen flying high over the mountains, along with mourning doves, hummingbirds, San Clemente Island sage sparrow, finches, meadowlarks, and ravens. Seabirds include pelicans, gulls, and the black-footed albatross, plus many more varieties. Seals, sea lions, and elephant seals don't seem to mind the Navy bombardments, since their numbers are growing. As many as three hundred elephant seals use San Clemente as their hauling ground.

HISTORY

It's presumed that what Cabrillo's party first called "La Victoria" on October 7, 1542, was actually San Clemente. During Vizcaino's travels along the west coast in 1602, he also sighted the island, and renamed it San Clemente.

Indians

Although archaeologists have not conducted as many investigations on San Clemente as on some of the other Channel Islands, archaeology classes from local Mainland colleges have uncovered over 1,000 midden sites. The Indians used the huge caves scattered around the island as living quarters. San Clemente Indians traded widely with the other islands and Mainlanders; many artifacts from neighboring Catalina Island have been found on San Clemente, along with other proof that these Indian mariners traveled the channel extensively. San Clemente Indians suffered the same indignities at the hands of the Aluet otter hunters as did the rest of the Channel islanders. Only after the populace was almost totally destroyed did they move to the Mainland in the 1820s to San Gabriel Mission.

After the Indians left, the island was largely uninhabited. The Chinese collected abalone from San Clemente, dried them and shipped them from about 1890 to 1910. Documents indicate that a Spanish land grant was awarded to Pio Pico, but the grant was never claimed. Several ranchers with interests on the other Channel islands also used San Clemente to raise sheep, but the island's single owner has been the United States government since the Hidalgo Treaty in 1848.

Island People

Over the years a variety of people have touched the island in some way. After the Indians were gone the island was used at various times as a hiding place for pirates and then bootleggers that would hide their illegal liquor in the many caves along the shore. Later a number of hermits found the island soothing for short periods of time, but those that stayed the longest were the sheep ranchers.

Navy

In 1934, the U.S. government assumed management of San Clemente Island. During World War II, the island, under Navy jurisdiction, was used as a fleet training base and artillery target.

PRACTICALITIES

Boating

There is anchorage at Pyramid Cove, but as part of the Navy target area, it's off limits to boaters during periods of bombardment, which usually take place on Tuesday, Wednesday, and Thursday of each week. For detailed information contact The Commander, Amphibious Force, the Pacific Fleet, Naval Amphibious Base, Coronado, CA, tel. (619) 437-2231, or the 11th U.S. Coast Guard District, 400 Oceangate, Long Beach, CA 90822.

Fishing

Thick kelp beds grow directly off the lee side of the island, where steep cliffs drop to the sea. The ocean bottom deepens quickly here. Sports-fishermen, divers, as well as the commerical fishing fleet come together at these rich fishing grounds. The Navy allows fishing and diving except in target areas but prohibits landing on any part of the island. Undersea caves hide abundant sealife including swarms of game fish and elusive lobster that have managed to stay away from the ever-present lobster traps of Mainland fishermen.

BOOKLIST

FICTIONALIZED HISTORY

Dana, Richard Henry. *Two Years Before The Mast.* New York: Airmont, 1965.

Eaton, Margaret Holden. *Diary Of A Sea Captain's Wife.* Santa Barbara: McNally & Loftin, 1980.

Kallman, Robert and Eugene Wheeler. *Shipwrecks, Smugglers, and Maritime Mysteries of the Santa Barbara Channel Islands.* Santa Barbara: McNally & Loftin, 1984.

NATURE STUDIES

Miller, Daniel J. and Robert N. Lea. *Guide To The Coastal Marine Fishes of California.* California: University of California, 1982.

Udvardy, Miklos D.F. *The Audubon Society Field Guide to North American Birds, Western Region.* New York: Knopf, 1977.

HISTORY

Johnston, Bernice Eastman. *California's Gabrielino Indians.* California: Southwest Museum, 1962.

Hillinger, Charles. *The California Islands.* California: Academy, 1958.

Holder, Charles F. *The Channel Islands of California.* McClurg, 1910.

Bolton, Herbert E. *Spanish Exploration In The Southwest.* New York: Scribner's Sons, 1916.

Kroeber, A.L. *Handbook of the Indians of California.* Dover Publications, 1976.

Landberg, Leif C.W. *The Chumash Indians of Southern California.* California: Southwest Museum, 1965.

Moore, Patricia Anne. *The Casino.* California: Catalina Island Museum Society, 1979.

Overholt, Alma. *The Catalina Story.* California: Catalina Island Museum Society, 1962. Edited and updated by Jack Sargent, 1971.

Windle, Ernest. *Windle's History of Santa Catalina Island.* California: Catalina Islander, 1940.

BOATING/FISHING

Berssen, Capt. William, USCGR (Ret). *1987 Pacific Boating Almanac.* California: Western Marine Enterprises, Inc., 1987.

Davis, Charlie. *Hook Up.* California: Charles Davis, 1977.

Fagan, Brian M. *Cruising Guide To California's Channel Islands.* California: Western Marine Enterprises, Inc., 1983.

INDEX

Index abbreviation key: SB = Santa Barbara Island; SN = San Nicolas Island;
ANA = Anacapa Island; SM = San Miguel Island; SR = Santa Rosa Island;
SC = San Clemente Island; SCZ = Santa Cruz Island. Place names not identified, except those on
the Mainland, are on Catalina Island.

Boldfaced page numbers indicate the primary reference; *italicized* numbers refer to information in
maps, charts, illustrations, photos, or captions.

ABOUT THE AUTHOR

Chicki Mallan never forgets that she is one of the "lucky people" who grew up on Catalina Island. Growing up on a small island is an experience that has colored her entire life. Traveling since childhood, Chicki has logged thousands of miles around the world, first with her parents, then with her own large family. Chicki and children have lived in the Orient and Europe, but she still counts Catalina as the number-one island in the world. When not traveling, lecturing, or giving slide presentations, Chicki, husband Oz, and teen-age twins Patti and Bryant live in Paradise, a small community in the foothills of the California Sierra Nevada. She does what she enjoys most, writing magazine and newspaper articles in between travel books. In June of 1987, Chicki was awarded the *Pluma de Plata* ("Silver Pen") writing award from the Mexican government for articles she has written and published about Mexico. She has been associated with Moon Publications since 1983, when the first edition of *Guide to Catalina* was published. Presently Chicki is working on the second edition of her *Guide to the Yucatan Peninsula.*

Oz and Chicki Mallan

ABOUT THE PHOTOGRAPHER

Oz Mallan has been a professional photographer for the past 36 years. Much of that time was spent as chief cameraman for the *Chico Enterprise-Record.* Oz graduated from Brooks Institute of Santa Barbara in 1950. His work has often appeared in newspapers across the country via UPI and AP. He travels the world with wife, Chicki, handling the photo end of their literary projects, which include travel books, newspaper and magazine articles, as well as lectures and slide presentations. The photos in *Guide to Catalina Island and California's Channel Islands* were taken on the many trips to Catalina as well as the Southern California coast.

ABOUT THE ILLUSTRATORS

Kathy Escovedo Sanders is an expert both in watercolor and the stipple style which lends itself to excellent black-and-white reproduction used in all of Chicki Mallan's books. Kathy is a 1982 Cal State Long Beach graduate with a BA in Art History. She exhibits drawings, etched and woodcut prints as well as her outstanding watercolor paintings. In the April 1982 issue of *Orange Coast Magazine,* a complete photo essay illustrates Kathy's unique craft of dyeing, designing, and etching eggs. Her stipple art can also be seen in Chicki Mallan's *Guide to the Yucatan Peninsula.*

Diana Lasich Harper is a Moon Publications regular, with illustrations in many Moon books. She received her degree in Art from San Jose State University and continued studying as she traveled through Japan, where she learned wood-block printing, *sumie,* and *kimono* painting.

Louise Foote is a talented artist, as well as official mapmaker for Moon books. She is also an archaeologist and has spent some interesting time on various digs at Indian sites around Northern California. Louise executed all the maps in Guide to Catalina and California's Channel Islands.

When in Catalina- stop here first

- ❏ All sightseeing tickets (see page 111)
- ❏ Reservations for Pavilion Lodge and Hotel Atwater
- ❏ Displays and videos highlighting Catalina's activities
- ❏ Free map of Avalon ❏ Restaurant information
- ❏ Group and Senior rates

Visitor's Information Center

Look for the Visitor's Information Center in the center of town across from the green Pleasure Pier. For more information call (toll free in CA) 1-800-4-AVALON or (outside CA) 1-213-510-2000 from 8 a.m. - 5 p.m.

Look for the "Saludos" girl ~ Your assurance of satisfaction.

Did You Enjoy This Book?

Then you may want to order other MOON PUBLICATIONS titles.

Like the guide you're holding in your hands, you'll find the same high standard of quality in all of our other titles, with informative introductions, up-to-date travel information, clear and concise maps, beautiful illustrations, a comprehensive subject/place-name index, and many other useful features. All Moon Publications' guides come in this compact, portable size, with a tough Smyth-sewn binding that'll hold up through years of hard traveling.

The Americas Series

GUIDE TO CATALINA: and California's Channel Islands
by **Chicki Mallan**

Twenty-six miles across the sea from Los Angeles, Santa Catalina Island offers a world of vacation opportunities right in Southern California's back yard. A complete guide to these remarkable islands, from the windy solitude of the Channel Islands National Marine Sanctuary to bustling Avalon, *Guide to Catalina* covers hiking and birdwatching; the best locations for scuba diving and snorkeling, fishing, swimming, and tidepooling; and activities for children. Boaters will especially appreciate the comprehensive listing of marinas and other boating facilities in the area. 8 color pages, 105 b/w photos, 65 illustrations, 40 maps, 32 charts, booklist, index. 275 pages. **$8.95**

GUIDE TO THE YUCATAN PENINSULA: Including Belize
by **Chicki Mallan**

Explore the mysterious ruins of the Maya, plunge into the color and bustle of the village market place, relax on unspoiled beaches, or jostle with the jet set in modern Cancun. Mallan has gathered all the information you'll need: accommodations and dining for every budget, detailed transportation tips, plans of archaeological sites, and accurate maps to guide you into every corner of this exotic land. The new section on Belize helps open up this delightful, little-known Caribbean getaway just over the border from Mexico. 8 color pages, 154 b/w photos, 55 illustrations, 57 maps, 70 charts, appendix, booklist, Mayan and Spanish glossaries, index. 400 pages. **$11.95**

ARIZONA TRAVELER'S HANDBOOK by Bill Weir

Arizona, the sunniest state in the Union, is a land of dazzling contrasts, packed with as much history and natural beauty as one state can hold: giant saguaro cactus and shimmering aspen, ancient pueblos and sophisticated cities, the lofty peaks of the San Francisco Range, and of course, the magnificent Grand Canyon. This meticulously researched guide contains a comprehensive introduction, motel, restaurant, and campground listings, trail maps and descriptions, and travel and recreation tips—everything necessary to make Arizona accessible and enjoyable.8 color pages, 250 b/w photos, 81 illustrations, 53 maps, 4 charts, booklist, index. 448 pages. **$11.95**

UTAH HANDBOOK by Bill Weir

Three states rolled into one, Utah has the pristine alpine country of the Rockies, the awesome canyons of the Colorado Plateau, and the remote mountains of the Great Basin. Take in cosmopolitan Salt Lake City, ski Utah's "greatest snow on earth," and explore the spectacular rock formations in Zion, Bryce, Capitol Reef, Canyonlands, and Arches national parks. Or choose among the many national monuments and other special areas for outstanding scenery, geology, Indian lore, and pioneer history. Weir gives you all the carefully researched facts and background to make your visit a success. 8 color pages, 102 b/w photos, 61 illustrations, 30 maps, 9 charts, booklist, index. 468 pages. **$11.95**

NEVADA HANDBOOK by Deke Castleman

Nevada—born of Comstock si......, and prospering from casino gold. Fastest-growing and second-most-visited, Nevada is also the wildest state in the Union, indoors and out. You can get married on a whim and divorced in a flash, freely partake of the world's oldest profession, protest nuclear testing and dumping, and turn your hands black feeding one-armed bandits. Basque ranchers and cowboy poets, tuxedoed high-rollers and topless showgirls, nine residents per square mile and 30 million visitors—Nevada has it all, and then some. *Nevada Handbook* puts it all into perspective and makes it manageable and affordable. Color and b/w photos, illustrations, 40 maps, charts, booklist, index. 300 pages. **(Available Fall 1989) $10.95**

NEW MEXICO HANDBOOK by Stephen Metzger

New Mexico is a haunting and magical land of gorgeous mountains, fertile river valleys, broad expanses of high desert, and breathtakingly beautiful skies. This guide takes you from prehistoric Indian ruins to 16th-century Spanish settlements, to ghost towns and 20th-century artists' colonies. Explore the badlands where Billy the Kid roamed, wander through the stark redrock plains of Navajo country, ski the high peaks of the southern Rockies. *New Mexico Handbook* offers a close-up and complete look at every aspect of this wondrous state, including its geology, history, culture, and recreation. Color and b/w photos, illustrations, 40 maps, charts, booklist, index. 400 pages.

(Available Fall 1989) $11.95

BRITISH COLUMBIA HANDBOOK by Jane King

British Columbia is snowcapped mountains and shimmering glaciers, dense green forests and abundant wildlife, mirror-perfect lakes and mighty rivers teeming with salmon and trout, thriving cosmopolitan cities and fun-filled resorts. *British Columbia Handbook* introduces you to the province's colorful history, geography, flora and fauna, and more. With an emphasis on outdoor adventures, this guide covers mainland British Columbia, Vancouver Island, the Queen Charlotte Islands, and the Canadian Rockies, and includes attractions, good-value restaurants, entertainment, transportation, and accommodations from tentsites to luxury hotels. Color and b/w photos, illustrations, 60 maps, charts, booklist, index. 300 pages. **$11.95**

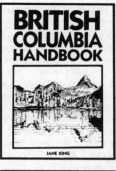

WASHINGTON HANDBOOK by Dianne J. Boulerice Lyons

Few states are as geographically diverse and rich in recreational opportunities as Washington. Volcanos, deserts, rainforests, islands, glaciers, lakes, rivers, and seashore offer outdoor diversions from mountain climbing to clam digging, cycling to sun worshipping. Seattle and other cities offer such urban delights as award-winning restaurants, world-class shopping, and myriad cultural and historical attractions. *Washington Handbook* covers sights, shopping, services, and transportation, hot spots for hiking, boating, fishing, windsurfing, birdwatching, and other outdoor recreation, and has complete listings for restaurants and accommodations. Color and b/w photos, illustrations, 81 maps, charts, booklist, index. 425 pages. **$11.95**

ALASKA-YUKON HANDBOOK: Including the Canadian Rockies
by Deke Castleman & David Stanley

Alaska occupies a special place in the geography of the imagination; its mystery and magnetism have compelled adventurers northward for over a hundred years. *Alaska-Yukon Handbook* guides you to North America's tallest mountains, wildest rivers, greatest glaciers, largest wilderness parks, and most abundant wildlife. Castleman and Stanley provide the inside story, with plenty of well-seasoned advice to help you cover more miles on less money, tips on working in Alaska, plus what the Alaskans themselves do for recreation and where they take visitors for fun. 8 Color pages, 26 b/w photos, 92 illustrations, 90 maps, 6 charts, booklist, glossary, index. 375 pages. **$10.95**

BACKPACKING: A HEDONIST'S GUIDE
by Rick Greenspan and Hal Kahn

Imagine yourself hanging out in an alpine meadow high up in your favorite mountains, enjoying the sunset and reflecting that the strenuous hike ended at the second most beautiful campsite in the world; that the bubble-and-fly bagged a panful of trout; that the bread rose, and the brandy chocolate warmed your very soul. If this sounds enticing, then *Backpacking: A Hedonist's Guide* is for you. This humorous, handsomely illustrated how-to-guide will convince even the most confirmed naturophobe that it's safe, easy, and enjoyable to leave the smoggy security of city life behind—in style. 90 illus,. annotated booklist, index. 200 pages. **$7.95**

The Pacific/Asia Series

HAWAII HANDBOOK by **J.D. Bisignani**
This definitive travelers' resource to the magnificent archipelago takes you beyond the glitz and high-priced hype and leads you to a genuine Hawaiian experience. It offers a comprehensive introduction to the islands' geography, history, and culture, as well as inside tips on the best sights, entertainment, services, food, lodging, and shopping. This is also the guide for the outdoor enthusiast, with extensive listings for land and water sports of every sort. 12 color pages, 318 b/w photos, 132 illustrations, 74 maps, 43 graphs and charts, Hawaiian and pidgin glossaries, appendix, booklist, index. 788 pages. **$15.95**

MAUI HANDBOOK: Including Molokai and Lanai by **J.D. Bisignani**
Maui is one of the most enchanting and popular islands in all of Oceania. Luxuriate on glistening beaches, swim and snorkel in reef-protected waters, dive into the mysteries of a submerged volcanic crater, or challenge the surf at world-famous beaches. Discover unspoiled Molokai, where ethnic Hawaiians still work the land, and sail the "Lahaina Roads" to Lanai for beauty and solitude. Bisignani offers "no fool-'round" advice on these islands' full range of accommodations, eateries, rental cars, shopping, tours, and transport, plus a comprehensive introduction to island ways, geography, and history. 8 color pages, 60 b/w photos, 72 illustrations, 34 maps, 19 charts, booklist, glossary, index. 350 pages. **$10.95**

KAUAI HANDBOOK by **J.D. Bisignani**
From its dazzling chain of uncrowded beaches to its highest peak, Hawaii's "Garden Island" bows to no other for stunning scenery. Kauai is where Hawaiians come when they want to get away from it all. *Kauai Handbook* introduces you to the island's history, culture, and natural features, and takes you into a world away from the hustle and crowds of Waikiki. With up-to-date facts on accommodations, dining, shopping, entertainment, and services, plus detailed coverage of outdoor recreation, *Kauai Handbook* is the perfect antidote to the workaday world. Color and b/w photos, 15 maps, 4 charts, 12 illustrations, Hawaiian and pidgin glossaries, booklist, index. 200 pages. **(Available Fall 1989)** **$9.95**

BLUEPRINT FOR PARADISE: How to Live on a Tropic Island
by **Ross Norgrove**

This one-of-a-kind guide has everything you need to know about moving to and living comfortably on a tropical island. Derived from personal experiences, Norgrove concisely explains: choosing an island, designing a house for tropical living, transportation, installing electrical and water systems, adapting to the island lifestyle, successfully facing the elements, and much more. Norgrove also addresses the special concerns of "snow-birds"—those Northerners who escape to an island getaway to leave winter far behind. Whether you're an armchair Robinson Crusoe dreaming of faraway beaches, or your gear is packed and you're ready to leave the mainland behind, you'll find *Blueprint for Pardise* as entertaining as it is practical. 8 color pages, 40 b/w photos, 3 maps, 14 charts, appendices, index. 202 pages. **$14.95**

SOUTH PACIFIC HANDBOOK   by **David Stanley**

Here is paradise explored, photographed, and mapped—the original comprehensive guide to the history, geography, climate, cultures, and customs of the 19 territories in the South Pacific. A finalist for the prestigious Thomas Cook Travel Guide Award in 1986. No other travel book covers such a phenomenal expanse of the Earth's surface, and no other traveler knows the South Pacific like David Stanley. 12 color pages, 195 b/w photos, 121 illustrations, 35 charts, 138 maps, booklist, glossary, index. 588 pages. **$14.95**

GUIDE TO TAHITI-POLYNESIA   by **David Stanley**

Legendary Tahiti, isle of love, has long been the vision of "La Nouvelle Cythere," the earthly paradise. All five French Polynesian archipelagoes are covered in this comprehensive new guidebook by Oceania's best-known travel writer. Leap from the lush, jagged peaks of Moorea and Bora Bora to the exotic reefs of Rangiroa and Paul Gauguin's lonely grave on Hiva Oa. Rub elbows with the local elite at the finest French restaurants and save francs by sleeping in a lagoonside tent, then take in the floor show at a luxury resort for the price of a drink. This handy book shows you how to see Polynesia in style for under $50 a day. Color and b/w photos, illustrations, 29 maps, 6 charts, booklist, glossary, index. 250 pages.
(Available Fall 1989) $9.95

MICRONESIA HANDBOOK:
Guide to the Caroline, Gilbert, Mariana, and Marshall Islands
by **David Stanley**

Midway, Wake, Saipan, Tinian, Guam—household words for Americans during WWII, yet the seven North Pacific territories between Hawaii and the Philippines have received little attention since. Enjoy the world's finest scuba diving in Belau, or get lost on the far-flung atolls of the Gilberts. With insight into island culture, leads on the best diving locales and other recreation, and creative accommodation and dining suggestions, *Micronesia Handbook* cuts across the plastic path of packaged tourism and guides you on a real Pacific adventure all your own. 8 color pages, 77 b/w photos, 68 illustrations, 69 maps, 18 tables and charts, index. 300 pages. **$9.95**

INDONESIA HANDBOOK   by **Bill Dalton**

This one-volume encyclopedia explores island-by-island Indonesia's history and geography, her people, languages, crafts and artforms, her flora and fauna, ancient ruins, dances, and folk theater. It's a gypsy's manual packed with money-saving tips, pointing the way to Indonesia's best-value eating and accommodations, and guiding you through the cities, mountains, beaches, and villages of this sprawling, kaleidoscopic island nation. The *Sunday Times* of London called this "one of the best practical guides ever written about any country." 30 b/w photos, 143 illustrations, 250 maps, 17 charts, booklist, extensive Indonesian vocabulary, index. 1,050 pages.   **$17.95**

BALI HANDBOOK   by **Bill Dalton**

Since the early 20th century, foreigners have been drawn to Bali, an island so lovely that Nehru called it "the morning of the world." They're seldom disappointed, for Bali's theater-stage scenery, its spectacular music and dance, its highly developed handicrafts, its baroque temples, its tropical climate, glorious beaches, and colorful religious festivals have no equal. This comprehensive, well-informed guide has detailed travel information on bargain accommodations, outstanding dining, volcano climbing, surfing and diving locales, performing arts, and advice on exploring beyond the crowded southern beach resorts. Color and b/w photos, illustrations, 35 maps, glossary, booklist, index.
400 pages.   **(Available Fall 1989) $12.95**

NEW ZEALAND HANDBOOK   by Jane King

New Zealand is nature's improbable masterpiece, an entire world of beauty and wonder jammed into three unforgettable islands. Pristine fjords, icy waterfalls, smoldering volcanos, lush rainforests, and tumbling rivers, all bordered by sun-drenched beaches and an aquamarine sea. New Zealand's got it all. This information-packed guide introduces you to the people, places, history, and culture of this extraordinary land, and leads you to reasonably priced accommodations, restaurants, entertainment, and outdoor adventure—all the best that only New Zealand can offer. 8 color pages, 99 b/w photos, 146 illustrations, 82 maps, booklist, index. 512 pages.   **$14.95**

SOUTH KOREA HANDBOOK   by Robert Nilsen

A land of haunting beauty, rich culture, and economic promise, South Korea neatly weaves the warp and woof of tradition and modernity. This definitive guide to the once-hidden "Hermit Kingdom" leads you into the heart of Seoul...and beyond to the heart and soul of the country, with an emphasis on exploring and understanding the many facets of Korean society. Whether you're visiting on business or searching for adventure, *South Korea Handbook* is an invaluable companion. 8 color pages, 78 b/w photos, 93 illustrations, 109 maps, 10 charts, Korean glossary with useful notes on speaking and reading the language, booklist, index. 548 pages.   **$14.95**

JAPAN HANDBOOK   by J.D. Bisignani

This comprehensive guide dispels the myth that Japan is too expensive for the budget-minded traveler. The theme throughout is "do it like the Japanese" and get the most for your time and money. *Japan Handbook* is a cultural and anthropological encyclopedia on every facet of Japanese life, an indispensable tool for understanding and enjoying one of the world's most complex and intriguing countries. 8 color pages, 200 b/w photos, 92 illustrations, 112 maps and town plans, 29 charts, appendix on the Japanese language, booklist, glossary, index. 504 pages.   **$12.95**

The International Series

EGYPT HANDBOOK   by Kathy Hansen

Land of ancient civilizations, diverse cultures, and sharp contrasts, Egypt presents a 5,000-year-old challange to all comers. *Egypt Handbook* leads you through the labyrinth of sprawling Cairo, along the verdant Nile, across the desert, and into the far oases. With a deeper appreciation for Egypt's profound cultural legacy than any other guidebook, *Egypt Handbook* helps the traveler to unravel the complexities of the "Gift of the Nile," from prehistory to the present. An invaluable companion for intelligent travel in Egypt. Color and b/w photos, illustrations, over 40 detailed maps and site plans to museums and archaeological sites, Arabic glossary, booklist, index. 500 pages.
(Available Fall 1989) $14.95

IMPORTANT ORDERING INFORMATION

PRICES: All prices are subject to change. We always ship the most current edition. We will let you know if there is a price increase on the book you ordered.

SHIPPING & HANDLING OPTIONS:
1) Domestic UPS or USPS 1st class (allow 10 working days for delivery): $3.00 for the 1st item, 50¢ for each additional item.

Exceptions:
- **Indonesia Handbook** shipping is $4.00 for the 1st item, $1.00 for each additional copy.
- **Moonbelts** are $1.50 for one, 50¢ for each additional belt.
- Add $2.00 for same day handling.

2) UPS 2nd Day Air or Printed Airmail requires a special quote.
3) International Surface Bookrate (8-12 weeks delivery): $3.00 for the 1st item, $1.00 for each additional item.

FOREIGN ORDERS: All orders which originate outside the U.S.A. **must** be paid for with either an International Money Order or a check in U.S. currency drawn on a major U.S. bank based in the U.S.A.

TELEPHONE ORDERS: We accept Visa or Mastercard payments. **Minimum Order is U.S. $15.00.** Call in your order: (916) 345-5473. 9:00 a.m.—5:00 p.m. Pacific Standard Time.

How did you hear about Moon guides?_____

Are Moon guides available at your local bookstore?_____

If not, please list name of store and we will follow up:_____

_____

_____

_____

MOONBELTS. A new concept in moneybelts. Made of heavy-duty Cordura nylon, the **Moonbelt** offers maximum protection for your money and important papers. This pouch, designed for all-weather comfort, slips under your shirt or waistband, rendering it virtually undetectable and inaccessible to pickpockets. Many thoughtful features: 1-inch-wide nylon webbing, heavy-duty zipper, and a 1-inch high-test quick-release buckle. No more fumbling around for the strap or repeated adjustments, this handy plastic buckle opens and closes with a touch, but won't come undone until you want it to. Accommodates travelers cheques, passport, cash, photos. Size 5 x 9 inches. Available in black only. **$8.95**

ORDER FORM
(See important ordering information on opposite page)

Name: _____ Date: _____

Street: _____

City: _____

State or Country: _____ Zip Code: _____

Daytime Phone: _____

Quantity	Title	Price

Taxable Total	
Sales Tax (6%) for California Residents	
Shipping & Handling	
TOTAL	

Ship to: ❑ address above ❑ other _____

_____

_____

Make checks payable to:
Moon Publications, Inc. 722 Wall Street, Chico, California, 95928, USA
We Accept Visa and Mastercard
To order: Call in your Visa or Mastercard Number, or send a written order with your Visa or
Mastercard number and expiration date clearly written.

Card Number: ❑ Visa ❑ Mastercard
❑❑❑❑ ❑❑❑❑ ❑❑❑❑ ❑❑❑❑

expiration date: _____

Card Name:
❑ same as above ❑ other _____

signature_____

18-2

WHERE TO BUY THIS BOOK

Bookstores and Libraries:
Moon Publications, Inc., guides are sold world-wide. Please write sales manager Donna Galassi for a list of wholesalers and distributors in your area that stock our travel handbooks.

Travelers:
We would like to have Moon Publications' guides available throughout the world. Please ask your bookstore to write or call us for ordering information. If your bookstore will not order our guides for you, please write or call for a free catalog.

MOON PUBLICATIONS, INC.,
722 WALL STREET
CHICO, CA 95928 USA
tel: 916/345-5473